ADVANCE PRAISE

"**A highly informative and absorbing read**. With the help of extensive research, this book brings to the fore a completely new perspective on global problems and their solutions. A monumental work by a real polymath."

—Ibrahim B Syed, ScD, PhD, DSc, FACR, FInstP, FAIC, FRSH,
Clinical Professor of Medicine,
Director of Nuclear Medicine Sciences,
University of Louisville

"**This book is a remarkable undertaking**! Though unlikely in its wide ambition, it actually succeeds in seamlessly linking the wisdom (and also corruption) of the world's many seemingly unrelated systems of religion, philosophy, politics, education, psychology-- and especially the world's most profound poetry—within a deeply thoughtful and respectful work of both scholarly and personal reflection. It is so readable that even the clarifying footnotes are enlightening! Grounded in spirituality as well as in solid research, ***Radical Revolution of Values* is a hopeful book, compelling readers to rethink and challenge some surprisingly basic assumptions.**"

—Elizabeth Aaronsohn, EdD,
Associate Professor Emerita, Teacher Education Department,
Central Connecticut State University

"**Compelling and inspiring. *Radical Revolution of Values* covers key burning topics of our time—highlighting the relationship between society and its commercial institutions**. The incisive analysis in this book brings a new perspective to the very definition of corporate social responsibility. Mr. Saeed makes a clear case: "Don't be evil" and other such slogans have to go beyond lip service; they need principled manifestations in the role an institution plays within a society. **Even in the midst of today's global concerns, this book provides a sense of hope and future. A must-read for business executives who desire to be responsible citizens and leaders**."

—Idris T Vasi,
Head of Nokia CNS - Asia-Pacific

"An excellent resource for helping us understand the backstory to the major socio-political and religious issues of today."

—Miriam Therese Winter, PhD
Medical Mission Sister, Professor Emerita,
Hartford International University for Religion and Peace

"In this persuasive and meticulously researched work, Azam Saeed delves into matters that are at the heart of humanity's suffering. While his thoughtful analysis of the geopolitical woes of the world is soul-wrenching and even frightening, he eases the reader's anxiety by offering attainable alternatives to free humankind from its cycles of self-imposed crises. His haunting call for a "radical revolution of values" provides a blueprint to preserve freedom and reclaim true spirituality. This book is a must-read for those who are searching for ways to move our world toward a more enlightened state."

—Carol Shaw Austad, PhD,
Professor of Psychology, Co-coordinator of Peace Studies,
Central Connecticut State University

"Few writers can marshal the **impressive command of history, psychology, religion and spirituality** that Azam Saeed tackles in his masterful analysis of (nothing less than) the state of international and interpersonal conflict. Saeed insistently pulls every sort of polarity into question in the search for an overarching, more-encompassing truth; a truth which demands self-awareness, contrition and confession from all systems—from the human personality to the organizing structures of governance. …

Mr. Saeed invites us to apply the same wide-angle lens on our inner evolution. He brings **a beautiful interplay of spiritual voices, images and practices**. The whole of the book is infused with an integrative worldview—interweaving informed practical action in the world alongside the necessary growth of self-awareness. Inspiring and informed."

—Rabbi Andrea Cohen-Kiener,
Temple Israel, Greenfield MA

"*Radical Revolution of Values* is **a wide-ranging and multi-layered memoir** of Azam Saeed, a Pakistani-American which takes us on a stimulating exploration of his much-examined life. Inspired by Dr. Martin Luther King's call to work toward a more just and compassionate world through a radical revolution of many prevailing ideas and values, Saeed undertakes an Odyssean venture to find a solution to critical contemporary issues particularly in the context of his dual identity as a Pakistani Muslim and an American citizen. He believes that the solution lies in religion which is foundational and central to human life, and looks at it in the framework of various disciplines including history, philosophy, sociology, literature, political thought, and science.

An exceptional feature of this book is the author's strong affirmation of all religions which he sees as different pathways to the same spiritual goal. His well-selected citations from a variety of religious and wisdom traditions are truly appealing as are the precious nuggets of personal memories imbedded in the expansive narrative.

"*Radical Revolution of Values* is a scholarly book but its message of **love, compassion, justice, and inclusion, which is much-needed today, is for all people**. I am very pleased to give it my highest endorsement."

—Dr. Riffat Hassan,
Professor Emerita, Islamic Theology,
University of Louisville

"Azam Saeed has tackled **the big topics we all confront** today in our divided culture: religious exploitation, tribalism, threats to our freedom, domestic terrorism. He **skillfully dissects these and provides solutions in clear, easy-to-understand language**. He reveals himself to be a man with an open mind and heart whose cultural insight is impressive and whose writing is very much worth reading."

—Cynthia Parzych,
Author and Publisher,
Cynthia Parzych Publishing, Inc.

"We humans face the challenge today of living with freedom without compromising on the spiritual values of our predecessors. To realize this ideal, the message of the great world religions has to be made socially and intellectually relevant to our times. The biggest threat in the way of achieving this goal is posed by the terrorism that seeks its justification from the religious text. Azam Saeed's *Radical Revolution of Values* is a **well-researched, skillfully-written, and thought-provoking book that is an important attempt at refuting the disturbing claim that religion promotes terrorism**. He deserves the gratitude of all people who are seriously concerned about the claim that seeks to relate terrorism with religion. The book rebuts the claim thoroughly and convincingly."

—Khalid Zaheer, PhD,
Islamic scholar and academic

Radical Revolution of Values

Reclaiming Our Spiritual Heritage, Preserving Our Freedoms, and Countering Terrorism

Radical Revolution of Values

Reclaiming Our Spiritual Heritage, Preserving Our Freedoms, and Countering Terrorism

Azam Saeed

Durham, NC

Radical Revolution of Values: Reclaiming Our Spiritual Heritage, Preserving Our Freedoms, and Countering Terrorism
Azam Saeed
AzamSaeedAuthor@proton.me
www.AzamSaeedAuthor.com

Published 2022, by Torchflame Books
an Imprint of Light Messages Publishing
www.lightmessages.com
Durham, NC 27713 USA
SAN: 920-9298

Paperback ISBN: 978-1-61153-482-5
Hardcover ISBN: 978-1-61153-501-3
E-book ISBN: 978-1-61153-483-2
Library of Congress Control Number: 2022915392

Unless otherwise noted, most of the Qur'an quotations are taken from *The Message of The Qur'an* translation by Muhammad Asad, and Bible quotations are predominantly taken from the *Authorized King James Version* (KJV).

To my high school teachers Haji Fazl Ahmed and Shumshaad Mohammad Lodhi, whose facility in seeing love and beauty through their religion and whose dedication to raising responsible citizens informed my worldview at an early stage.

To the 9-year-old stranger who, in a 5-minute interaction decades ago, taught a lesson about spirituality and education that has become an integral part of my being.

CONTENTS

ACKNOWLEDGMENTS

In addition to my family, I have been lucky to have had exceptional teachers at every stage, beginning at primary school level. This book is dedicated to two of my secondary school teachers, Haji Fazl Ahmed and Shumshaad Mohammad Lodhi, who helped me understand the spirit of my religion (even though they did not teach religion per se). Imtiaz Ahmed was my flight instructor at the PAF Academy in Risalpur. Even in the highly disciplined field of aviation, the message was that checklists were not meant to be followed blindly, but rather with conscious discernment and thoughtful judgment.

The closest I have ever come to taking a college-level course in English (literature or otherwise) was at the University of Washington when I took two classes in business writing from Judith Kalitzki. She took a lot of personal interest in helping me develop an understanding of the basics. Later, at the University of Michigan, being the president of student government there, I had a lot of interaction with B. Joseph White, the dean of University of Michigan Business School, and Ted Snyder, the associate dean. While I did not take a formal course from either, the interaction alone was educational in its own way. White was a Jesuit priest before he entered the field of business. My first job after MBA was essentially because of White. Several years after graduating, I had called Snyder to seek his help in reaching some people. He was then the dean of the Darden School at the University of Virginia. He graciously took my call and then sent introductory emails to create the connections for me.

Mentioning these teachers also expresses my gratitude to all others who have come into my life and who are far too many for me to list here. To me, it is such individual and personal transmission of values that is the actual source and vehicle of education.

I am grateful for the help I received from my friend Liz Aaronsohn at an early stage when converting my initial thought into words. Her feedback was instrumental in my ability to shape and refine the book's concept and turn the raw ideas into an organized, thematic format.

Another friend, Rabbi Andrea Cohen-Kiener, was very kind to review the first draft and provide valuable observations about the content.

As a first-time author, I have been fortunate to have Torchflame Books as the publisher. Given the unusual nature of this book, it was essential to have a publisher who approached it with a sense of purpose. At Torchflame, that's what I got from the first day. I received remarkable support and attention with professional expertise of a high caliber in various departments: editing, cover design, layout, and marketing. My special thanks to Wally Turnbull for project direction and Vivian Turnbull for insightful editing. Credit for so many aspects of this book goes to the Torchflame team.

And finally, I would like to acknowledge the pivotal role played by my wife, Aysha. To begin with, this book was her idea. I initially told her it would be impossible to combine these disparate themes as a coherent thesis. She wouldn't take no for an answer and, as always, proved me wrong. Her ideas and advice at every step of manuscript development have been pivotal in my ability to complete this project.

One of the great liabilities of history is that all too many people fail to remain awake through great periods of social change. Every society has its protectors of the status quo and its fraternities of the indifferent who are notorious for sleeping through revolutions. But today our very survival depends on our ability to stay awake, to adjust to new ideas, to remain vigilant and to face the challenge of change.

—Rev. Dr. Martin Luther King, Jr.

Analysis is the distinguishing of things that exist sound and true in combination—but that have become confused in the mind—in such a way that each of them is rendered separate from the others in its potential and in the definition, or in such a way that each of them comes to indicate the existence of the other, so that when one considers the state of one of them, one is transported from one to the other.

—Al-Shaykh al-Ra'is Abu Ali Ibn Sina (Avicenna)

INTRODUCTION

Know truth as truth and untruth as untruth.

—Dhammapada 12

You will know the truth,
and the truth will set you free.

—John 8:32

Yes, the human race today faces unprecedented existential challenges. No, looking the other way is not the most convenient option. Disentangling symptom from source, effect from cause, and solution from problem makes clear the global and local pictures of the problems and their solutions. A bold encounter in this regard empowers us to solve even problems that seem daunting, complex, and perhaps beyond our reach. A journey towards such an engagement is the purpose of this book.

At the global level, we see crises induced by chronic structural problems such as climate change, nuclear threat, socio-economic inequity, war, terrorism, degradation of human freedoms, and now pandemics. At the individual level, we struggle with material pursuits, search for meaning and identity, dissatisfaction, dysfunctional relationships, unhealthy and unsustainable family structures, fear, happiness, and the raison d'être questions that arise everywhere.[1]

Religion is often projected as part of the problems we face today, or even as the source of some of them. It is also frequently used to create or exacerbate polarization on issues purely political in nature. Throughout history, people have turned to religion for help in their search for meaning and understanding of our human condition.

Sadly, rather than a path to greater insight, religion has sometimes been used to divide us, even blind us to the truths that surround us.

Socrates wisely concluded that an unexamined life is not worth living. Amid the present-day socio-politico-economic tumult, ignoring this guideline is singularly perilous. In that sense, it would be prudent to rethink the place of religion as part of the solution, not just part of the problem. If we fail to do that and allow the very concept of religion and even spirituality to remain a vehicle for psychological exploitation by political forces, religion will further lose the struggle for legitimacy and relevance.

Friedrich Nietzsche begins the preface to his seminal work *On the Genealogy of Morality* with a pertinent observation, "We are unknown to ourselves.... We have never looked for ourselves—so how are we ever supposed to find ourselves?"[2] If so, this condition opens the door to mischief by others. But then, it also opens the door to true enlightenment.

The exploitation of our identities, especially religious, in the creation of the "other" (out-group) amounts to an abuse of our religions for promoting myriad goals that often are contrary to scriptural teaching. The cages and fiefs will always be created to exploit our identities—by the projection of raw, and often chauvinistic, tribalism—in the service of one agenda or the other.

How willingly we confine ourselves into those prisons shall remain our own choice. The freedom from these imposed boundaries of thought allows us not just to witness the reality, it also allows us to be true to our identity. Our scriptures provide us all the needed guidelines to find our real identity, which may often be different from the way our identities (especially religious and national) are promoted by various establishments. The negative historical place of our religions in such exploitation simply indicates how easily those who control the power structures have been able to manipulate the basic human needs to belong and to believe in something greater than our own selves.

A 2018 Chapman University *Survey of American Fears* indicates that 49 percent of Americans are afraid or very afraid of Islamic extremists. The same exact percentage is also afraid or very afraid of

White supremacists.[3] (White supremacy does derive its validity from certain forms of belief in Christianity.) The concern in both cases is highly valid and relevant in today's world. This book unfolds the religio-political drivers of "Islamic" terrorism, exposing its intimate connections with geopolitics.

While forces within religion sometimes play a catalytic role in exacerbating social discord, religion may still be the most reliable vehicle available to the human race in addressing some of the most difficult issues we are dealing with. When, however, the institutions of religion are corrupted to serve the agendas of power, religion itself loses its potential to bring about a positive change in the society.

The conversion of these concerns into instrumental understanding and effective policymaking is all but absent within the public discourse. A critical mass of ordinary citizens would be needed to ignite such a public debate actually geared towards finding solutions. Indeed, shouldering this responsibility becomes an imperative for the ordinary citizen in a democracy.

Over a half century ago, the Reverend Dr. Martin Luther King provided the diagnosis of the human world's ailment: "the evil triplets" of racism, militarism, and extreme materialism. His prescription of the solution was equally concise and precise with two components: the need for "restructuring" our systems and a "radical revolution of values" so we have a better and balanced framework to guide the individual and the collective in various domains of life. The problems—left unaddressed, without an earnest effort to resolve them—have now become much more intricate and severe. Yet King's prescient and prophetic solution is still as applicable today as it was fifty years ago. Human wisdom and will—individual as well as collective—is all that stands as the barrier between an insightful future and an ignoble one. The choice is ours to make!

The thesis of this book revolves around Dr. King's call for a Radical Revolution of Values. King called for this "revolution" so we would avoid a "spiritual death." Over half a century later, I fervently believe the task lies in the present moment—now.

Throughout this book's framework, I quote and draw inspiration from the eclectic, essential, vital, and dynamic concepts and teachings that we have inherited from our various spiritual traditions: Buddhism, the Baha'i Faith, Christianity, Confucianism, Hinduism, Islam, Jainism, Judaism, Sikhism, Taoism, and Zoroastrianism. Among others, these concepts include *Agape* (love), *Aparigraha* (non-attachment), *Ihsan* (beauty in action), *Panna/Prajna* (discernment), *Santosha* (contentment), *Seva* (service), *Te* (moral force), and *Tikkun* (repair).

This book's purpose is not to provide an exhaustive comparison of various religions on specific themes. Rather, it is to provide a basic understanding of convergences or, sometimes, divergences. Two points are important here: First, the abundance or scarcity of scriptural teachings and quotations in this book from various traditions is not a function of my belief in the primacy of one over the other. In my opinion, and as this book demonstrates again and again, all these paths provide perfect avenues towards one's spiritual destination. I see nothing but beauty in the diversity and nuances.

Second, the intent and nature of scriptural references and religious teachings in this book is primarily informational, not exegetical. I have tried to limit explanations of the scriptural text or religious teaching. In some cases, though, I found it appropriate to provide a brief explanation.

I have spent much of the past four decades in the United States. That's why most of the examples provided are from the United States; the focus of the message would also seem to be rooted here. Yet, the message is global and the observations in the book are applicable at the international level.

The mental models and thought patterns we so readily accept need to be challenged. Enlightenment philosophy, at least on the surface, divorced faith from practical life, thus creating a separation between "ceremonial belief" and "pragmatic reality." Such attitude relegates spirituality to a weekend activity with no bearing on the week. The church (of any religion) thus tends to become more of an identity-based club with a parochial orientation underneath a spiritual gloss. The narrow-mindedness enshrined in such a dichotomy between the sacred and the secular is perhaps one of the allusions made by theologian and philosopher Rabbi Abraham

Joshua Heschel when he says that "it is the weekday in which the Sabbath is reflected."[4]

Enlightenment philosophy, combined with the conceptual and legal framework of the nation-state, created the secular-religious binary. It also seems to have broken the expectation of reason from the practice of religious faith. The split creates thought-patterns that remove the anticipation of moral and ethical behavior from the societal culture—making such an expectation mostly a domain of the state and the legal system. Such a binary also establishes science/knowledge as almost entirely rational, and spirituality as almost entirely non-rational. When looked upon critically from the societal and civilizational viewpoint, these developments pose a plethora of detrimental consequences. As the influential Italian philosopher Roberto Calasso[5] summed up the place of religion in modern times: "Theology ended up being transferred into politics, while theology itself was relegated to universities."[6]

It would be no exaggeration to say that the conceptual guidelines developed during the Enlightenment (the Age of Reason, circa seventeenth to eighteenth century) still dominate the current thought-patterns in all walks of life—academic, political, legal, sociological, economic, etc. With its reliance on reason, evidence, and ideals such as liberty, many good ideas came forth from this intellectual movement (and from the preceding Renaissance period, the fifteenth and sixteenth centuries). This book features areas of weakness that get glossed over in the study, application, and impact of this philosophy.

Seventeenth-century English philosopher Thomas Hobbes's doctrine "war of everyone against everyone" still resonates in our societal structures. The role of his philosophy has been especially evaluated in understanding how our sociopolitical systems have evolved. The place of imperialism and colonialism—and their undermining, if not outright destruction, of amazingly rich spiritual systems and cultures—is also not commonly and adequately understood in Europe and North America. Without understanding this historical bequeathal, we will not be able to address the sources of human problems.

The theme in this book clearly deals with human nature—the good and evil that is inherent in it. Yet it is also important to realize the place of the "polluted barrel" (not just the "bad apple") in our evaluation. We also see that the current socio-politico-economic paradigm and the central role played by the institutional structures under the aegis of the nation-state have drastically diluted the concept of culture—if not the very concept of society. Yet, the problems created by the power play of economic and political interests are not transparently highlighted in their true colors. Given the consequent misreading of the global situation by most people, these liabilities of our institutions pose serious threat to human wellbeing. This book presents a unique framework comparing the attributes of culture in relation to those of a structured institution.

My tendency to look at religion in a contextual framework that includes sociology, science, literature, politics, etc. is simply a reflection of the mode in which I understand this world and religion's place in it. Also, the way I was taught religion is that, while there may be some tension among these concepts, there really is no mutually exclusive conflict among them. However, in our social, cultural, psychological, and spiritual naivety, we humans find it difficult to deal with paradox. The book attempts to capture these various facets of our understanding of knowledge and existence.

This book intends to show the reader that, given the complicated nature of global problems, it is only by looking at the world through diverse lenses (from various fields of knowledge) can we get a holistic picture and find realistic solutions. The purpose of this book, however, is not to prescribe solutions in every chapter or for every problem discussed. On the other hand, the depth of understanding developed through this book will enable the reader to explore potential solutions on their own depending upon their outlook and concerns.

This book uniquely and deliberately assembles information from various disciplines: religion, politics, and philosophy to show the multifarious connections in the creation of our problems. With this non-traditional approach, it is important to expect occasional difficulty in connecting these topics, by the author or by the reader.

These challenges result from our natural difficulty in comprehending the interconnected sociological developments behind these problems.

Humans experience their spiritual essence and connect with their inner truth through one or multiple of various modalities or pathways: religion, nature, humanistic, experiential, devotion to a higher purpose. The willingness to accord validity to diverse sources of inspiration broadens our horizon in learning from the other, and in being one with the other. Conflicts and political ideologies distort and disappear the wisdom and beauty within our religions. And this wisdom and beauty is what may contribute towards a solution to the present-day human condition.

The content of this book is organized in six parts. The first four of them show various dimensions of the problems we humans face. The last two parts highlight the potential of religion as a source of inspiration in our attempt at dealing with these challenges.

Part 1 presents the world's problems at the most macro level. By addressing the common geopolitical perils of war, terrorism, and the corruption of our systems, part 1 shows the connections between religion and geopolitics. It would be highly naive for people of faith to not be aware of those inseparable connections.

Part 2 brings the problems more to the level of a single country or even an individual. Here too, though, we can see the global connections. These chapters explain the centrality of Hobbes's adversarial ethos in social structures and its consequent effect on our cultures of living and education systems. Following the basic thesis of this book, the chapters in part 2 emphasize that the source of most of the problems in these areas are traceable to the economic and political power structures across the globe.

Parts 3 and 4 address the most common modes of exploitation of religion as well as the barriers that thwart religion from becoming a source of harmony. Even though these concerns are often presented as endemic to (or emanating from) religion, it is clear that these matters find their connections into the topics discussed in parts 1 and 2.

Finally, parts 5 and 6 provide a solution-orientation by showing the similarities as well as differences in the teachings of different religions. The radiance emanating from our spiritual teachings can provide the beacon and guiding light towards solutions in any domain of human endeavor. Chapters in parts 5 and 6 also clarify how spiritual traditions have effectively brought humans together to work towards common goals of peace and justice.

As noted in the endnotes, I have myself translated much of the non-English poetry into English. Transliteration of the original is also provided in the endnotes. Appendix B provides a glossary of foreign words representing relatively unfamiliar persons, places, and concepts.

This book makes no attempt at providing a universal approach to solving the problems the human race faces today. Instead, the book endeavors to create a framework within which the reader can deploy different lines of reasoning—within their spiritual traditions—to reach their own theoretical or practical conclusions. This understanding provides the stepping-stones towards tactics and strategies for effective solutions.

Despite proclamations to the contrary by some, there can be no question religion has a place in our lives. In fact, as human history and psychology dictate, there is a basic human need for spiritual belief—a need that can neither be denied nor eradicated.[7] This need is absolutely essential because every individual as well as society requires a reliable moral compass.

Over the centuries, religions have been—and continue to be—exploited and abused by political forces to foment war, violence, and other atrocities. This can end only when we open our minds and hearts to sincerely recognize the right of the "other" (the out-group) to follow a different path. This acknowledgment of *volo ut sis* (I want you to be),[8] accepting the validity of the "other" is what, in turn, will allow us to prevent the exploitation of our own religion.

Religion is in the middle of many of the problems we face today. If we allow the status quo to determine our future, we face a dire prognosis. The effort to understand how religion has come to occupy a central place in our societal problems is essential for us to be able to harness its innate power to heal. Indeed, this book is written entirely on that premise.

PART ONE:

GLOBAL REALITY: CORRUPTION AND TERRORISM

The masters of avarice have become the claimants
as well as the judges;
Whom do we besiege for representation,
whom do we beseech for justice?[9]

—Faiz Ahmad Faiz

CHAPTER 1:

TRAVERSING THE LAYERED COMPLEXITY OF GEOPOLITICS

A man's foes shall be they of his own household.
—Matthew 10:36

He should elevate himself by the self,
not degrade himself;
for the self is its own friend
and its own worst foe.
—*Bhagavad Gita* 6.5

The difficulty of grasping the various facets of global crises is undeniably formidable and cannot be overstated. Yet, there never was a time when comprehending this geopolitical complexity was more important for the ordinary citizen than it is today because the solutions to the problem, and their implementation, fall squarely on the collective shoulders of the informed and responsible citizenry. And without an adequate understanding of the intricacy of the problem, finding a feasible solution becomes an unrealistic prospect.

A concept in chaos theory known as the *butterfly effect* shows the amplified impact over time of a small and supposedly insignificant change within a system. In a reductionist information environment, therefore, finding connections between seemingly unrelated affairs becomes pivotal in our understanding of various global problems.[10] That, nevertheless, is neither how information is generally available, nor is it the human instinct to approach a problem that way. Our weak understanding caused by these limitations is further exacerbated by the one-sided and misleading blame game that is propagated by the institutions from whom we expect solutions. By bringing the reader's attention to such connections, this chapter guides a deeper understanding into the complexity of global reality.

Among the various "identities" I carry, two stand out in high relevance in relation to geopolitics. My Muslim identity informs me of the spiritual angle to my responsibilities, whereas being a citizen of the United States posits responsibilities from the civic perspective. The tumult within, and globally in the name of, these two identities is remarkable. As examples in this book show, it is also remarkable that a lot of what happens in the name of these identities is against the interest of an overwhelming majority of ordinary US citizens or Muslims. That's why, for the concerned and responsible citizen, it becomes important to realize the knottiness of geopolitics.

This book generally limits the discussion only to these two identities. Many religious and national identities do face analogous crises. The reader can use examples in this chapter to evaluate applications of their own identities. The human inclination to more clearly see problems with others limits most people from seeing components of these global crises that may impact their own identities. And that's why a clear understanding of the analysis in this chapter (and the following two) is so crucial in developing a deeper picture of global human concerns.

Ideological And Economic Forces Threatening Human Heritage and Civilization

In 2001, the Taliban's deliberate destruction of the Bamiyan Buddha statues in Afghanistan came as a shock to the world. Over a decade later, ISIL's heinous destruction of massive religious and cultural heritage in Iraq and Syria also startled the world. None of it should really have been a surprise. The basic connections of these events with the prevalent religio-political ideology and the geopolitical forces driving the destruction of human heritage in recent history are fairly straightforward.

Since the mid-twentieth century, a massive crime against human heritage and history has been taking place with relatively little notice by the international community at large. The Saudi government has destroyed innumerable historical structures sacred to Islamic history, many of them going back to the time of Prophet Muhammad. The sporadic and capricious desecration of religious and cultural heritage began when the land was militarily conquered by the Saudi-Wahhabi[11] alliance in the 1920s.[12] Since the 1970s, however, the trend became a systematic Saudi policy fully displaying its contemptuous attitude towards Islamic history. The house of the Prophet's first wife, Khadijah, has been turned into a toilet block.[13] The fate of the house the Prophet was born in is uncertain, and so is the future of his tomb and related mosque.[14] The damage to Islamic heritage is incalculable and irreversible. Within recent history, an estimated 95 percent of historical sites in Mecca and Medina have been obliterated.[15]

Besides the commercial interests involved in Saudi Arabia, the fanatic ideology driving the Saudi derby of desecration and depredation is also the inspiration behind the diabolical actions taken by the Taliban and the ISIL. (Even when the facade is nonidentical,[16] the source and essence of the force are exactly the same.) If the Saudi-Wahhabi ideology "rejects the history, culture, philosophy and learning of Muslim civilizations as deviant and degenerative,"[17] how could it be expected to value any other human heritage?

This easy connection should have been inescapable. That, for reasons of pragmatic convenience, the human race chooses to reductively separate these movements is a choice we make. But then, shouldn't we also be willing to accept the price we are paying for such choices?

We would be remiss if we did not briefly cover another geopolitical angle to the destruction of culture in the Middle East.

Iraq, with around 10,000 years of known Mesopotamian history, is considered the cradle of human civilization. Not only did we receive cursive writing and the wheel from it, that land has been home to some of the world's greatest cultural treasures—so rich that it has been known as one large archaeological site. In addition to the great capitals of Babylon, Nimrud and Nineveh, Iraq's archaeological treasures include over 150 ancient Sumerian cities. Combined, there are some 12,000 sites in the country.[18]

ISIL's sudden appearance from nowhere and its takeover of large parts of Iraq seemed to have caught everyone by surprise. In addition to ancient monuments from before the current era—such as the Temples of Baalshamin and Baal as well as the Asad al-Lat—ISIL's ruination included Christian, Shi'a, Sunni, and Yazidi heritage. Even the mosques of Prophet Jonah and Prophet Seth were not spared. (In Syria, after destroying the Mar Elian Monastery, ISIL released a video showing the exhumation of the remains of Saint Elian.[19]) The financial incentive wasn't so hidden either. ISIS would search churches and mosques prior to their destruction and would remove all valuables—to be sold on the black market.[20]

ISIL, however, was not the pioneer in the looting and destruction of our Mesopotamian cultural heritage. A decade earlier, that project had already begun in earnest. In 2003, the US-led coalition invaded Iraq. As the prospect of the war became tangible, some of the world's leading scholars of archaeology, art, and history issued vehement warnings of the civilizational loss from the foreseen destruction and looting of the cultural heritage.[21] The premonition of the scholars seems to have fallen on deaf ears.

However, the then newly-formed American Council for Cultural Policy (ACCP), with strong connections within the White House,[22] seems to have received much more official reception. ACCP, a lobbying coalition of antiquities collectors and arts lawyers was created in 2002, months before the invasion of Iraq. Its influence was such that it would have meetings with "US defence and state department officials before the start of the war."[23]

Ostensibly, it seems that ACCP's meetings must have been productive. The expression "condoned looting,"[24] used by an official at the British Museum, aptly sums up what transpired in Iraq soon after the 2003 invasion. From the Baghdad Museum alone, some 15,000 objects were stolen, including dozens of renowned objects.[25] Three members of the U.S. Cultural Property Advisory Committee (appointed by the president), including its chairman, resigned to protest the US government's responsibility.[26] However, Donald Rumsfeld, the then US defense secretary, dismissed the reports of cultural devastation as misplaced and exaggerated.[27]

Commenting on the premeditated and targeted nature of the looting, the chief US investigator opined that "the thieves had advance 'orders' from international dealers."[28] The trafficking of this human cultural treasure continued well after the invasion. Between 2007 and 2009 alone, "customs officials at Heathrow [London airport] confiscated 3.4 tons of antiquities looted from war zones in Iraq and elsewhere, intended for sale on the international market."[29]

The US military also built bases on the sites of ancient cities of Ur and Babylon, where the construction involved the use of heavy earth-moving equipment.[30]

In a report released by the British Museum, Dr. John Curtis, an authority on Iraq's archaeological sites, discusses the "substantial damage" caused by the US military at Babylon: "This is tantamount to establishing a military camp around the Great Pyramid in Egypt or around Stonehenge in Britain."[31] On his visit to Babylon, Curtis saw a 2,600-year-old brick pavement "crushed by military vehicles, archaeological fragments scattered across the site" as well as "cracks and gaps where somebody had tried to gouge out the decorated bricks forming the famous dragons of the Ishtar Gate."[32]

"Outrage is hardly the word," reflected Lord Redesdale, an archaeologist. "This is just dreadful."[33]

Destruction or looting of cultural heritage is a serious breach of international law: It violates the 1949 Geneva Convention (Article I) and the 1954 Hague Convention. It also constitutes a war crime under Article 8 of the Rome Statute (International Criminal Court's Statute). An act of this nature may even fall under "cultural cleansing" because it effectively destroys the means of collective memory and connection with one's beliefs, history, and identity. That's why "discriminatory intent against a cultural community can be charged as a crime against humanity."[34]

Additionally, as the United Nations Special Rapporteur's report titled *Cultural Rights* points out, "The qualification of intentional destruction may also be applied in cases of willful neglect of cultural heritage either during armed conflicts or in times of peace, including with the intent of letting others destroy the cultural heritage in question, for example, through looting."[35]

Raphael Lemkin, who drafted the 1951 Genocide Convention, coined the word "genocide" to broadly encompass "destruction of the political and social institutions of culture, language, national feelings, religion, and the economic existence of national groups...."[36]

When we consider the international laws involved, the destruction of our human heritage in Afghanistan, Saudi Arabia, and Iraq (among various other global locations) has grave implications for the culpable entities. The purpose of this book, however, is to understand this in terms of our own responsibility and ability to find solutions. Broadly speaking, cultural destruction is an expression of contempt for our human commonality and essence—because it annihilates the shared bonds that bind us together. Our human heritage is a trust whose integrity we all share as a common responsibility.

> The ultimate titulaires [administrators, trustees] of the right to the safeguard and preservation of their cultural and spiritual heritage are the collectivities of human beings concerned, or else humankind as a whole.[37]
>
> —Judge Cançado Trindade, International Court of Justice

The scenarios here generate some instructive questions that will be helpful in understanding this chapter and the next.:

1. What did the governments of the "Islamic" countries do to stop the destruction of the common Islamic heritage by the Saudi government? What if this atrocity had been committed by a European colonizing power? What if it were committed by the state of Israel? Would the information then be on the radar of the ordinary Muslim? How would the information be used then, and what would be the geopolitical implications?

2. Why are the governments of Europe and North America the bulwarks of the Saudi-Wahhabi religio-political empire? Why did the British Empire help establish the Kingdom of Saudi Arabia in the early twentieth century? (Winston Churchill, then the British colonial secretary, was the prime mover of this policy—even though he had labeled the Saudi-Wahhabi alliance as "bloodthirsty" and ready to "kill all who do not share their opinions."[38])
3. Why, in the past quarter of a century or so, has Saudi Arabia been the world's second-largest spender in the area of armament (second only to the United States)? How many hundreds of billions of dollars a year go to large corporations (especially in the name of "defense") from these Middle Eastern countries[39] and even the so-called third-world countries that face serious problems of hunger, disease, etc.?
4. How many of these European and North American mega corporations would be immediately put out of existence if it weren't for this funding? What would happen to the European and the North American economies[40] if there were no wars, no armed conflict, and no international weapons sales or deliveries in the world for just one year?
5. Would it be acceptable to say that all humans should be considered equal—in their dignity and pursuit of happiness according to their own culture and way of life—without the forced imposition of some "client" government or external ideology?

These complex issues are beyond the scope of this book. Even when we don't have the information to readily or accurately understand the picture, just asking the questions can widen the lens and help shift our focus away from the narrow and prevalent identity-based narratives.

Geopolitical Agendas Exploiting Religion

The complexity of religion's role in the global political and economic power play is quite confounding. Here, however, it is important to understand the place of global conflicts in their historical contexts. It would be more realistic and constructive to realize that such conflicts are not battles between good and evil, but rather part and parcel of the tussle for resources, power, and dominance. Religion is simply another pawn in this complicated project.

The connections between global politics and the involved economic interests have resulted in the world's economic system becoming heavily reliant upon sales of arms and ammunition—creating a perpetual scenario of large-scale conflicts. The result seems to be the distortion of the very nature of human existence and its meaning. The decoupling of this connection between global economy and constant global conflict that King and Heschel pointed out half a century ago has become even more urgent.

Besides the inherent intricacy, the opacity surrounding various global phenomena make some people explain them in what's become known as "conspiracy theories." However, we have to realize that highly complex phenomena are relatively difficult to reconcile in terms of some overarching conspiracies. The global system produces equally dystopian results when it revolves around an obsession with the growth of power and profit. Indeed, we can adequately understand most developments by the evaluation of their origin and causality via available[41] information. The transpiring events can thus be viewed as the cumulative effect of tactical maneuvers by disparate entities with conflicting interests trying to achieve their strategic objectives.

The connection of geopolitics with realpolitik (position and advantage in domestic politics) is usually straightforward. What is not commonly understood is the unpredictable and uncontrollable nature of the genies that are released in such power plays.[42]

The events set in motion by the Soviet invasion of Afghanistan provide a rather instructive example of the human inability to even comprehend, let alone control, the consequences of geopolitical policies and maneuvers. It is also a good example of how religion has been exploited, blamed, and corrupted to serve geopolitical agendas.

In 1979, the Soviet Union invaded Afghanistan to establish a government there that would be more favorable to their interests. The waves from that military invasion spread all over the world and the consequent ripples can still be felt in myriad ways. The effort opposing the Soviet military expansion was led by the United States, whose Operation Cyclone is considered the most expensive intelligence operation undertaken in the world's history. The project created a complicated syndicate of sometimes conflicting geopolitical actors. A whole slate of players—some of them unaligned in the Cold War—were engaged in the purpose of fighting the Soviet influence in Afghanistan.

It would be fair to say that the deliberate recruitment, brainwashing, and military training of tens of thousands of Muslim civilians from all over the world had a big role in the creation of the present global movement of violent "Islamic" extremism. In the span of a decade, over 100,000 militants[43] were groomed to fight the Soviet forces in Afghanistan. In addition to the United States, the governments of Britain, Pakistan, Egypt, and Saudi Arabia were the most involved in that effort.

Initially, the surface-to-air missiles to be used by the guerillas were provided by China and Egypt; but they were highly ineffective. The British-made Blowpipe missiles, and even the US-made Redeye had a high rate of failure.[44] Thence the latest US-made surface-to-air Stinger missiles were added to the arsenal of the guerillas. Ironically, the United States would not sell the Stinger missile to Saudi Arabia even though the kingdom was paying for the Stingers being supplied to Afghan guerillas.[45] Another irony is that the United States later had to pay to buy back some of these Stingers.[46]

Even communist China,[47] as one of the major suppliers of weapons to the guerillas,[48] was involved against the communist regime of the Soviet Union: "[China] worked hand in glove with the United States in supplying the guerillas with rocket launchers and other weapons."[49] Here, it is important to notice and remember how alliances shift in the unprincipled realm of geopolitics.

Needless to say, the so-called mujahideen were "the best-equipped guerilla force in the world."[50] Over the period of a decade, somewhere in the vicinity of ten billion dollars were spent—equally shared by the United States and Saudi Arabia. As the *New York Times* tells us: "The Government of Saudi Arabia has generally matched the United States' financial contributions.... In addition, several wealthy Saudi princes, motivated by a sense of religious duty and solidarity, gave cash contributions to the guerrillas."[51]

In our understanding of the spread of extremism within Islam, however, it would be important to realize that Operation Cyclone was not an exception. Throughout the Cold War, soon after WWII, the United States had promoted militant Islam as a counterforce to the socialist or communist movements within Muslim countries.[52] At the end of the Cold War, as British historian Sir Richard J. Evans points out, when it was "determined that Russia could no longer serve as the antithesis of civilization ... Islam provided a handy substitute."[53] When an enemy is needed, as George Orwell pointed out in *1984*, the enemy is created. Though there is even more to it than that.

Zbigniew Brzezinski, President Carter's national security adviser, was a central figure in the creation and implementation of Operation Cyclone. In a 1998 interview with French magazine *Le Nouvel Observateur*, he was asked if he regretted supporting the Islamic fundamentalism that has given rise to terrorism. Brzezinski's response was, "What is more important in world history? The Taliban or the collapse of the Soviet empire? Some agitated Moslems or the liberation of Central Europe and the end of the Cold War?"[54]

It is instructive to see that just three years before 9-11, this leading authority on geopolitics and the begetter of "some agitated Moslems" was so unaware and dismissive of the problems his policy had unleashed in the world. That should come as no surprise though because, in how well he perceived the consequences of such policies and operations, Brzezinski was the rule and not the exception. In the same interview, Brzezinski also verified the claim by Robert Gates (former CIA director and defense secretary) that the United States had begun to mobilize and support fighters in Afghanistan six months before the Soviet intervention. In Brzezinski's words:

> According to the official version of history, CIA aid to the Mujahiddin began during 1980, that is to say, after the Soviet army invaded Afghanistan on December 24, 1979. But the reality, closely guarded until now, is completely otherwise: Indeed, it was July 3, 1979 that President Carter signed the first directive for secret aid to the opponents of the pro-Soviet regime in Kabul ... in my opinion this aid was going to induce a Soviet military intervention.[55]

This is consistent with the information that "British covert aid to the Afghan resistance began to flow even before the Soviet invasion."[56] As indicated earlier, such geopolitical battles are best understood when looked upon as amoral tussles for resources, power, and dominance—and not as battles between good and evil. In their magisterial book about the Soviet invasion of Afghanistan, UN Undersecretary General Diego Cordovez and journalist Selig Harrison forthrightly conclude: "Although both superpowers invoked noble objectives, both treated Afghanistan in reality as a pawn in their global struggle."[57]

In this power struggle, religion was recruited as a foot soldier for political and military advantage. During a visit to Pakistan in October 1984, the then CIA Director (William Casey) offered to provide 10,000 copies of the *Qur'an* in Central Asian languages to his counterpart in the ISI (Pakistan's intelligence agency). The purpose? To "stick it to the Russians," Casey urged the ISI to carry the war into the USSR by conducting operations inside the Soviet territory. The copies of the *Qur'an* were to be used in Soviet territories with ethnically Muslim populations.[58]

Ultimately, the mental, psychological, and ideological landmines[59] laid at the time (in the name of Islam) would prove even more explosive than the billions spent on ammunition. In connection with Operation Cyclone, the role played by academia and charity in promoting these perilous agendas is also noteworthy. For example, the USAID (a US federal agency that administers over half of all U.S. foreign assistance and promotes "peace" as its mission[60]) provided over $50 million to the University of Nebraska-Omaha, which produced textbooks in the Dari and Pashto languages.[61] These books were then used to educate Afghan children and adults.[62] In a 2016 article titled *Both Arsonists and Firefighters*, the *New York Times* elaborated the nature of the USAID-dispensed "education" in Afghanistan during that time:

> In fact, the United States spent $50 million from 1986 to 1992 on what was called a 'jihad literacy' project—printing books for Afghan children and adults to encourage violence against non-Muslim 'infidels' like Soviet troops. A first-grade language textbook for Pashto speakers ... used 'Mujahid,' or fighter of jihad, as the illustration: 'My brother is a Mujahid. Afghan Muslims are Mujahedeen. I do jihad together with them. Doing jihad against infidels is our duty.'[63]

Now, these people are known as Jihadists!

Extremist Ideologies Hijacking Religion

The reality of the abduction of religion by ideological extremisms was captured by Eqbal Ahmad, a globally renowned political scientist. In evaluating the motives of modern Islamic zealots, he clarified that they "are concerned with power, not with the soul; with the mobilization of people for political purposes rather than with sharing and alleviating their sufferings and aspirations. Theirs is a very limited and time-bound political agenda."[64]

Incidentally, Ahmad is pointing to the raison d'être of religious extremism in general, not just its Islamic variety. Echoing a similar sentiment, David Shulman of the Hebrew University highlights: "As has been the case throughout Jewish history, humane voices such as Hillel's are today at war with sanctimonious, atavistic ones such as those that now dominate the public sphere in Israel. But ... 'the fight isn't over.'"[65]

Our myriad identities are brought into the middle of all kinds of confrontations and political games. Our religious identity will almost always be one of them, and we should be well aware of that. When we know the agendas in play, we will have the capacity to not allow our religions to be bartered in the marketplace of money and power.

Many religions are facing their own crises of extremism today Given the human tendency to stay in denial, however, most followers of these religions also may not see or understand the signs and parameters of such phenomena. Greatly contributing to our obliviousness is a concept known in the field of psychology as "attribution bias" in which, cognitively, we humans tend to attribute different reasons to ourselves than we would to others—for the same action. What Rabbi Heschel said decades ago is still valid: "The religions of the world are ... no more isolated than individuals or nations. Energies, experiences, and ideas that come to life [for one] ... continue to challenge and to affect every religion. Horizons are wider, dangers are greater. No religion is an island."[66]

Whether the extremisms are promoted in the name of Buddhism, Christianity, Hinduism, Islam, Judaism—or an entirely other belief system (democracy, freedom, human rights, free market, technology, values)—we have to be able to see them through the shrouds within which they are packaged. That's important because these extremisms pose a threat to the common human civilization, heritage, and well-being. And the route to this eventuality goes through serious spiritual as well as intellectual depravation.

The Evil Promoted by the Hobbesian Mindset

There is no denying that we live in a world that is highly adversarial—perhaps much more so than ever before on most dimensions. Even the system of nation-states[67] as well as the legal systems worldwide seem to have been built upon that very assumption of the fundamentally adversarial nature of human relationships. By marginalizing the role of culture, the current politico-economic institutional system also weakens the concept of society in our lives. The collective and individual patterns of thought and behavior seem to have evolved in recent history to follow the guidelines of Thomas Hobbes, the influential Enlightenment philosopher.[68] The assertion of Hobbes's outlook on human nature is unambiguous: "There Is Alwayes Warre Of Every One Against Every

One .... So the nature of War, consisteth not in actuall fighting; but in the known disposition thereto ..."[69]

Because this Hobbesian human disposition is expected to be the norm, ideas and systems must effectively function within a very narrow set of objectives. And this applies to the current geopolitical scenario. As the discipline of anthropology tells us, "there is no actual reason to assume that war has always existed. Technically, war refers not just to organized violence but to a kind of contest between two clearly demarcated sides."[70]

In that sense, the Cold War itself can be looked at as essentially a military conflict between the "religions" of capitalism and communism. The tussle between these two ideologies, each with exclusive claims over how to organize a society and its politico-economic structures, came at a very large cost to the human race (as evidenced by the conflicts in the second half of the twentieth century. Even the "local" price for the principal contestants can be tantamount to a weakening of the moral compass, as pointed out by the eighteenth-century writer Samuel Johnson: "Among the calamities of war may be justly numbered the diminution of the love of truth, by the falsehoods which interest dictates, and credulity encourages."[71]

An ideology such as nationalism plays a similar role in damaging human well-being. Since the global entrenchment of the nation-state concept, this prejudice seems to have taken over all others. Almost a century ago, just before the onset of WWII, it is this exploitation of human passion that forced writer Aldous Huxley to wail: "All that we can be sure of is that nationalistic feeling was never so acutely inflamed as it is today and the expenditure on armament never higher."[72]

Nationalistic ideology as currently promoted identifies a person with a nation-state. It further places that state beyond right and wrong, good and bad—advocating that the specific state's interests have primacy over all other considerations. It then demands blind loyalty, and attachment to such objectives, from all those upon whom it affixes the identity label. Much else—including fact, reason, truth, independent thought, and even moral consideration—is to be suspended, or subordinated to the nationalist ideology.

The ideology itself thus assumes the status of the prime and incontrovertible truth, effectively making the state a sacred object of devotion and worship. In George Orwell's elaboration of the phenomenon in *1984*: "Whatever the Party holds to be truth is truth. It is impossible to see reality except by looking through the eyes of the Party.... It needs an act of self-destruction, an effort of the will."[73]

Aldous Huxley also clarified that nationalism elevates "the ugly reality of prejudice and passion to the rank of an ideal."[74] Such "vicarious triumph in the religion of nationalism"[75] all over the world poses serious perils to the human race. It provides all the disadvantages of the traditional religion, and absolutely none of the advantages. And it tends to be combined with the traditional religion to yield a potent tool for political exploitation and control. For a democracy, the bipartisan prevalence of nationalism in the United States is rather daunting and is used quite effectively to steer the trusting public.

With powerful ideological and economic forces continuously jockeying for dominance, both the collective and the individual thus become the losers. In societies constantly at war with this or that enemy, would information and truth get weaponized? With intense power play among so many politico-economic contestants, is it even reasonable to expect information integrity within the political system? In his famous essay ("An outline of Intellectual Rubbish") Bertrand Russell made a pointed observation: "There is no nonsense so arrant that it cannot be made the creed of the vast majority by adequate governmental action."[76]

Despite all the misgivings in various quarters, the political system in the United States is still considered a democracy in much of the world. Yet there are no guarantees the image or the reality would remain what it is today. Dr. King's provident observation a generation ago is still presciently valid: "if American democracy gradually disintegrates, it will be due as much to a lack of insight as to the lack of commitment to right."[77] Thus, the predicament staring us in the face demands insight, not just intelligence; conscience, not just conception; resolve, not just resource; wisdom, not just wit; and courage, not just comprehension.

In the societal context, a dream becomes potentially fulfillable only when we realize and accept that it will always be unfulfillable. Complacency in preserving democracy, for example, does not just risk deteriorating the institution; it could destroy it. The downward slide may have become more apparent in the recent past, yet it can only be looked upon as the accumulation of various changes in the past. *Democracy in America*, written almost two centuries ago by Alexis de Tocqueville, is still considered a seminal treatise on the political system of the United States. Tocqueville's observations are rather astute for having been made almost two hundred years ago.[78] More importantly, they may be equally valid today.

> I had remarked during my stay in the United States, that a democratic state of society, similar to that of the Americans, might offer singular facilities for the establishment of despotism.... A more accurate examination of the subject, and five years of further meditation, have not diminished my fears.... If despotism were to be established amongst the democratic nations of our days, it might assume a different character; it would be more extensive and milder; it would degrade men without tormenting them.[79]

A clear understanding of the detrimental impact of the Hobbesian mindset on our individual and collective well-being makes us less vulnerable to manipulation, thus augmenting freedom in our thought and action. It is time the ordinary citizen took notice.

Unrecognized Civilizational Impact

A few decades ago, terrorism was not an everyday word. Today it is. When growing up as a child in Pakistan some half a century ago, I wouldn't have been able to identify known terrorists (even though I was a relatively well-informed child). Today, a lot of children in the United States would be able to point to "domestic terrorists"—

terrorists within us—let alone those of the international variety. (In the recent past, most Americans were successfully convinced that "terrorism" is limited only to Arabs or Muslims. That spell is breaking at a rapid speed.) Yet, we don't seem to ponder, or even realize, the significance of how these concepts are evolving within a lifetime. Similarly, other consequential phenomena pass us by without much notice. The handful of people who observe such a progression usually get ignored, even when they are heard.

Being continually in an environment of conflict and manipulated information can clearly have a highly disconcerting impact on a society—whether based on religious or national identity. And such impact could include a negative influence on a society's cognitive abilities. We can find highly astute people who have pointed to such developments in both the American as well as the Muslim societies (here, one is a national society, the other a religious one at the global level).

Shahab Ahmed,[80] who taught at Harvard University, was arguably the most insightful modern-era scholar in the field of Islamic Studies. He had succinctly captured the latent civilizational developments within the Islamic world by highlighting the "*radical diminution*" in various intellectual domains within the "*societies of modern Muslims.*"[81] One of the drivers as Ahmed judged was that the intellectual and spiritual environment has been effectively choked:

> It would appear that the public sphere in modern societies of Muslims has, on the whole, emerged as an intimidating and censorious space where speech-acts that contradict or challenge monovalent prescriptive norms are more likely to be persecuted by the public or prosecuted by the state for blasphemy than to be received with equanimity and explorative interest.[82]

Neil Postman chaired the Department of Culture and Communication at NYU. Referring to the reductionism and disconnections created by how the media deliver the message, Postman wrote the following in the mid-80s:

> Americans are the best entertained and quite likely the least well-informed people in the Western world… I am saying something far more serious than that we are being deprived of authentic information. I am saying we are losing our sense of what it means to be well informed. Ignorance is always correctable. But what shall we do if we take ignorance to be knowledge?[83]

Postman's picture of the information landscape begins to emerge when we ponder his definition: "Disinformation does not mean false information. It means misleading information—misplaced, irrelevant, fragmented, or superficial information—information that creates the illusion of knowing something but which in fact leads one away from knowing."[84]

When the careful layers of courtesy in the words by the two scholars are peeled away, it is easy to see that the concern being expressed by both Ahmed and Postman is that of an unusual dumbing-down process in the American as well as the Islamic societies. And it would not be so difficult to understand the dynamics.

To begin with, such cognitive decline would be an inescapable result in any social system where some inherent superiority or exceptionalism is promoted. It is also an essential side effect in any society where some external or internal "enemy" seems to be lurking, creating an ever-present menace. The presence, or creation, of enemies results in the atmosphere of fear and conflict (military or otherwise). However real or imaginary the "enemy" may be, this atmosphere of being under siege (even when self-created) becomes debilitating—physically, emotionally, psychologically, spiritually, as well as intellectually.

What's important to realize is that the creation of this debilitating atmosphere is usually an internal phenomenon within a society, not an external one. The unwillingness to face that internal reality reduces a society's capacity to find equitable and moral solutions—further perpetuating the Hobbesian war. To paraphrase preeminent twentieth-century historian Arnold Toynbee, empires and civilizations fail not due to some external physical threats but rather the inability to deal with internal moral dilemmas.[85]

Can any civilization that, collectively, is on a downward slope on so many dimensions (e.g., emotional, spiritual, and intellectual) expect to enjoy a meaningful democracy—or even freedom? My writing this book expresses my hope that both Americans and Muslims would especially pay attention to such questions.

CHAPTER 2:
COUNTERING GEOPOLITICAL TERRORISM

Those who have great realization about delusion are buddhas.
Those who are greatly deluded within realization
are sentient beings.[86]
—Dogen Zenji, *Shobogenzo Genjokoan*

No fork is to be found in the road to gnosis,
the path leading to bliss also goes to the abyss.[87]
—Dr. Mahboob Alam Khan

At a gathering in the United States several years ago, I came across a professor who taught Middle Eastern studies. The discussion soon came to the goings-on in Iran, especially the influence of the theocracy there. To clarify a point, I gave the example of the 1953 overthrow of Mohammad Mosaddegh, the elected Iranian prime minister (Operation Ajax,[88] a plot involving the governments of the United States and the United Kingdom). He looked at me and said, "We don't have to bring in conspiracy theories."[89] I was taken aback. Since before I was a teenager in Pakistan, I had been aware of the conspiracy (which is different from a "conspiracy theory") by the two governments in overthrowing Iran's democratically elected government and the installation of the shah.

Remarkably, helping the CIA and the MI6 in this 1953 coup was Ayatollah Kashani—one of whose disciples was the young Ruhollah Khomeini, the supreme leader of the 1979 "Islamic" revolution in Iran. Declassified British government documents show that both the British and the US governments had even considered installing Ayatollah Kashani as their puppet leader of Iran after the coup.[90] Even concepts such as "blowback" cannot do justice to how just one event or decision can alter the course of history. As Mark Curtis, a British analyst of international affairs, opines: "The British public has been deprived of key information to understand the roots of current terrorism and the role that government institutions, who pose only as our protectors, have played in endangering us."[91]

There is nothing exceptional about the British public in this regard. Curtis's observation, in general, applies to all nationalities; the nation-state system is structured to function that way.

Whether or not one classifies Operation Ajax as terrorism, it is still an example that shows how the commonly unknown information keeps us from understanding such phenomena. On the other hand, if two Asian governments conspired and orchestrated a violent coup d'état in North America or Western Europe, would it be called terrorism?

How could an experienced professor who taught subjects related to Middle Eastern affairs pretend that he was not aware of Operation Ajax, dismissing it as conspiracy theory? Obviously, one can locate a myriad of reasons that would lead one into such a denial of an evident and well-documented historical reality, not to mention the very complex scenarios of the consequences for a society. Here, let's just assess five simple implications.

First, if there is a sizable number of faculty members who have this mindset and attitude, the knowledge and attitudes of the droves of students who go through such an "education" is easy to foretell. Second, could such an education process be called indoctrination? Propaganda? Conditioning? Third, what if a lot of policymakers and public intellectuals also follow similar thought patterns? Fourth, it gives us a remarkable glimpse into how policies are made and how the public is kept "informed" by our politico-economic machinery.

And, finally, could the use of violent activity to overthrow a democratically elected government be classified as terrorism?[92]

Defining Terrorism

The Turkish government and the PKK (Kurdistan Workers' Party) call each other terrorist. How can we know who is correct? Could they both be?

Defining a phenomenon that is controversial—and useful fodder for political opportunism—can be tricky business. All kinds of vested interests come into play. That there is no universal agreement on defining the meaning of a crime so significant in national and international politics shows the utility in keeping the vagueness alive. Some "experts" would brush this off by claiming that terrorism is so complex as to preclude a universal definition. I have even seen arguments bordering on the so-called logic that you know it is terrorism when you see it, or that terrorism is like beauty, residing in the eyes of the beholder.

Such "logic" simply does not add up. How can we have such a loaded concept that is universally projected to be so heinous as to be more serious than anything else in its moral turpitude—and yet have no inkling of how to place a definition for it? Would we accept a similar logic to say that "murder" is not definable? How can we convict someone of murder if we cannot define what murder is? Maybe the need to keep the concept of terrorism nebulous and subjective serves a political purpose for many players.

So then, the human world is waging a war against something we cannot even identify—effectively a war against an abstract phenomenon, a phantom? As the US House of Representatives Permanent Select Committee on Intelligence discovered in the early 2000s, "practically every agency in the United States government with a counterterrorism mission uses a different definition of terrorism."[93]

This section does not come up with a firm definition, though it does attempt to provide a solid framework of understanding for the benefit of the reader. It also highlights how the term "terrorism" is subjectively used to aim at whatever it is the state finds useful to make a target of, regardless of how many laws already exist to deal with those crimes. (State, in political language, denotes the governmental system.) Using the "terrorism" label affords wide leeway to states in skirting due process, constitutional rights, and even human rights. (In the United States, the Guantanamo prison camp provides an example. Going back a few decades, the FBI's actions against the Black Panthers would be another good example.)

The following subsections provide some classifications of how the non-definition of terrorism opens the door for abuses that are intended to remain obscure.

1. Subjectively Targeting Individuals & Groups: Broadly or Specifically

The benefits of keeping the concept of terrorism as a nebulous and malleable phenomenon become clear when we evaluate how different countries and authorities create laws around the crime.[94]

SAMPLING OF TERRORISM-RELATED LEGAL CODES

Arab Convention for the Suppression of Terrorism: "Any act or threat of violence, whatever its motives or purposes, that occurs in the advancement of an individual or collective criminal agenda ..."[95]

Turkey (Article 1, Anti-Terror Law 3713): "[A] ny kind of act done by one or more persons belonging to an organization with the aim of ... eliminating fundamental rights and freedoms, or damaging ... public order or general health by means of pressure."[96]

United States (US Code Title 22, Chapter 38, § 2656f): "[T]he term 'terrorism' means premeditated, politically motivated violence perpetrated against noncombatant targets by subnational groups or clandestine agents."[97]

Pakistan: A terrorist is one who, amongst other things, "commits an act of civil commotion as specified in section 7A."[98]

Kingdom of Saudi Arabia: Article 1: "Calling for atheist thought in any form, or calling into question the fundamentals of the Islamic religion on which this country is based."[99]

Article 2: "Anyone who throws away their loyalty to the country's rulers, or who swears allegiance to any party, organization, current [of thought], group, or individual inside or outside [the kingdom]."[100]

Insert 2:1

Here, one can see how these laws subjectively define the crime of terrorism, creating a broad net so as to arbitrarily target individuals and groups as the state chooses. The question of the government itself being a threat to rights and freedoms is completely skirted, even though it is the state that often poses the real threat to such freedoms. (The excerpted pieces from Turkey and KSA provide the most instructive examples.) As this section amply demonstrates, the concept of terrorism has just become an opportunistic football in the hands of states—virtually all of them. And they are only happy to be playing it to the hilt for their own narrow purposes.

2. The Irony of Computer Crime as Terrorism

The 2016 French *Code Pénal* (Article 421-1), in the very beginning of the law, includes "infractions on computerized information" (*les infractions en matière informatique*)[101] in its definition of terrorism.

The United Kingdom's Terrorism Act 2000 similarly begins by defining terrorism as "the use or threat of action" that, among others, "is designed seriously to interfere with or seriously to disrupt an electronic system."[102]

UK's law clearly says that "action" includes "action outside the United Kingdom." We have to realize the irony here. States (governments) are the cardinal perpetrators of clandestine computer crime across the world. A lot of such activity goes on all the time to intrude, disrupt, and sabotage computer systems of other states. In the United States, for example, it is commonly believed (especially among Democrats) that some Russian players influenced the 2016 presidential elections. Some even name Putin's direct involvement in this scenario.

Even close allies are not spared in this business. The leaks of the National Security Agency documents by Edward Snowden, for example, indicated that the US government had been eavesdropping on the mobile phone of Angela Merkel, the German chancellor. Using the French and British definitions, that certainly sounds like terrorism.

Then there was Stuxnet, a malicious computer worm, widely believed to have been developed by the US and Israeli governments to disrupt Iranian nuclear facilities. This program, codenamed Operation Olympic Games,[103] was developed during the era of President George W. Bush. As the *New York Times* reports, however, it was launched on the orders of President Obama.[104] Stuxnet caused immense havoc all over the world to all kinds of computer systems. The *Times of Israel* quoted the head of Kaspersky Lab[105] in reporting that Stuxnet had infected a Russian nuclear plant before spreading to the International Space Station.[106]

There is nothing Olympian about Stuxnet, and it certainly was no game. It was clearly cyberwarfare of the worst kind (involving nuclear facilities). According to UK and French law at least, Stuxnet was also a clear and undeniable instance of international terrorism.

Did the governments of the United Kingdom or France formally announce the extent of the mayhem Stuxnet caused within those countries? Did they do anything to deal with this act of international terrorism that violated their own laws so clearly (in addition to causing damage to their own computer facilities)? Did their investigation confirm that the governments of the United States and Israel were the instigators of this menacing attack on the world's computer systems? Was any effort made to seek accountability from the perpetrators? Would the United Kingdom and France have dealt with the situation the same way if this devastating computer worm had been unleashed on the world by Russia and Iran, or by China and North Korea? Why or why not?

3. Is It Really Impossible to Come Up with a Universal Definition?

Not at all, at least not conceptually or linguistically. The difficulty is largely a diplomatic one because the very concept of terrorism is bound up in the exercise of power by the entities that wield it. Even if the world ever has a consensus on the definition, it will be one that is highly favorable to the prevailing political, military, and economic powers of the time. In the meantime, the reader may use the following two authentic guidelines to create one's own framework of this complex concept.

The Encyclopedia Britannica presents a concise but meaningful definition: "Terrorism, the calculated use of violence to create a general climate of fear in a population and thereby to bring about a particular political objective."[107]

In 1985, the Office of the Joint Chiefs of Staff of the United States adopted the following definition of Low Intensity Conflict ("LIC"):

> A limited politico-military struggle to achieve political, social, economic, or psychological objectives. It is often protracted and ranges from diplomatic, economic, or psychosocial pressures through terrorism and insurgency. Low intensity conflict is generally confined to a geographic area and is often characterized by constraints on the weaponry, tactics, and the level of violence.[108]

In the above iteration, the word "terrorism" is used almost casually. Yet, it is clear that the description of LIC in the full paragraph covers the various components of terrorism. This seems to be an attempt to create two separate buckets: one for violence of a certain kind perpetrated by non-state militants and the other for the same activity committed by or on behalf of the military. We, therefore, have to analyze the whole definition (of LIC) as a tool to provide us a solid framework in defining terrorism. What is called LIC in military parlance thus may itself be the same thing as terrorism.

Violence begets violence and is not its own cure. Modern-day states celebrate the success of their violence in one guise or another. Yet, no genuine problems can be solved by labeling others with the word "terrorist" when the universal definition of the word has been unachievable—for the selfish reasons of governments, who would have to agree on such a definition. If a consensus is reached on a definition, one would hope that it would hold states culpable for the terrorism (and unconstitutional or illegal violence, mayhem, etc.) they are responsible for. Until then, it is perhaps best not to be swayed by the subjective and mostly manipulative use of the word.

Beyond Terrorism as We Know It

The term "terrorisme" was coined in France at the time of the French Revolution. It signified a sense of government intimidation of people. For reasons that serve the state and other political interests, the denotation of the expression has been turned on its head. Currently, the "terrorism" label is reserved almost exclusively for non-state actors who engage in a certain type of violence (as well as those governments that are on the "wrong" side of the desired track). Such meaning and usage of the term, while dubious, provides highly useful discretionary tools to governments who can now label any undesirable element as "terroristic" and can craft special laws for such elements. Maybe that's why no universal consensus has been achieved in defining the term.

This approach (to a subjective definition of terrorism) also extends an open license for exploitation in different ways all over the world. And such a license is readily leveraged, especially by those in power. There is the situation where Richard Perle, an influential political intellectual and a Pentagon official, accused Seymour Hersh, the Pulitzer-winning legendary journalist, of being "a terrorist."[109] Hersh's crime? Writing an exposé for the *New Yorker* magazine in which he "accused Perle of inappropriately mixing business and public office in dealings with Saudi Arabia."[110] *The Independent*, a British paper, goes on to point out that, after much denial of wrongdoing, Perle's situation became untenable, and he suddenly resigned his official post as chairman of the Pentagon's Defense Policy Board (DPB). Such blatantly false use of the word "terrorist," however, was not invented by Perle and would not end with his resignation.

In the geopolitical arena, all kinds of players are involved in the sponsorship or direct execution of what would be objectively classified as "terroristic" activity. This includes governments all over the world. Operation Satanique,[111] the 1985 sinking of the *Rainbow Warrior*, a Greenpeace ship, by the French government is a good example of state-executed terrorism that gets hushed up within the geopolitical system. There is strong evidence that the authorization for this act of terrorism came from Francois Mitterand, the French president at the time. Mitterand was said to have personally authorized the operation[112] by Pierre Lacoste, the head of the French DGSE[113] spy agency, who was involved in the plan's execution. Yet, this global scandal was swiftly swept under the rug. Operation Northwoods[114] would be another interesting example. How many Americans are aware that, in the 1960s, the chairman of the Joint Chiefs of Staff sought JFK's approval to execute this operation?

Regarding Operation Satanique, we have to keep in mind that it is just one example of terrorism by one government.[115] Besides, the disclosure of its terrorism did not seem to shake the conscience of the French government. Colonel Jean-Claude Lesquer, the "brain" behind the operation at DGSE headquarters in Paris, was promoted to major-general and commanded the Daguet division in the 1991 Gulf War. And in 1995 he was given the honorific title of "grand officier de la Légion d'honneur."[116]

Who should the "terrorist" label be applied to in the Operation Satanique situation? Given the loss of human life involved in this instance, would it be fair to use the word "murderer" to describe everyone involved? What percentage of the French people would be fully informed about this instance of terrorism committed by their government? What percentage would entertain the possibility that this may not be the only instance of terrorism their government has engaged in, presumably on their behalf? Some would surely defend President Mitterand or his government for having authorized the operation. Would the same people accept similar apologetics or excuse-making by supporters of non-French state-sponsored terrorism?

When the source and implementor of the legal system has to resort to terrorism despite all the laws available to it, it becomes reasonable for those without such power to argue that terrorism is justified. The way the human psyche works can sometimes be rather strange. (This can be understood using the concept of attribution bias, see chapter 1, section "Extremist Ideologies Hijacking Religion.")

Another example is much more intricate in terms of the allocation of responsibility. As mentioned in chapter 1, the United States supplied the Stinger ground-to-air missiles to the Afghan guerillas in the mid-80s. The SAS (the British equivalent of the US Delta Force) is believed to have been directly involved in training the guerillas in using these missiles,[117] which were used not just against the Soviet forces, and not just against military targets. "These missiles were used by the mujahideen to shoot down several passenger aircraft, with heavy loss of life."[118]

Would the use of Stingers to shoot down passenger airplanes be considered terrorism or a war crime? Should the two sponsoring governments share the responsibility for such activity? (A latter section, "Multi-dimensionality of the Sources of Extremism ...," further highlights this aspect of the terrorism phenomenon.)

Understanding the Geopolitical Roots of Religious Extremism

The prevalent image in many parts of the world today is that extremism is limited to Islam. This viewpoint, especially its systematic propagation in Europe, North America, South Asia, and the Middle East, creates dangerous complacency in terms of solving related problems and ignoring extremism in other religions and ideologies in these and other regions—not to mention the denial of the geopolitical drivers of such extremism.

The acceptance of the outcomes and unintended consequences of geopolitical power play become unsettling when we try to delve into the complexity and interconnectedness of global affairs. The human tendency, especially in the modern political environment, is to become attached to identities.[119] Institutional conditioning through the promotion of human doctrines as unquestionable truth is the basis of such attachment. Misinformation and misleading perceptions can then be selectively used to advance hidden agendas. The marriage of identity with the current socio-political system creates an impossible task of separating the actual drivers of extremism from the opportunistic projections that serve the schemes on one side or the other.

The truth and reality of global affairs is often discomfiting, becoming subversive when sincerely pursued. The subversion being referred to here is against the mental icons one has created for one's own comfort, the false images that assure us that the problem is always and completely with the "other." As history tells us, a blind belief in such assumptions makes us vulnerable to easy deception in a climate of misinformation. What is needed is the drive to overcome the identity-based conditioning that keeps us from identifying or acting upon the truth.

When we examine these "icons" in the religious context, it is common to hear people allocate certain attributes to particular religions. Since 9/11 especially, Muslims and their allies have promoted Islam as a "religion of peace," whereas anti-Muslims and some others have referred to it as a "violent religion." It would seem that those promoting such classifications, if not driven by political agendas or sheer malice, may not be adequately informed about the history of war and other human pursuits for power and profit.

Thus, perhaps the very attribution of "peaceful" or "warlike' to what we call religion is a misguided idea—and that arose from our knowledge of the medieval-era Crusades. The Northern Ireland conflict provides another good example. Despite the persistent use of terms such as "Catholic" and "Protestant," the underlying issues were not primarily about religious disagreements but other socio-politico-economic concerns.

This is not to say that we should deny the noticeable religious component of such events; that would be a gross mistake. The need is to change our reflex thought-habits of affixing the "religion" label to things with more complicated roots and sources. Thus, it would be wrong to call the crusades as wars between "Christianity" and "Islam." It would be more effective to understand these conflicts as contests for power and territorial aggrandizement between or among empires (controlled by Europeans and Muslims). In a political context especially, the word "religion" is an abstraction that is edified into a monolith. The practice is effective for slogans but not for comprehension.

Religion's presence, however, in these human problems cannot be denied. It would be difficult to find a religion today in which some adherents and even clergy are not involved in activities gravely violating its fundamental teachings and then justifying such violations using religious reasoning.

These nuances need to be kept in mind to fully comprehend the role of religion in relation to other politico-economic factors in the prevalent geopolitical reality.

The Multi-dimensionality of the Sources of Extremism and Terrorism

Extremism and terrorism are not produced exclusively in the minds of fanatical religious militants. The picture is more convoluted. It is this complexity that has to be addressed to solve the "terrorism" problem. For that, we'd have to begin by questioning the existing mental models of individuals and groups. Such mindsets may be related to various areas: politics, economics, sociology, and science, as well as religion. When a society enlarges the space within which pre-conceptions can be questioned, it has also enlarged the space within which problems and solutions can be meaningfully understood. Everyone has a contribution to make in that regard.

In that context, the ability and willingness to look at things from multiple lenses yields a more meaningful education. If we examine the phenomenon of terrorism using various lenses, we may obtain a fuller grasp on the subject. It is important to realize that to understand something is not to condone it but to comprehend the variables that drive it. The examples in this section serve to clarify points, not to prove or disprove any specific instance. That's why the elaborations are somewhat simple and succinct, not conclusive and comprehensive.

Not all scenarios fall exclusively in one classification or the other as defined below. It is common for various instances or movements to fall into multiple categories. Examples highlight the variety and complexity of what we are dealing with.

1. "Freedom" Fighters

President Ronald Reagan had famously created a moral equivalency between the founding fathers of the United States and the initial Afghan freedom fighters[120] who were precursors to Taliban and al-Qaeda. "Freedom fighters," when they turned their guns on the Soviet Union, were not just lionized—they were actively supported and funded. They only became "terrorists" when they turned against the United States. Reagan had also made a similar comparison on behalf of the Nicaraguan Contra rebels. The Iran-Contra hearings, however, created a major "memory malfunction" for a lot of witnesses—including Reagan—showing the precariousness and fragility of such opportunistic euphemisms.

QUIZ: TERRORIST OR NOBEL LAUREATE

One of the following four heads of government received the Nobel Peace Prize. Two of these four were officially, at one time, considered terrorists by authorities / governments.

1. Yasser Arafat
2. Menachem Begin
3. Nelson Mandela
4. Yitzhak Shamir

(Answers available at Endnote #: [121])

Insert 2:2

The place of genuine resistance simply cannot be brushed aside, even if laws are created to criminalize it. The resistance by the ANC in South Africa is a good example. The role played by the clandestine National Council of the Resistance (*Conseil National de la Résistance*) in France to defy the Nazi occupation (and the Vichy regime) also seems clear. We have to be cognizant, though, that what's perceived to be so clear comes from the context within which history is now understood. The challenge will always be to make such judgments, of current or past phenomena, when such context of right and wrong is twisted within the narratives of geopolitical conflicts and tussles for power. Therein lies an immense difficulty.

It is also important to realize that those labeled terrorists often don't view themselves as such. They believe they are fighting for a cause. Putting right and wrong aside, at least for the moment so as to understand this subject, such people may perceive that they are undoing an injustice—even if that antidote comes in the form of targeted or random violence. Others, especially the victims of such violence, have a viewpoint that is quite the opposite. Agents who work for a government and engage in terroristic activity or other violence (Operation Satanique, for example) on behalf of it usually believe they are serving their nation. That is precisely the reason those engaged in terrorist activity are able to garner support from a certain percentage of those for whom they perceive themselves to be fighting.

2. Sponsorship: International & Domestic

The image that terrorist groups simply spring out of nowhere is simplistic and, often enough, patently wrong. Frequently, it turns out, such entities have powerful and wealthy benefactors (usually states) whose interests they serve.[122] Such groups, when they have gained power and resources of their own, may however spin out of the control of their initial sponsors.

All kinds of unsavory extremist elements were trained and supported in the conduct of Operation Cyclone. Casper Weinberger[123] was the secretary of defense in President Reagan's administration. In a 1994 interview, Weinberger said, "We knew we were involved with Islamic fundamentalists. We knew they were not very nice people, that they were not attached to democracy. But we had this terrible problem of making choices."[124] Al-Qaeda came into being to frustrate the Soviet Union's presence in Afghanistan. In their infancy, al-Qaeda and other such groups were nursed by support from, among others, the governments of Saudi Arabia, Pakistan, the United Kingdom, and the United States.[125] Even with its origins in the Wahhabi-Saudi religiopolitical ideology, al-Qaeda ultimately turned against the Saudi establishment as well as against the United States and Pakistan.

The case of the Taliban, which began as a small group of religious students, is equally curious. Pakistani military intelligence agency supposedly exerted significant operational influence on the organization. After gaining power and control in Afghanistan in the mid-1990s, however, the Taliban functioned relatively independently; yet they remained the operatives of choice for the Pakistani government. There is a further twist to this picture as clarified by Adam Thomson, the British Foreign Office's director of South Asia and Afghanistan. Thomson informed a parliamentary inquiry that "historically—at our behest, in part—the ISI [Pakistan's intelligence agency] developed relations with Islamic groups [in Afghanistan]."[126]

It is also commonly known internationally that Hamas, in its initial stage, was fully supported by Israel as a counter to the Palestine Liberation Organization's Fatah; the *Wall Street Journal* quoted Avner Cohen, a former Israeli official: "Hamas, to my great regret, is Israel's creation."[127] Cohen should know; he worked in Gaza for two decades and, until 1994, was responsible for religious affairs in the region. Israel's government, blaming others, now acts as if the existence of Hamas is a complete surprise—there is no acknowledgment or acceptance of who effectively created the bête noire.

The place of covert operations by governmental elements is also important to understand. The governments of India and Pakistan, for example, blame each other for all kinds of violent activities that take place in those countries. While we, the ordinary people, can never be sure who is behind what activity, we can be fairly certain that governments are involved in such instances. Sometimes, governments may even internally initiate such violence for their own purpose—blaming another state to intensify a brewing conflict or to get a tactical advantage over the adversary. Operation Northwoods (mentioned earlier) provides such an example in the United States. Another important point is that different agencies within the same government often have differing agendas, and such an operation may be sponsored by one department against the interests (or desires) of another.

In today's world, the rules are the same whether the state is capitalistic or communistic. According to journalist Masha Gessen, the 1999 "apartment-building bombings in Moscow and elsewhere were organized and carried out by the FSB, the [Russian] intelligence agency, in order to shore up Putin's power grab."[128]

And, in a 2018 piece in the *London Review of Books*, Francis Wade provides an instructive example of the genocidal terrorism against the Rohingya Muslim minority by various elements—Buddhist religious establishment, political establishment, military, police, etc.—within the Myanmar (Burmese) society. An October 2016 editorial in the *New Light of Myanmar*, a state paper under the control of the Information Ministry, used the following to describe the Rohingya: "... fleas that we greatly loathe for their stench and for sucking our blood."[129]

Such brainwashing can turn an otherwise decent human being into a monster. Aung San Suu Kyi was the country's leader at that time. Instead of the Nobel Peace Prize she possesses, a trial for crimes against humanity might have been more appropriate. The world, alas, works differently!

3. False-Flag (and Other Covert) Operations

Terroristic operations are sometimes created to implicate an opponent or a party to be discredited. That is why it is always a good idea to ask the quintessential "*Cui bono*?" question. When we can see who benefits from a certain instance of terrorism or violence, we are in a better position to estimate the source and further developments. Yet, this aspect can be only one component of various factors to be evaluated. For an event to yield a favorable outcome for someone does not, on its own, mean they are responsible for it.

The Second World War's initiation was justified entirely by the use of false flag operations (known as Operation Himmler or Operation Konserve). The Reichstag fire of 1933 provides another good example. Even though a young man, Marinus van der Lubbe, was found and arrested inside the building, the Nazis immediately declared the fire to be a Communist conspiracy. Mass arrests began and an emergency decree suspended civil rights. Within weeks, Hitler would have absolute legislative power. The Communists were acquitted at the trial, though van der Lubbe was promptly executed upon conviction. It is now commonly believed that the Nazis themselves may have been involved in the fire. While there may be no certain way of knowing the truth, it is clear that Hitler and his party used this instance to greatly consolidate power within a short time. The possibility, therefore, cannot be dismissed. The 1964 Gulf of Tonkin incident is another example of how an attack by the enemy can be "manufactured" to be leveraged for political purposes, even, as here, in escalating a war.[130]

On the domestic front in various countries, law enforcement is known to have used provocateurs to cause or initiate wanton violence, looting, rioting, etc. (When it comes to violence, it takes a minor spark to start a major conflagration.) This is a highly effective technique to discredit a group in the public's eyes. Various other techniques are used by governments to sabotage and undermine "undesirable" groups or movements. In the United States, the history of the FBI's COINTELPRO is a good example.[131]

The relationship between propaganda and false-flag operations is critical. Aldous Huxley deemed propaganda to be "largely at the mercy of circumstances."[132] Emerging circumstances, thus, are to be fully exploited. And, where necessary, exploitable circumstances must be made to emerge.[133]

4. Globalization of "Islamic" Terrorism: Understanding Kosovo[134]

The violent movement begun in Afghanistan in the 1980s (chapter 1) became portable and transcendent in the 1990s. The focus of the Great Game,[135] begun in the nineteenth century, had now shifted to Central Asia and the Balkans. In addition to weakening Moscow's influence in the former Soviet-influenced regions, the oil and gas reserves in the Caspian Basin also provided strong reasons. Extremist groups from far off with experience in Afghanistan were deployed. (Harkat ul-Ansar from Pakistan is an example.) Now we'll turn to the activities in Kosovo.

Tito's death and the disintegration of the Soviet Union led to the break-up of the Yugoslav republic. After the Dayton Accords in the mid-90s, the locus of action and attention in the Balkans shifted from Bosnia to Kosovo where the rebel force was known as the Kosovo Liberation Army (KLA), which "took on the role of Western proxies, carrying out some of the dirty work that NATO could not."[136]

Al-Qaeda's involvement in the wars in Bosnia and Kosovo is well known. Bin Laden himself is reported to have visited Bosnia and Albania several times during the 90s.[137] In addition to likely involvement in heroin smuggling and other links to organized crime, KLA's operations and finances were quite integrated with foreign allies. Regional players aside, this conflict attracted the involvement of global forces. Significant armament, funding, and training came from Saudi Arabia, the United Arab Emirates, Turkey, Pakistan, Iran, the United Kingdom, and the United States.

In June 1993, Saudi Arabia funded the building of a Bosnian base for guerillas to be sent into Kosovo, although the Serbia-Kosovo conflict did not begin until 1998. This leads to the conclusion that "the Islamist penetration of Kosovo and Albania had long been planned."[138] The coordination at high levels is revelatory. For example, media reports indicate that "several KLA leaders had the mobile phone number of General Wesley Clark, the NATO commander."[139] Meanwhile Robin Cook, the United Kingdom's foreign secretary, was in direct phone contact with the KLA commander Hashim Thaci.[140] (Thaci held several high positions; and resigned as the president of Kosovo in late 2020 to face charges of crimes against humanity.)

James Bissett, a former Canadian ambassador to Yugoslavia, stated that the early US training of the KLA (in 1998) involved sending them back into Kosovo "to assassinate Serbian mayors, ambush

Serbian politicians and intimidate hesitant Kosovo Albanians."[141] The ethnic hatred, thus heightened, seems to have been "an integral part of London and Washington's strategy."[142] As Ambassador Bissett clarified: "The hope was that with Kosovo in flames NATO could intervene and ... provide the aging and increasingly irrelevant military organization with a reason for its continued existence."[143]

5. Growth of Religious Extremism by Proxy: Understanding Syria[144]

In a 2015 interview, President Barack Obama admitted that "ISIS is a direct outgrowth of al-Qaeda in Iraq [AQI] that grew out of our invasion."[145] A 2012 document[146] by the US Defense Intelligence Agency (DIA) stated that "events are taking a clear sectarian direction. The Salafist, the Muslim Brotherhood, and AQI [al-Qaeda in Iraq] are the major forces driving the insurgency in Syria" and "the West, Gulf countries, and Turkey support these insurgent forces."[147] The document goes on to discuss the strategic consideration of "establishing a declared or undeclared Salafist principality in eastern Syria ... and this is exactly what the [insurgency's] supporting powers want in order to isolate the Syrian regime, which is considered the strategic depth of the Shia expansion (Iraq and Iran)."[148]

According to the DIA document, Syria's destabilization "creates the ideal atmosphere for AQI to return to its old pockets in Mosul and Ramadi, and will provide renewed momentum under the presumption of unifying the jihad among Sunni Iraq and Syria, and the rest of the Sunnis in the Arab world against what it considers one enemy, the dissenters."[149]

The same strategy was acknowledged in 2016 in a leaked audio tape by the then US Secretary of State John Kerry: "We saw that Daesh [ISIS] was growing in strength, and we thought Assad was threatened. We thought, however, we could probably manage [ISIS]..."[150]

Alastair Crooke, a former MI6 officer elaborated that the strategy effectively was to "inject hydraulic fracturing fluid [radical Sunni Muslim extremists] into eastern Syria" to disrupt "the bridge between Iran and its Arab allies, even at the cost" of the other outcomes.[151] The strategy, with some nuances here and there, was commonly shared by the anti-Assad governments involved in the conflict. Yet, history tells us time and again that these forces almost always spin out of control within a short time.

The covert operation in Syria (led by the U.S. and the UK), begun around 2011, "resembled the larger covert action in Afghanistan in the 1980s, involving a huge CIA programme, vast amounts of money, mainly from Saudi Arabia and Qatar, British-funded propaganda operation and a coalition of Arab and European intelligence agencies, notably France, Turkey and Jordan."[152] Qatar, Saudi Arabia, and the United States had spent several billion dollars each.[153] Joint spending of the coalition partners in Syria may have reached the level of US-coalition spending in Afghanistan.[154]

In this context, referring to the Syrian operations at the 50th Munich Security Conference in February 2014, the late Senator John McCain famously pronounced: "Thank God for the Saudis and Prince Bandar, and for our Qatari friends."[155] Perhaps it would be wise not to thank God on this account until we have carefully evaluated the immense human misery and further conflict spawned by this project.[156]

Heavy quantities of weapons were brought in from Libya (from the arsenal of Qaddafi, who had just been deposed and killed) and Croatia (including as part of Operation Timber Sycamore). In September 2012, for example, a Libyan ship with 400 tons of weapons docked in Southern Turkey.[157] Turkey's goal in the Syrian conflict was summarized by Graham Fuller, a former CIA official, who wrote that President Erdogan "preferred strengthening ISIS against Damascus than deepening Turkish ties with the Kurds."[158]

Around early 2013, the US, the UK, and other European allies coordinated around 75 planeloads (over 3,000 tons) of weapons from Zagreb airport in Croatia to Jordan.[159] Lord Ashdown, a British politician, clarified that these weapons were "left over from the Bosnian war" and that they were going "almost exclusively to the more jihadist groups."[160] Photographic evidence indicates that some of these weapons ended up in the arsenal of ISIS.[161]

Virtually all of the direct sustenance and training of ISIS came from three governments: Saudi Arabia, Qatar, and Turkey. Indeed, before it developed its own "education" curriculum, ISIS used regular Saudi textbooks.[162] That the Saudi curriculum met ISIS requirements should be no surprise; the ideology is the same.

In confirming the support from Qatar and Saudi Arabia, a senior Qatari official clarified that supporting al-Nusra (al-Qaeda's Syrian branch) was Qatar's focus, whereas "ISIS has been a Saudi project."[163] Even Prime Minister Nouri al-Maliki of Iraq accused Saudi Arabia of being a direct supporter of ISIS.[164]

As the *Financial Times* reported, former Saudi Foreign Minister Prince al-Faisal accepted the obvious when he said to Secretary Kerry: "Daesh [ISIS] is our response to your support for Da'wa [the Shia "Islamist" party the US installed in Iraq]."[165] British General Jonathan Shaw, however, asserted that the US/UK bombing of ISIS was "not addressing the fundamental problem of Wahhabi Salafism as a culture and a creed, which has got out of control and is still the ideological basis of ISIL ..."[166]

So what is this "culture and creed" the general is referring to, and how is it practically brought about? The "religious creed," of course, was derived by the founder of Wahhabism from his deviant interpretation of Islam in the eighteenth century. Besides intense indoctrination, the "culture" (and its enforcement) is accomplished through a draconian sociopolitical system whose understanding is also important. In its practical implementation, this ideology dovetails with another sister ideology—the northern Italian city of Bolzano still houses the former headquarter of the National Fascist Party. Its façade features a very large frieze with a clear message: *credere, obbedire, combatare* (BELIEVE, OBEY, FIGHT).[167] And it is this "culture," in addition to the financial largesse causing the global spread of the Saudi-Wahhabi ideology, that the British general is grumbling about.

Richard Dearlove, the former head of MI6, United Kingdom's intelligence agency, was commenting on a meeting with Prince Bandar Bin Sultan, formerly the head of Saudi intelligence. Dearlove recalled what the prince said to him: "The time is not far off, Richard, in the Middle East when it will be literally, 'God help the Shias.' More than a billion Sunnis have simply had enough of them."[168]

It is all of humanity, not just the Shias, who face a direct nemesis in the Saudi-Wahhabi religiopolitical ideology.

6. Propaganda[169] in Covert War & Terrorism

Terrorism, covert war, and LIC are all related[170] concepts (LIC is covered under the subtitle "Is It Really Impossible ... Universal Definition.?"). Propaganda is an integral companion to this type of warfare, as it is to conventional warfare. The success of covert wars can therefore be significantly dependent on propaganda.

In December 1979, when the Soviet Union invaded Afghanistan, Brzezinski sent a memo to President Carter stating, "we should concert with Islamic countries both a propaganda campaign and a covert action campaign to help the rebels."[171] Brzezinski's sentiment is echoed by the British ministry of defence (MoD) whose doctrine classifies information as "so prevalent, potent and unavoidable that it forms as much a part of the strategic environment as the terrain or weather" and thus needs to be managed by "strategic communications."[172]

This euphemistic jargon seems to be trying to convey a simple idea: Truth can be an enemy in the attainment of geopolitical objectives; it thus needs to be managed and, if need be, neutralized. An example each from Afghanistan and Syria shows the extent of such propaganda operations in those two covert operations.

We earlier discussed the plan to carry the Afghan war into the Soviet Union executed by the CIA, MI6, and ISI (see chapter 1, subtitle "Geopolitical Agendas Exploiting Religion"). Thousands of copies of the *Qur'an* with propagandistic translations were distributed in Central Asian languages.

Available information indicates that funding from MI6 for this project was channeled through the Jamaat-e Islami (JI) of Pakistan.[173] JI was well connected into the militant leaders such as Gulbuddin Hekmatyar (see the next subtitle "The Company We Keep"), whose group was the main force executing the sabotage operation inside the Soviet Union. It is worth repeating that MI6 funded the JI to funnel the funds to Hekmatyar and other warlords.

British documents from the 1950s describe the JI as a "reactionary force," an "extreme right-wing Islamic party" and "a potentially dangerous movement, comparable in many ways to the Muslim Brotherhood." The same document also described JI's founder and leader (Abul A'la Maududi) as a "clever, ambitious and unscrupulous man."[174]

Given this scenario, why are both the government of an Islamic country as well as a globally-influential Islamic organization conspiring with the CIA and the MI6 to grotesquely abuse the *Qur'an* as a propaganda tool to promote militancy, violence, lawlessness and international terrorism? Could such abhorrent abuse of the *Qur'an* by Muslims be classified as intentional blasphemy and treachery against God and God's Book?

Second, why is MI6 so fondly working with an organization it has itself labeled reactionary, extremist, and dangerous? Would it be fair to say that the label "unscrupulous" applies equally to the UK government?

In 2013, as part of the covert operation against the Assad regime, Britain launched a major propaganda campaign on behalf of the rebel groups in Syria. This "information warfare" project cost millions of dollars to the British government, which hired private contractors to work out of Istanbul, Turkey.[175] While hired by the Foreign Office, the contractors, Register Larkin and InCoStrat, were overseen by the MoD. The mission included the production of radio broadcasts, military reports, videos, photos, print products, and social media posts—all branded with the logos of the various rebel groups for whom the creatives were produced.

The contract documents required Register Larkin and InCoStrat to "select and train a spokesman able to represent" all of the rebel groups with a unified voice. The contractors were also expected to provide media coaching to "influential officials" of such groups—in addition to, of course, running a round-the-clock "central media office."[176] It would perhaps be fair to say that, for several years, the British government was running a PR firm for the rebel groups.

Harakat al-Hazm, a rebel group supported by the US, was one of the beneficiaries of this program. The group collapsed in 2015, and its weaponry (including US-provided anti-tank missiles) ended up in the safe custody of al-Nusra—an al-Qaeda clone and affiliate. Then there was the Saudi-supported Jaysh al-Islam, another program beneficiary, which faces charges of documented war crimes.[177]

The intended audience of the propaganda produced by this program includes Syrian civilians as well as military personnel, though the propaganda is also deemed to be useful to sway the funders of these rebel groups. A video of a shoulder-to-air missile shooting down a Syrian government helicopter can be "good PR to go back to the Pentagon."[178]

Samuel Johnson ends one of his famous essays with the following words: "I know not whether more is to be dreaded from streets filled with Soldiers accustomed to plunder, or from garrets filled with Scribblers accustomed to lie."[179]

7. The Company We Keep

While the assignment of guilt by association can be highly unfair and inaccurate, a consistent pattern of association does say something about the shared inclinations; and, perhaps, the nature of the partners in collaboration. In this regard, the case of Afghan "freedom fighter" Gulbuddin Hekmatyar is particularly instructive.

Singled out in the 1970s as a useful proxy by the administration of Pakistan's then Prime Minister Zulfikar Ali Bhutto, Hekmatyar kept his most-favored status with General Zia ul-Haq's regime. At the inception of Operation Cyclone, Hekmatyar's Hezb-i Islami organization received the largest share of "support" from all the benefactors. Both the United States and Saudi Arabia gave Hekmatyar hundreds of millions of dollars each. It is likely this poor man in God's service raked in "aid" in excess of a billion dollars towards his mission.[180] (The profits from narcotics trade would fatten his endowments even more. A US Congress report described Hekmatyar's organization as "the most corrupt of all Afghan resistance groups."[181])

In the mid-80s, Hekmatyar's organization was the main proxy, chosen by the ISI, the CIA, and the MI6, to carry out guerilla attacks inside the Soviet territory proper. Commando squads created for this purpose carried out sabotage missions, including train derailments, powerline disruption, and blowing up factories, fuel storage depots, and military installations.[182] The hawks in Pakistan were ascendent despite vociferous opposition from within its power establishment, and despite public opinion in the country being strongly in favor of peace and negotiation. This was the first time since the 1950s of direct Western action inside the Soviet Union,[183] and Hekmatyar was the man to be entrusted with this sacred mission of freedom for the Afghan people.

There seems to be a consensus that Hekmatyar was an unusually sadistic man. He was known for skinning humans alive, and his group committed some of the worst atrocities of the war. During the civil war in the early 90s, after Soviet withdrawal from Afghanistan, Hekmatyar came to be known as the "Butcher of Kabul" for the destruction he wrought upon his own land, and the human carnage he caused upon his own people.

In 1986, Hekmatyar visited 10 Downing Street to meet with Prime Minister Margaret Thatcher.[184] In 1988, he met Foreign Office officials in London.[185] In 1985, the CIA flew him into Washington, where he was hosted by the State Department.[186] Hekmatyar was invited to meet with President Reagan, but he refused. At this occasion, ironically, it was one of the most vicious men in human history who exercised his judgment in determining a worthy partner.

8. Serving God and Humanity—Do-gooders on a Sacred Mission

Religions frequently promote various doctrines of afterlife, salvation, reincarnation, reward and punishment, heaven and hell, etc. Curiously, it seems that the binary created by the Enlightenment philosophy has been adopted by some religious establishments towards the notion of a "completely otherworldly religion" that can be leveraged to make a "strange distinction between body and soul, the sacred and the secular."[187] Obviously, such notions are misused for exploitation and recruitment of the zealous or the innocent.

Besides, many who are engaged in extremism (even its violent variety), at the bottom of their hearts, usually believe themselves to be providing a service on behalf of a worthy cause—especially on behalf of those who are being wronged. This point has to be understood because many of these actors are willing to make great sacrifices—including even the sacrifice of their lives—in fulfilling such an "obligation."

Gempo Yamamoto (early twentieth century) was one of Japan's most famous modern Zen masters. Nissho Inoue was Yamamoto's lay disciple who created a militant organization (*Ketsumeidan* or the League of Blood). In the 1930s, the organization engaged in assassinations of high officials, including Prime Minister Inukai Tsuyoshi. At Inoue's trial, Master Yamamoto testified in Inoue's favor. Without understanding the socio-politico-economic context, it is not easy to understand why such an acclaimed Zen master testified in favor of his terrorist disciple.

In the United States, the bombings of abortion clinics and murder of physicians providing service there would provide another angle to looking at such instances. Here we have to begin with the brainwashing that comes from the religious establishments involved, as well as the exploitation of political forces that leverage such indoctrination to justify pure crime.

Then there is the 2011 assassination of Salman Taseer, the governor of Punjab province in Pakistan. Taseer openly opposed the imposition of "blasphemy laws" and lobbied for the pardon of Aasia Bibi, a Christian Pakistani who was accused of "blasphemy." Taseer's bodyguard executed him with an AK-47. Hundreds of Muslim clerics in Pakistan voiced support for the murder, and the killer was showered with rose petals when he arrived at the court for his hearing.

The complexity of these examples should not be underestimated. The responsibility in these instances, however, is directly shared by religious establishments and the dogma they promote. Even universities, whether it is al-Azhar in Cairo or its counterparts in other religions all over the world, shoulder the responsibility to understand their role in the problem as well as the solution.

9. Organizational Structures: Affiliate or Affinity

While ideological, extremist, or terrorist groups may share goals and strategies, they are often wrongly projected or perceived to be mutual affiliates, meaning that they are somehow organizationally or operationally connected (or that one takes orders from the other). This is usually not the case. Al-Qaeda in one country may have nothing to do with al-Qaeda in another. They may not agree with the goals and tactics of the other. The Hezbollah in Turkey, for example, may not have a direct linkage with its namesake in Lebanon. And Jundullah in Pakistan's Waziristan may be an ideologically-different group from Jundullah in Iran / Baluchistan. Sometimes, affiliated groups may not even use the same name. Jabhat al-Nusra of Syria, or al-Nusra, is an al-Qaeda affiliate but with a different name. Overall, it is best to view them mostly as affinity groups that may have been inspired by the other or may share some aspects of ideologies or goals with the other.

Frequently enough, ideologically extremist groups may even have no "affinity" for one another. Expediency, pragmatism, and lust for power may be all that keeps them together. The "Peshawar-Seven" coalition of Afghan militant groups during the Soviet occupation of Afghanistan, for example, was comprised of entities that loathed one other. Gulbuddin Hekmatyar led one of these groups. Hekmatyar had the reputation of investing more time and effort in destroying other rebel groups—his coalition partners—than fighting the Soviet forces. In the early 1990s, after the Soviet departure from Afghanistan, it was these same groups that engaged in a civil war, horribly disfiguring their country.

Sometimes, confusingly-similar names can trip up even a subject-matter authority. For example, Pakistan's Jamaat-e Islami (founded by Abul A'la Maududi in the 1940s) is a different organization from Afghanistan's Jamiat-e Islami (founded by Burhanuddin Rabbani in the 1970s). Yet I have seen a highly-qualified expert mix the two up in formal writing.

Identity-based commonality or "brotherhood" are also important in our understanding of development and sustainability of militant groups that fight injustice on behalf of those fighting for their rights and freedoms. Where there is oppression (real or perceived), some form of resistance would be unavoidable (and may even be justified by international law in many instances). Ethnic and religious identities create bonds of kinship where none might exist otherwise. That is why such identities provide good vehicles for mobilizing resistance and organizing movements. Muslims from all over the world were recruited by various intelligence agencies to fight against Soviet and Russian forces in Afghanistan and Chechnya. And more recently, the power of propaganda lured some European Muslims to support ISIS by joining the outfit. It is simply this bond of commonality that is leveraged in these situations.

An apt observation comes from Martha Gellhorn, the legendary war correspondent then covering the European front of WWII. She suggested that "the men who run the world" should "get to know the people who only live in it."[188]

Validating the "Other" and Recognizing the Prevalent Narratives

Extremism doesn't generate in a vacuum. It needs a psychological breeding ground. It also needs exploitative interests that benefit from the creation of division and hate. There need not be a conspiracy here; it just works that way. As conscientious citizens in a democracy, we are responsible for recognizing the mechanisms commonly employed to create and enhance divisions based upon our various identities, ideologies, or perceived interests. This is imperative because "democracy demands responsibility, courage, and the will to freedom from all ..."[189]

As this book frequently highlights, the concept of the "other" may be primed to create divisions where none might otherwise exist. The colonial systems were known to use divide et impera (divide and rule) strategies to keep the colonized under their control. Current political systems in sovereign nation-states, all over the world, may function in similar ways.

In the United States, some followers of the two dominant political camps may now use words such as "terrorist," "traitor," and "enemies," against each other.[190] In his 2021 Inauguration Address,

President Biden referred to an "uncivil war that pits red against blue ... conservative versus liberal."[191] The mutual detestation, intensifying over time, seems to have now reached a crescendo.[192] And this mutual hatred is no longer reserved to the party officials. Polls by the Pew Research Center indicate that 76 percent of Democrats view the Republican Party as "too extreme," and vice versa.[193] Clearly, the tussle for power between the two parties, accompanied by other politico-economic forces, has created an environment of mutual loathing, seriously dividing society by creating an internal "other," so much so that family structures and relationships are being damaged.

As the split becomes wider, either side becomes less capable of grasping its own reality, let alone the validity of the other. Political opportunism and ideological power play necessitate the generation of artificial divisions—such that the supporters of these two parties come across as having mutually incompatible interests. Yet that is not the case. The social, political, and economic interests and factors that concern the ordinary US citizen—liberal or conservative, Republican or Democrat—are not so different at their roots. Even decades ago, a June 1990 Gallup poll indicated that the "dream" of a vast majority of Americans is simply a "decent and secure life."[194]

Clearly, the ordinary American seeks the same economic objectives as any other ordinary person elsewhere: to feed, house, educate, and provide for the basic necessities of life. Even in terms of governance, a survey by Chapman University indicates that some 75 percent of US citizens are concerned about corrupt government officials.[195] The sociological differences between liberal and conservative platforms often tend to be illuminated and amplified, if not downright created by politicians' needs to benefit from a divide.

It should be no surprise that the disillusionment and distrust of both public and non-public institutions is also commonly shared by groups that are seemingly on the opposite ends of the political spectrum. And yet, the common citizen within this or that camp, as within a Hobbesian system, refuses to connect with the reality of the "other." Arguably, ordinary citizens are being won over to political agendas that run counter to their interests and values.

If the political system within the United States has succeeded in creating such drastic polarization and mutual disconnection within the domestic political terrain, imagining the reality behind international polarization should not be so difficult. Neither should be the realization of the artifice behind it all. Nevertheless, even overcoming such artificial gulfs requires insight, ingenuity, and courage. Perhaps we can begin with trying to accept that the "other" may have genuine concerns. As King pointed out, however, "a more difficult but no less necessary task is to speak for those who have been designated as our enemies.... For from his view we may indeed see the basic weaknesses of our own condition, and if we are mature, we may learn and grow and profit from the wisdom of the brothers who are called the opposition."[196]

The unquestioning acceptance of prevalent narratives becomes a hindrance in our ability to solve problems. One of the sources of this hindrance is internal: the human tendency that wants psychological comfort. The other source, of course, is the flood of "information" that keeps trying to drown us in its convoluted and sometimes disingenuous and deceptive nature. Political forces play a role in framing the very discussion by throwing fuel on opportunistic topics, or "disappearing" those deemed undesirable.

To effect a solution, we would have to understand and overcome these hurdles so we may locate the real sources of the problem. Besides, as Rabbi Heschel pointed out, "morally speaking, there is no limit to the concern one must feel for the suffering of human beings,[197] ... in regard to cruelties committed in the name of a free society, some are guilty, while all are responsible."[198] Dr. King, however, made it clear that a meaningful change will not come "through the complacent adjustment of the conforming majority." Such a change only comes "through the creative maladjustment of a non-conforming minority."[199]

Leveraging Information in Comprehension; Transcending Identity in Action

Extremism, and especially terrorism, whatever type it may be, has to be understood in its causality and defining characteristics,[200] not in terms of the identity of the perpetrator. The forces creating extremism in many religions today are variants of the same geopolitical paradigm, following similar patterns of the pursuit of power.

Identity-based extremism would often be presented by its instigators as a battle against an outsider. This strategy assures support (unity) of the target audience. And yet, while the fire rages to destroy the external "enemy," it ultimately burns those in whose name it is lit. It is akin to contaminating one's own well to poison the perceived adversary. For example, Wahhabism (including its cognates and analogs that may use different names) are not just engaged in their war against the "non-Muslim West." Their project is effectively destroying Islamic societies—in the name of Islam. History provides countless such examples: Germany, Rwanda, and the Balkans in the twentieth century, to name a few. Even today, the same can be seen with other extremist movements—especially religious and nationalistic ones, especially in the Middle East, South Asia, Europe, and North America.

Attachment to identity, especially national and religious, in the present-day world has become a great hurdle in our ability to even comprehend the sources of the problem, let alone deal with the solutions. In a world that "has to" be adversarial on so many fronts, the promotion of identity is intense, and thus the conditioning is rather unavoidable.

One need not throw away one's identities altogether. It is really about the freedom from the prison that social conditioning creates around identities. The "prison" being referred to here is the creation of the "other" based upon a label—national, racial, religious, ideological—regardless of the principles held by the "other." The prevalent non-validation of "others" is that license taken by the intolerant to promote their agendas.

Choice: Individual and Collective

Our religions provide the guiding light that can continue to illuminate our individual and collective life paths towards greater harmony, peace, and justice. And yet, there are forces that have perverted these same teachings to create division, hatred, and violence. From the darkness of a "belief" (or ideology) that someone inculcates in us to hate, kill, and die for, to the ever-expanding light of the "internal truth" that illuminates our life path, the religious tapestry today has many colors. Those who understand and realize the guided path of illumination need to stand up for their choice. Otherwise, the risk is that we are unduly influenced by forces working against our collective interest.

CHAPTER 3:

IMPERILED SOCIETAL AND INSTITUTIONAL STRUCTURES

"Incentives for academic scientists have become increasingly perverse in terms of competition for research funding ... Furthermore, decreased discretionary funding at the federal and state level is creating a hypercompetitive environment ... the combination of perverse incentives and decreased funding increases pressures that can lead to unethical behavior. If a critical mass of scientists become untrustworthy, a tipping point is possible in which the scientific enterprise itself becomes inherently corrupt and public trust is lost, risking a new dark age with devastating consequences to humanity."[201]

—Marc Edwards and Siddhartha Roy

The epigraph above is from an academic article published in the journal *Environmental Engineering Science* (January 2017, vol. 34, No. 1). The concerns here are not some future projections. The article talks about immediate action needed to deal with "perverse" problems in the present such as "pressures to 'cut corners' throughout the system"[202] and "troubling level of unethical activity, outright faking of peer review and retractions"[203] and that the "Misconduct is not limited to academic researchers. Federal agencies are also subject to perverse incentives and hypercompetition, giving rise to a new phenomenon of institutional scientific research misconduct."[204]

The authors go on to quote a 2010 piece in *The Economist*

with the following inference: "The modern academic research enterprise, dubbed a 'Ponzi Scheme' by *The Economist*, created the existing perverse incentive system, which would have been almost inconceivable to academics of 30–50 years ago."[205]

This piece underlines the importance of discerning how structures (or institutions) work and why they are so easily corrupted. (Appendix A shows a useful chart comparing the essential attributes of cultures and structures. These differences help in understanding how structured institutions may degenerate, fail, or work against the society's interest.)

If the current politico-economic environment is causing corruption within the academic[206] realm, what can we assume about the commercial, media, health, legal, governmental, and legislative arenas? As the examples in this chapter indicate, the answer may not be so encouraging. That's why it is crucial to understand the implications of this development. The blackout of the "new dark age" that Edwards and Roy are referring to, if or when it happens, would go well beyond just the academic domain.

For the excerpt in the epigraph, a few salient observations, opinions, and hypotheses are worth considering.

- The incentive system being described exists, by and large, with good intentions and is being implemented with good intentions. The system is really meant to be in the interest of the society (unlike various other situations where the interest of the institution is advanced at the cost of the society).
- There is no intent in the policies of these institutions to create corruption in the system. If anything, the intent is to minimize a tendency towards chicanery within the system.
- The unethical and corrupt behavior has to be understood in terms of the "interests" within the system. In general, it is not driven by any overarching malevolence by anyone. There certainly is no conspiracy going on.[207]

- The most curious thing is the employees of the institutions in many of these cases are explicitly acting against the tactical and strategic interests of the institutions they work for and represent. Such a scenario (of the agent working against the principal's interest with virtual impunity) is antithetical to most systemic cases of corruption that a system tolerates. Systemic corruption usually benefits several components of the system, especially the powerful components—even if such corruption is not directly beneficial to the overall structure. When an agent works against the system, the reaction is generally guaranteed. The structure always protects itself. (Systemic is different from systematic, see glossary.)
- There is nothing fundamentally bad about the individuals involved in the corruption. They are the product of the system. On the average, they are not morally different from any of us. If anything, these academic professionals may have higher ethical standards than the agents in various other professional domains (such as commerce, legal, government, and political).
- It would be fair to say that the institutions and those who run these institutions are aware of the problem. What is it then that makes it so difficult to take an action and ameliorate the problem? While there may be exceptions, the answer here is that the situation emanates from the very nature of a structure. Along with the content of this chapter, Appendix A, which highlights the attributes of structure vs. culture, will help us answer that question.

This chapter will define the concept of "structure" and will provide examples to emphasize the corruption of structures at the global level.

It's Not the Apple, It's the Barrel!

Within the global rubric of law and justice, especially in the United States, the functioning mode of our penal system and political processes condition us to think of even the concept of justice in extremely limited terms (guilty/not-guilty, for example), even creating a direct connection between justice and retribution/punishment.[208] As this chapter shows later, Dr. King equated the philosophy of *lex talionis* (law of retaliation) to "worship[ing] the god of revenge" and to "bow[ing] before the altar of retaliation."

No wonder, the societal mindset in facing any problem is to allocate the blame to someone—oftentimes to the entire exclusion of any deliberation of assessing causes—and not even to differentiate between guilt and blame. Everything else aside, this model has not helped us overcome any basic problems.

Philip G. Zimbardo is an emeritus professor of psychology at Stanford University. In 1971, he masterminded and directed the notorious Stanford Prison Experiment, which may well be the best-known study in the field of psychology. Student volunteers in this simulation of a prison role-played guards and prisoners. Even though the participants knew that it was a study, their shocking behavior forced termination of the planned two-week long study after six days. After the repulsive disclosures about Abu Ghraib prison, Zimbardo wrote an op-ed titled "Power turns good soldiers into 'bad apples'" for the *Boston Globe*. In this writing, he described the study and a few lessons he learned.

STANFORD PRISON EXPERIMENT

Good boys chosen for their normalcy were having emotional breakdowns as powerless prisoners. Other young men chosen for their mental health and positive values eased into the character of sadistic guards inflicting suffering on their fellow students without moral compunction. And those "good guards"

> who did not personally debase the prisoners failed to confront the worst of their comrades, allowing evil to ripen without challenge.
>
> The terrible things my guards did to their prisoners were comparable to the horrors inflicted on the Iraqi detainees. My guards repeatedly stripped their prisoners naked, hooded them, chained them, denied them food or bedding privileges, put them into solitary confinement, and made them clean toilet bowls with their bare hands.
>
> As the boredom of their job increased, they began using the prisoners as their playthings, devising ever more humiliating and degrading games for them to play. Over time, these amusements took a sexual turn, such as having the prisoners simulate sodomy on each other. Once aware of such deviant behavior, I closed down the Stanford prison.[209]
>
> —*Boston Globe*, 9 May 2004
>
> Insert 3:1

Zimbardo's op-ed provides other highly pertinent lessons that we should summarize here. Referring to what happened at the Abu Ghraib Prison, he denounced the tendency to blame the "bad apples" without learning the "dynamics of why." Referring to the forces that can transform "ordinary people into evil perpetrators," he declared that the once-good apples had been "soured and corrupted by an evil barrel." Human behavior, as Zimbardo highlighted, is substantially more under the control of situational forces than we realize or acknowledge. Circumstances that allow humans to suspend their moral discernment can morph virtually anyone "into creatures alien to our usual natures." Research in psychology, as Zimbardo highlighted, has already catalogued the conditions for "stirring the crucible of human nature in negative directions."[210]

Many others, such as philosophers Hannah Arendt and Elizabeth Minnich, have reached similar conclusions. Given George Orwell's observation that "the further a society drifts from the truth, the more it hates those who speak it," speaking one's truth on such matters often becomes a rather courageous stance.

Besides, the modern concept of justice seems to have been linked so closely to punishment and revenge that people such as Zimbardo or Arendt may even get serious backlash from otherwise well-meaning people.[211] Yet, as a society we become capable of finding solutions only when we realize and accept human vulnerabilities; when we accept that, at the end of the day, we may not be so much different from the participants in the Stanford Prison Experiment or the guards and prisoners at the Abu Ghraib Prison—that "many of us can be morphed into creatures alien to our usual natures."

This understanding also helps us appreciate those—politicians, lawyers, educators, police officers, nurses, students, and others in all walks of life—who stand up for their inner truth despite the hurdles created by the systems they function in. What comes to mind is the viral image of the "tank man" in the Tiananmen Square protest in 1989, who stopped a column of tanks. Such an effort and its effect may sometimes be mundane, nominal, or temporary; it is the spirit in the effort that keeps alive the spark for the monumental difference just one individual can make.

This "tank man" aspect of human impact needs to be highlighted. Otherwise, our evaluations of circumstances are more likely to yield thought processes bordering on nihilism, thus tending to malign a whole category of individuals such as politicians, police officers, lawyers, doctors, etc. What we sometimes seem not to realize is the courage and integrity, within these structures, of those who fight for society at a cost to their own interests. That's why assimilating Zimbardo's assessment is so important. It's the barrel, not the apples, we need to change. The good apples are the best bet we have in that effort, and still they may well be in the majority within these systems!

Structure and Corruption: Defining and Grasping the Concepts

Structure and corruption being somewhat nebulous words, we should provide a clear explanation for them.

"Corruption," in a broad sense, captures how political and economic power is used especially by those in the higher echelons, to benefit themselves or their agendas. In this sense, even intellectual dishonesty within the societal context would classify as corruption.

The word "structure" involves more complex interpretations and applications. The way the word is used in this book often comes close to the way we understand the word "institution"—a corporation, a governmental agency, a university, an NGO—entities and organizations usually with an established hierarchy, infrastructure, or legal existence.

Distinction also should be made between the aspect of an institution that is an abstraction and that which is hierarchical. This book mostly refers to problems created by the hierarchical structures and institutions, not institutions that have no "physical" or "legal" presence and are thus mainly abstractions.

For example, Catholicism (the religion) is an institution without a legal or physical existence that can be looked at as an abstraction. The Catholic Church, however, is a centralized and hierarchical organization based at the Vatican and operating all over the world. The two can be mixed up in our thought processes. A Muslim, similarly, may just be following her understanding of Islam (an abstract institution) that may have nothing to do with this or that religious establishment purporting to represent Islam. Thus, the use of the word "structure" would not apply to the religions of Christianity and Islam, but rather the hierarchical religious establishments that claim to represent those religions. Similarly, when we talk about "the university," we are usually referring to academia in general (an abstraction in this context). But when we talk about Yale University, we are referring to a hierarchical organization with a legal or physical presence (a structure in our context).

As another example, the word "America" is used as the name of a country (especially in the United States). When we contemplate the "interests" of America (the land mass and its people), they may not be so different from those of what we know as "China."[212] That's because the names of the two countries are being used in a context that is something of an abstraction. But when we compare the "interests" of the two governments or two competing industries in these countries, the picture changes.

Even within the context of the government of a nation-state, which is a hierarchal structure, interests may vary from one entity to the other. The interests being pursued by the State Department may be very different from those of the Pentagon or the White House. The internal clashes and game-playing may be significant, though not so visible externally. It is, therefore, important to realize that the interests of these "American" institutions or their leaders may often be diametrically opposed to the interests of the average US citizen. The same would apply to any other country.

Corruption That Touches Everything

In a 2020 piece in the *New York Review of Books*, Hari Kunzru wrote: "[Trump's] family identifies its own interests with the national interest, and appears to see the presidency as a monetizable asset."[213] An informed and non-partisan person would find it difficult to argue with that assertion.[214] There is more to this "monetization," though. What if we measured the financial assets of the Clinton family in 1990 and then in 2020? What's the likelihood we would see an eye-popping difference? How about counting the Clinton Foundation in the mix also? How about every act of influence-peddling and personal gain besides the money creation / transfers involved in those acts?

All that aside, what's important to realize is that the game is much bigger than any individual player or specific society. In a 1998 special report titled *The House of Graft*, the *New York Times* reported the following about Pakistan's emblem of democracy:

> A decade after she led this impoverished nation from military rule to democracy, Benazir Bhutto is at the heart of a widening corruption inquiry that Pakistani investigators say has traced more than $100 million to foreign bank accounts and properties controlled by

> Ms. Bhutto's family. Starting from a cache of Bhutto family documents bought for $1 million from a shadowy intermediary, the investigators have detailed a pattern of secret payments by foreign companies that sought favors during Ms. Bhutto's two terms as Prime Minister.[215]

Professor Eqbal Ahmad knew Benazir Bhutto personally and worked with her. As his account indicates, the $100 million quoted by the *Times* is puny compared to the reality: "Benazir Bhutto, in the space of three-and-a-half years as prime minister, stealing nearly 2 billion dollars from a poor country like Pakistan. That's pathology. She doesn't need that kind of money. She was already a rich woman."[216]

And he may be right. What we are dealing with at the global level may well be a human-created pathology. Here, it is helpful to be clear on a few points that often are not covered in such journalistic reporting. First, this is only the tip of the iceberg for just the Bhutto family. After her assassination, her widower, Asif Ali Zardari, had a stint as the president of the country, and it's anyone's guess as to how much more was stolen. Second, we are discussing only one family and their misdeeds in billions of dollars. Then there is the Sharif[217] family and so many others. The *Times* may call this a special report, but there is nothing special about corruption; as indicated by examples in this chapter alone, corruption is common in today's world. Third, it's curious how the financial system in our world allows a single family to steal billions of dollars, from an "impoverished" country. It is thus conceivable that tens or hundreds of billions have been stolen from each of many impoverished countries.[218] Fourth, this gives us a glimpse of one of the major sources of poverty and deprivation faced by the so-called third world.

Most importantly, though, we have to realize that this network of corruption spans the globe and there may not be any corner of the world that is free of its tentacles. Through intricate connections—financial, monetary, economic, digital—virtually everything that happens is related to everything else, with or without design. As pointed out in chapter 1, the global systems would collapse in a relatively short time without all the grease that keeps the wheels churning. There is no conspiracy here, it is just how the systems have evolved, though when we can see what's in plain view, the picture can be completed without the details that are hidden or may not be so pronounced. To get an idea of how things work, we'll begin with a brief look at eighteenth-century Britain's active role in the slavery trade—which is quite contrary to the way Brits view it. In his book *Black and British: A Forgotten History*, David Olusoga, a British-Nigerian historian, says:

> It is important to remember how few voices were raised against slavery in Britain until the last quarter of the eighteenth century. The Church of England was largely silent on the issue, as were most of the politicians.... too much money, too many livelihoods and too much political power were invested; millions of British people lived lives that were intimately connected to the economics of slavery and the sugar business.[219]

The global system—economic, commercial, political, international—is exponentially more "intimately connected"[220] today than it was three centuries ago. Even though it may not seem that way on a day-to-day basis, all our systems are interdependent even when there may not be any direct connections.

Vulnerabilities of Our Societal Institutions

Raised in the epigraph of this chapter, the concerns about the "troubling level of unethical activity" and "institutional scientific research misconduct" come to life every day, all over the world—in virtually every walk of life. After a momentary blip on the radar, if that, they are neatly archived on some shelf where they will forever disappear into oblivion.

The inertia and the unwillingness to change the fundamental concepts around which everything revolves within the sociopolitical system can be overwhelming because "whole fields of knowledge—not to mention university chairs and departments, scientific journals, prestigious research grants, libraries, databases, school curricula and the like—have been designed to fit the old structures and the old questions."[221] With the psychological urge to not even notice the "bad barrel," the tendency is to simply talk about the "bad apple" momentarily and then move on to topics more palatable to all involved. The accumulated decline in the systems ultimately renders them too corrupt to remain redeemable.

The human cost of the systemic degradation spills over as soon as we scratch the coating. In the richest society ever in human history, for example, the massive reality of hunger and homelessness should dumbfound anyone who possesses a mind and a heart. Does such evidence of human misery highlight a systemic conundrum? We would be told that all systems have weaknesses and face problems that are detected and resolved. That ours is not a perfect system, but it's the best there is. That there will always be some price to pay for free market, that's the American way, etc.

This reasoning may provide some consolation, and that's the problem because the logic allows us to look the other way. For a people that is generous, resourceful, and purposeful, this situation indicates that the politico-economic structures have effectively incapacitated the collective agency, perhaps even the human solidarity, of over 300 million.

Theologian and scholar Charles Long had said about the United States that she faces "a hermeneutical situation."[222] The observation can be expanded today to all of the human race. The examples below from the medical and legal domains would show the prevalence of the "bad barrel" phenomenon which, one way or the other, applies globally to structured institutions.

1. Healthcare: the "Monumental Fraud"

Since the beginning of the COVID-19 pandemic, finding a cure or a method of prevention of some sort has become the most urgent imperative for the health/medical/pharmaceutical community. Clearly, there is quite a bit of financial incentive for the innumerable players involved. Given all we know about how these systems work, it should not surprise us to locate fraudulent activity running after money. Using information from various sources, Insert 3:2 provides an example that involves some of the biggest names in medicine.

SCANDAL INVOLVING THE HIGH PRIESTS OF MEDICINE

Lancet and *New England Journal of Medicine* (NEJM) are arguably the most prestigious journals in the global field of peer-reviewed medical research. In May 2020, major Coronavirus-related studies appeared in both. The study in *Lancet* was about the use of the anti-malarial drug hydroxychloroquine (HCQ) to treat Covid-19. The study falsely[223] claimed that the use of HCQ could cause serious harm without helping patients.

Within a week, an open letter from over 200 scientists to *Lancet* requested details of the data and an independent audit. The letter was "signed by clinicians, medical researchers, statisticians, and ethicists from across the world."[224] Within about two weeks of publication, the studies were retracted by both journals.

Both retracted studies had been led by a widely published and highly regarded professor of medicine at Harvard University, who is also the medical director of the Heart and Vascular Center at Brigham and Women's Hospital.[225]

The database used for the studies came from a US company called Surgisphere. The *Lancet* study claimed to include 96,032 patients from 671 hospitals across six continents.[226] Regarding Sugisphere, a *Guardian* investigation revealed that its "handful of employees appear to include a science fiction writer and an adult-content model" and that both the COVID-19 research studies were "co-authored by its chief executive."[227]

An investigation by the Alliance for Human Research Protection, a watchdog for ethical standards in medical research, revealed the following:

"[The] lead co-author, affiliated with Harvard and Brigham & Women's Hospital, and the Lancet failed to disclose that Brigham Hospital has a partnership with Gilead and is currently conducting two trials testing Remdesivir, the prime competitor of hydroxychloroquine [HCQ] for the treatment of COVID-19, the focus of the study."[228]

On 15 June 2020, the FDA revoked the emergency use authorization for hydroxychloroquine and chloroquine.[229] The FDA also updated the fact sheets for the emergency use authorization of Remdesivir, to warn that using chloroquine or hydroxychloroquine with Remdesivir may reduce the antiviral activity of Remdesivir.[230]

In interviews with the New York Times, Dr. Horton, the editor-in-chief of Lancet, called the paper retracted by his journal a "*fabrication*" and "*a monumental fraud*."[231]

—*New York Times* (2020-06-4 and 06-14),
Guardian (2020-06-03), et al.

Insert 3:2

This information brings with it a throng of questions and concerns. Let's consider just a few. First, this is not the first time the name of a pharmaceutical company has shown up in news of this nature. Second, it is curious but not surprising that almost everyone (including the media outlets) is throwing all the blame on Surgisphere, the only "bad apple." Third, it would be difficult to explain the decision by Brigham as well as Lancet not to disclose the possible conflict of interest that Brigham & Women's had in this study. For everyone involved to claim such innocence shows the condition and ethos of the ugly barrel. Finally, the problem may not be as unique as the idea we get from the coverage in the *Times* and the *Guardian*.

For a rather condensed look at other examples of human vulnerability and how it applies to otherwise ethical healthcare professionals, the reader may wish to read *Medical Apartheid* (by Harriet Washington), or watch the documentary *Belly of the Beast*, or look up the role of the medical community in nuclear testing on the Marshall Islands.

2. Justice v. the Legal System:

Being a "nation of laws" is a common refrain within the United States. It seems, however, that our pride may be seriously misplaced. A vibrant society would put its pride in its system of justice, not in the abundance of laws that no legal scholar seems to be able to count. It is clear that, however long ago, what we considered to be the "rule of law" had already been converted into "rule by law." The consequences are damning. As the Human Rights Watch points out, "The 'land of the free' has become a country of prisons."[232] The following statistics in criminal law alone would help us explore the implications:

1. According to a 2015 analysis by the Brennan Center for Justice ("BCJ"), as many Americans have criminal records as college diplomas. Using DOJ and FBI data, the BCJ cites the number to be over 70 million.[233]

2. The United States imprisons the highest percentage of its citizenry of any country. Close to a quarter of the world's prisoners reside within the USA even though she has less than 5 percent of the world's population.[234] Even more strikingly, in absolute numbers, the United States has the highest number of people behind bars than any other country. In 2020, the United States had almost 7 million[235] people in its "correctional" system. About 2.3 million of them were incarcerated.[236]

3. If every US state were a country, the Top-30 countries with the worst per capita incarceration rate in the world would all be US states.[237] All of the 50 U.S. States would fall within the Top-60 worst countries in per capita incarceration.[238] "Liberal" California and Oregon would beat communist Cuba when it comes to incarceration. Connecticut, New York, and Washington are all worse than Rwanda. Oklahoma's incarceration rate is over five times that of Saudi Arabia's, eight times Uganda's, nine times China's, and forty-five times Congo's.[239]

4. A 2014 Bloomberg op-ed states: "more than 70 percent of American adults have committed a crime that could lead to imprisonment."[240] Citing a book by legal scholar Douglas Housak of Rutgers University, the op-ed says that, in addition to the federal and state criminal statutes, "300,000 or more federal regulations may be enforceable through criminal punishment in the discretion of an administrative agency. Nobody knows the number for sure."[241] The op-ed goes on to say that "the criminal law can no longer sort out the law-abiding from the non-law-abiding."[242]

   Validating this information, Columbia Law School's professor Jeffrey Fagan states: "I've violated imprisonable offenses while fishing,"[243] while Professor David Gray of the University of Maryland School of

> Law says: "70 percent seems low to me. Once you factor in ... [numerous listed scenarios] I'd be surprised if the percentage wasn't much higher than 70 percent over the course of most adults' lifetimes."[244]

As the points above indicate, the system of justice seems to vastly fail even on simple metrics, let alone purely moral dimensions. While nobody can be certain of how many laws we have on our books, we can be fairly certain of another reality: If we ran a computer simulation to apply all the laws to every single utterance and deed of every citizen, there is an extremely high likelihood that both you and I will be criminally convicted of one thing or the other (likely multiple crimes) that we committed without knowing anything about their legal status.

To comprehend the workings of the legal system, we have to deliberate the implication of this profusion of laws: "Police and prosecutors effectively define what is prohibited by their discretionary decisions to arrest and charge individuals... Vesting such power in prosecutors stands on its head the distinctive criminal law idea of the principle of legality, which demands advanced legislative definition of crime."[245] And this discretion in the hands of the prosecutor and the police effectively becomes a weapon against the poor because about 95 percent of criminal cases settle without going to trial.

The late William Stuntz of Harvard—labeled a "seminal thinker" and a "giant among legal theorists"—made this observation in a 2001 paper: "[We] are likely to come ever closer to a world in which the law on the books makes everyone a felon, and in which prosecutors and the police both define the law on the street and decide who has violated it."[246] He then asked the question: "How did criminal law come to be a one-way ratchet that makes an ever larger slice of the population felons?"[247] And the conclusion to his worthy document provides a clear answer to that vexing question:

> Criminal law is, in other words, not law at all, but a veil that hides a system that allocates criminal punishment discretionarily.... The system by which

> we make criminal law has produced not the rule of law but its opposite. And the doctrines that aim to reinforce the rule of law only add to the lawlessness.... Not only is the current system lawless, but the doctrines that aim to prevent that state of affairs instead ensure that it will continue to exist.[248]

As Stuntz would tell us, it is justice that has collapsed, not the system that claims to deliver it. It is noteworthy that he was an outspoken evangelical Christian and a political conservative. His views, therefore, cannot be boxed in the usual ideological categories, making his opinion on this subject that much more salient.

Sanford Kadish, a preeminent legal scholar, was the dean of UC Berkeley School of Law and one of the drafters of the American Model Penal Code. In a well-known 1967 paper, he seemed to have already pre-empted his future colleagues in pointing to the dangers of the legal systems becoming the primary arbiter of good and bad:

> The use of criminal law to enforce morals ... has served to reduce the criminal law's essential claim to legitimacy ... It has also fostered organized criminality and has produced, possibly, more crime than it has suppressed... Finally, its use to circumvent restrictions on police conduct has undermined the principle of legality and exposed the law to plausible charges of hypocrisy.[249]

Even preliminary research on this subject exposes a system that is not merely unjust and inhuman, it is also economically insane.[250] The 2020 dissenting opinion by Chief Justice Bernette Johnson of the Louisiana Supreme Court sheds light on the case of Fair Wayne Bryant, a Black man sentenced to life in prison for an attempted (but unsuccessful) minor theft:

> Mr. Bryant was sentenced to life in prison for unsuccessfully attempting to make off with somebody else's hedge clippers. Since his conviction in 1997, Mr. Bryant's incarceration has cost Louisiana taxpayers

> approximately $518,667... If he lives another twenty years, Louisiana taxpayers will have paid almost one million dollars to punish Mr. Bryant at his failed effort to steal a set of hedge clippers.[251]

From Augustine of Hippo to Thomas Aquinas to Henry David Thoreau, the theme of unjust law finds abundant coverage, all seemingly following the lead of *Isaiah* 10:

> Woe to those who make unjust laws, to those who issue oppressive decrees, to deprive the poor of their rights and withhold justice from the oppressed of my people.

As an example, looking at the statistics relating to sexual offense against women, we find that the global socio-political systems and their legal mechanisms are failing the human race. We also see how the reported numbers often and effectively "disappear" the magnitude of the crisis.

A 2009-2010 survey of female students in the United Kingdom found that "68 per cent have been a victim of one or more kinds of sexual harassment on campus during their time as a student" and 14 percent have "experienced a serious physical or sexual assault."[252] Global numbers are also similar. Drawing on 104 studies from 16 countries, a 2021 analysis in the Lancet concluded that 17.4 percent of women students in higher education had been victims of an "attempted or completed sexual act obtained by force, violence, or coercion."[253]

Despite this reality, what gets reported is puny. A special report by the Guardian in 2017 revealed that for the six years from 2011 to 2017, 120 institutions of higher education in the United Kingdom had received only 169 allegations of staff-on-student sexual harassment.[254] (Almost half of those universities and colleges reported to have had zero such incidents during the six-year period.) Given the statistics quoted above, though, these numbers defy reason.

What's happening at universities is not an exception to the rule; it is a fair representation of reality in general. As philosopher Lorna Finlayson points out, "rates of violence are not significantly higher in universities than anywhere else."[255] In short, this is a massive concern in various domains. In the face of this global pandemic directed mostly towards a specific gender, the legal system's irrelevance comes from India where "an estimated 99.1 per cent of sexual violence cases are not reported."[256]

Does human history show such state of affairs prevailing in past societies? Does anthropology reveal that the human race has always been this misogynistic, with such criminal orientation towards its women—within the same society? It would arguably be reasonable to suspect that the Hobbesian socio-political system, including its legal component, is responsible globally for the problem—especially so because no serious effort towards a solution is visible.

Two clear conclusions seem to emerge statistically, signifying the socio-political system's culpability. First, the Hobbesian system is evidently failing to respect the rights of a specific gender. Second, the system is grossly underreporting the incidence of crime against the gender, effectively keeping the concern below the radar.

At a micro level too, it is easy to see the malfeasance, opportunism, careerism, corruption, persecution, and inhumanity prevalent in the legal system. Here's a good example: Ronnie Long was released in 2020 after forty-three years of captivity—for a rape he did not commit.[257] The moral bankruptcy of the system—and it appears continually—is that his conviction was the result of perjury by state officials and that evidence in his favor was wittingly suppressed. The color of his skin must have been incriminating enough to establish guilt. The list of such exonerations in the last quarter of a century alone is in the thousands, and there must be other tens of thousands who were not so lucky.

For more examples, the reader may wish to read about the cases against Aaron Swartz and Steven Donziger.[258] Some things do not change, unless, of course, society finds the spark in its heart that leads to the desired change. That, our society must!

In describing the natural human state as fraudulent and violent, Enlightenment philosopher Hobbes says: "The notions of Right and Wrong, Justice and Injustice have there no place. Where there is no common Power, there is no Law: where no Law, no Injustice.

Force, and Fraud, are in warre the two Cardinall vertues. Justice, and Injustice are none of the Faculties neither of the Body, nor Mind."[259]

Hobbes was trying to reason that a system without an all-subjugating law would be without the notion of right and wrong, just and unjust. What he did not realize is that when a society is run mostly on a system of law, a similar result is likely to be produced. Perhaps our politico-legal system is showing those symptoms.[260]

Legal Leviathan or The Radical Love of Jesus?

Justice is a central concept in the Qur'an and its exhortation is ubiquitous. In 16:90, the Holy Book says: "Truly, God commands Justice and Ihsan." We have to keep in mind that both Justice and Ihsan (beauty in action) become compatible (and second nature) only when based upon the foundations of love and service. Without love and service, they cannot be part of one's state of being.

This connection between justice, beautiful action, service, and love would seem strange. Yet, it should not be so. What makes this relationship odd is simply the legal backdrop of Roman law within which we seem to be setting it up for evaluation. This backdrop establishes our expectations of what we mean by justice, equity, fairness, freedom and other such concepts. Therein is our limitation because these conceptual frameworks may limit even our imagination.

Incompatibility is inevitable when we compare Roman law to Jesus' love or the Qur'anic concepts stated above. Even in a concept such as freedom, incompatibility is unavoidable when the "Roman Law conception of natural freedom ... implies freedom is essentially a state of primordial exception to the legal order."[261]

And it is this kind of an incompatibility that Dr. King is referring to in the excerpt below. Using the example of Jesus,[262] King makes it clear that our legal system, defying evidence and good sense, seems intent to "continue to go its disastrous way ... to worship the god of revenge and bow before the altar of retaliation."

> Man is slow to forgive. We live by the philosophy that life is a matter of getting even and saving face.... Society is even less prone to forgive.... Man has never

> risen above this idea of the lex talionis [Latin for "law as retaliation"]. In spite of the fact that the law of revenge solves no social problems, men continue to go its disastrous way. History is cluttered with the wreckage of nations and individuals that followed this self-defeating path. Jesus eloquently affirmed from the cross a higher law.... He overcame evil with good. Although crucified by hate, he responded with a radical love.[263] What a magnificent lesson! Generations will continue to rise and fall; men will continue to worship the god of revenge and bow before the alter of retaliation; but ever and again this noble lesson from Calvary will come as a nagging reminder that only goodness can drive out evil,[264] and only love can conquer hate.[265]

In order to understand King's reference to Jesus's love, we have to be able to grasp the all-encompassing place of love in all aspects of our life. In his *Epistle on Love*, Ibn Sina (Avicenna), the eleventh century Persian polymath,[266] expressed it thus: "Love is the manifestation of Essence and Existence."[267]

Naseer-ud-Din Tusi, the thirteenth century political and social philosopher, advocated an idea similar to Dr. King's. His highly circulated book *Akhlaq* (Ethics)[268] has a chapter titled "Virtue of Love, By Means of Which Societies Are Bound Together." The excerpt below is not about the need to replace hypocrisy, injustice, or the law with love. What this says is that love even replaces our concept of justice altogether: "The need for Justice ... arises from the absence of love, for if love were to accrue between individuals, there would be no necessity for equity and impartiality ... In this regard, the virtue of Love over Justice is obvious."[269]

What we are discussing here is difficult to absorb given the prevalent paradigms and thought patterns our modern societies are so used to. In the zeitgeist[270] of his time even, King stated "that law and order exist for the purpose of establishing justice, and that when they fail to do this they become dangerously structured dams that block the flow of social progress."[271]

Over the last century, we have also witnessed the profusion of the legal concept of human rights, whose definitional subjectivity has rendered it all but meaningless for the ordinary person, though the concept now is used to justify wars and conflict. In following King's approach, a better idea would be to replace the concept of "human rights" with the pursuit of a framework that includes non-hypocritical justice, informed[272] human agency, and equality of human dignity. (Dignity here implies the inborn value and spiritual worth of every human being.)

> And when they are told, 'Do not spread corruption on earth,' they answer, 'We are but improving things!'
>
> —Qur'an 2:11

> It is he who has empowered us as ministers of a new covenant, not written but spiritual; for the written law condemns to death, but the Spirit gives life.
>
> — 2 Corinthians 3:6

The word Leviathan in the title of this section is a pointer to Thomas Hobbes's magnum opus. It should be clear that our legal system, based upon adversarial animus, is now a leviathan that follows Hobbes's prescription. It would take some imagination, yet the prescription from Jesus is quite the opposite. A society whose principles and practices follow Jesus's socio-ethical philosophy, as elaborated by Dr. King, rather than those enunciated by the Enlightenment philosophers, can only be more humane and tranquil than the current legal order.

Historic Racism and Other Injustice Via Legal Structures

We would be remiss not to briefly discuss the place of racism and other forms of injustice inherent not just in our socio-political system but in the various facets of our legal system. For example, recent statistics indicate that the incarceration rate of Black citizens in the United States is over 600 percent above that of incarceration for Blacks at the zenith of the Apartheid regime in South Africa.[273] At one time or another in the history of our nation, virtually every minority has faced discrimination: LGBT, women, Catholics, Jews, Muslims, Irish, Italians, Japanese, Chinese, Latino, the indigenous ... among other "politically weaker" minorities of their time.

While bias, in some form, may have been part of our human nature, the last half a millennium saw some extreme manifestations of it all over the world. Much of it has more to do with systems of power and profit than with pure human nature. When we look deeper, we may find that it has been necessary to politically stoke and manipulate human weaknesses to achieve the outcomes that we have witnessed over this period. The role of structures pursuing financial and political gain has always been instrumental and instructive.

History tells us that for a millennium and a half, Jewish ghettos/quarters in Europe functioned under their own systems without help from the state or the official law. This was possible because of a strong culture that included an ethical code of how to live in society. The other side of the coin would be the *Limpieza de Sangre* (purity of blood) doctrine and laws in Spain, introduced in the fifteenth century, which remained on the books until centuries later. These laws were used against Christians who themselves or whose ancestors—Jews and Moorish Muslims—had converted to Christianity. This may have been the very beginnings of our modern notion of race, which was further modified by post-Enlightenment developments in science, philosophy, and commerce. It is interesting to note that, as evident here, the conceptual framework for race began with the desire by a group of Christians to deprive another group of Christians based upon their past or even lineage that connected or affiliated with two minority religions. Another inference is that the law or the state were not needed by minorities with a culture; yet it was law that was used as an instrument of oppression and persecution.

The current racism phenomenon in Europe and North America, we have to realize, is rather paradoxical (certainly so to this author). Having lived and worked on both continents, it would be fair to classify most of the countless people I have come across as inherently decent, sincere, humanistic, and non-racist. Yet the systemic problem is simply undeniable.

It would thus be the "polluted barrel" inherited from the past whose exploitation by certain forces continues its toxicity. Understanding and accepting history as it was become important in unravelling this dilemma because past and present inspire, and even justify, ideas in their domains. And it happens in a rather rotary form. As pointed out by a Yale law professor, for example, "when the leading Nazi jurists assembled in early June 1934 to debate how to institutionalize racism in the new Third Reich, they began by asking how the Americans did it."[274] Ironically, the inspiration now goes in the reverse: racist groups in the United States use the Third Reich as their inspiration! History can be a teacher only if we humans allow it to be. The depth of ignorance needed to create these bigotries becomes blatant as we realize that "the only thing we can say with real certainty is that, in terms of ancestry, we are all Africans."[275]

While the complex topic of racism is beyond the scope of this book, three brief ideas are in order. First, our religions have provided very effective guidelines in terms of prejudice, though their abuse is also common even within religions, as was seen in the example of the blood purity laws. Second, racism has no biological basis. It is entirely a social construct, and a relatively recent one at that. Besides, in its present state, we may not even be able to really understand racism unless we bring in classism, and androcentrism (patriarchy/misogyny), as well as other prejudices and their manifestations such as gross economic inequity. Socio-political systems have to be understood as a whole, not piecemeal. Third, as Zimbardo recommended, we need to shift the focus entirely towards the "evil barrel" rather than the "bad apple" even in understanding and undoing the undergirding of racism. Evidence tells us that too much emphasis on punishing the "bad apple" in a Hobbesian system creates polarization and is detrimental to society's interest. Dr. King would choose fixing the barrel rather than a fixation on the bad apples.

In Search of a Free, Functional, and Just Society

A salient intent of this chapter is to show the grossly unfair, and perhaps erroneous, emphasis on "law" as the fundamental, if not the only, constituent of what drives our society's concept of functionality, well-being, and justice. We know from history that a society encourages and exhorts using its code of moral rules, whereas it forces and compels using its code of legal rules. But a society is not formed or known by its laws, but rather by its morals.[276] For a living and functional society, a moral ethic is essential and cannot be replaced by even an abundance of books and universities, let alone an abundance of laws.

A free and functional society has to be one that is able to exhort without an undue reliance on compelling or goading through legal ordinances. When, however, a society is completely accustomed to being forced by legal rules, it loses its capacity for exhortation without the law. A people that is subject to the whip of the law (or policies) for their day-to-day living and decision-making cannot possibly be exercising free will, and thus is substantively not free.

Finally, the "lawlessness" in the presence of an overwhelming regime of laws is not limited to a single country; it is a global phenomenon and a feature of the fiat-driven system that controls every aspect of life. To gain a wholesome understanding of subjects such as society, culture, and law, it may be time we paid attention to our scriptures and the message we have had in our possession for millennia. Lao Tzu's opinion on the subject minces no words:

> The more legal affairs are given prominence, the more numerous bandits and thieves.
>
> —*Tao Te Ching* 57:12-13

Cumulative Impact on Our Systems of Living

Some of the current human dilemmas are best understood with examples at local and individual level (see chapters in part 2). While difficult and intricate, the symptoms and perils of the complex conundrums are also clear on various dimensions. A lucid understanding will facilitate the realization and acceptance of our responsibility: individual and collective. Let's set the stage by evaluating geopolitical commentator Pankaj Mishra's statement in the *New York Review of Books* (May 22, 2018). This analysis will bring together various forces in action and then show how religious identity is abused in the process of conditioning and exploitation.

Attributing the process of dehumanization in various parts of the world to "organized disgust for the religious/ethnic/civilizational 'alien'," Mishra comments on the deeper drivers of this condition and warns us that our faith in our institutions is misplaced: "Liberal detractors of Trump, Modi, and other elected demagogues set great store by democracy's impersonal institutions, and their checks and balances. But political and culture wars among groups sequestered in their hate have reached a new peak of ferocity, and faith in the rules, norms, and laws of liberal democracy seems too complacent."[277]

Referring then to the rape of an eight-year-old girl in India, and its politicization on sectarian and religious grounds, Mishra goes on to say:

> Faith in humanity is unlikely to survive contact with the politicians,[278] police officials, and lawyers who ideologically justify the rape of a child; and reason and logic will seem the slave of vile passions when manifested in the whataboutism, driven by fake news, of social media 'influencers,' who include a pioneering feminist publisher and an information technology tycoon.[279]

Mishra's excerpts highlight the corruption and degeneration of various socio-political structures at a global level working against our collective well-being. The dynamic forces in motion here are institutional, technological, commercial, political, ideological, and psychological. We can immediately see the tyrannies of identity and victory in action. Fear (of the "other") is inserted into such situations. We can also see the role of media and communication channels engaging in hateful propaganda. The structures of power and economic interests are fully involved too. All this is wrapped up in the Hobbesian "religion" of adversariness ("war of everyone against everyone"). Culture, obviously, is too delicate a thing to survive the forces unleashed by the power play of international and local politics.

Edmund Burke was an eighteenth-century Irish philosopher who is known as the founder of modern conservatism. In the *Reflections on the Revolution in France*, Burke wrote, "the most important of all revolutions ... [is] a revolution in sentiments, manners, and moral opinions."[280] Here, Burke is pointing to the French Revolution's negative impact on the psychology, education, and culture of society. That concern would be equally applicable today in the evident evolution our socio-political systems are going through globally. We should be equally watchful of the evolution underway in the "sentiments, manners, and moral opinions" of human societies—the evolution that has been caused by the global structures protecting their economic and political power. We should also be cognizant that the consequences of evolution are much more durable than those of a revolution.

When the very scale of values is turned upside down by societal institution, the concerns expressed by Burke and Mishra become palpable and imminent. The "faith in humanity" Mishra refers to can only be restored when we humans have relearned how to detach ourselves from our narrow material interests and have realized the fundamental weaknesses of human nature; and when we have dismantled our blind faith in institutions we have ourselves created. The work to repair would best commence once the root cause of the problem has been identified.

PART TWO:

HOBBESIAN ENLIGHTENMENT: UNDERSTANDING THE SOCIETAL DECLINE

Heartened by the naivete of simpletons like me,
what sacrilege have the false prophets
not pulled off?[281]

—Faiz Ahmed Faiz

CHAPTER 4:

SOCIETAL CONSTRUCTS EXACERBATING TYRANNIES OF HUMAN PSYCHE

Since he knows that self-mastery
means unbinding the bonds of dukkha,
he should practice self-mastery resolutely,
without despair dulling his reason.
—Bhagavad Gita 6.23

Of paths, the eightfold is the best.
Of truths, the four statements.
Detachment is the best of dhammas.
And of two-footed ones, the one endowed with eyes.
—Dhammapada 20.1

Economic models are usually based upon the assumption of what is referred to as "homo economicus." According to Investopedia, "The term 'economic man' (also referred to as 'homo economicus') refers to an idealized person who acts rationally,[282] with perfect knowledge and who seeks to maximize personal utility or satisfaction. The presence of an economic man is an assumption of many economic models."[283] This belief dovetails with Aristotle's classification of human as a rational animal (*zoon logon echon*). And yet this theory of the rational man is violated time and again.[284] In the consumer market alone, as this chapter shows, transition from *homo sapiens* to *homo economicus* to *homo consumericus* is rather easily achieved.

Before addressing the "tyrannies" of human psyche, we will set up the thought-framework upon the Enlightenment philosophy, especially the doctrine of Thomas Hobbes. Understanding Hobbes's creed and its influence on our social systems becomes instructive and instrumental in grasping the core of this chapter. Hobbes is not just recognized as a pivotal force in the post-Renaissance development of thought, he is still very much considered a towering and seminal sociopolitical thinker.[285]

Referring to Hobbes's central place in our social thinking, psychologist Adam Phillips and historian Barbara Taylor write in their 2009 book *On Kindness*: "Modern ideas ... effectively begin with Hobbes and his critics ... thus he is a key figure in this history, his insights providing a crucial bridge between past and present."[286]

As we explore the concept of "tyrannies," we'll see how the adversarial conception of Hobbesian relations can provide one of the basic underpinnings influencing today's thought patterns and perhaps even belief systems. His proclamation, "war of everyone against everyone,"[287] now ubiquitously resonates in all walks of human life. In consort with the proverb that declares man as a wolf to its fellow men (*homo homini lupus est*), Hobbes's doctrine has played a remarkably influential role in how our institutions are structured.

A careful reading of Hobbes's seminal texts *Leviathan* and *De Cive* shows that man is essentially worse than a beast because no other animal—not even the wolf quoted in the Latin proverb—behaves this way within its own species. For clarity, summarized below are two salient points in Hobbes's *Leviathan*:

Chapter XIII makes it clear that Man's known disposition is to be in a state of war with one another. There is no place for right/wrong, just/unjust in man's faculties. The individual has no conscience or moral sensibility. Thus, a controlling power is needed to keep all people in awe. Given this description of fundamental human nature, chapter XIV tells us that man has natural right to anything owned by another man (yes, even his body). Because an individual's honor cannot be counted upon, a coercive power is needed to compel performance of any agreement.[288]

Naturally, with *Leviathan* regarded as "the founding text of modern political theory,"[289] thinkers and socio-political influencers in recent history have promoted some version of Hobbes's theory. And the adversarial state of current human systems and conduct seem to be rather reflective of this doctrine.[290] This mindset contradicts not just our indigenous spirituality, traditional religions, and Greek philosophical tradition, but even modern science itself.[291]

The research of Michal Yakir, an Israeli botanist, provides clear evidence. Referring to what she calls *conscientious collaboration* within the world of flowers, Yakir expounds: "These collaborative strategies—where everyone gives some of itself for the greater good, yet benefits—was found to be the most advanced and efficient strategy of all."[292]

In the mammalian domain, this same observation has been emphasized by ethologist Frans de Waal, an expert in the evolution of animal behavior and human character:

> Western civilization ... seems saturated with the assumption that we are asocial, even nasty[293] creatures rather than the *zoon politikon* that Aristotle saw in us.... [We] are social to the core... Our social makeup is so obvious that there would be no need to belabor this point were it not for its conspicuous absence from origin stories within the disciplines of law, economics, and political science.[294]

De Waal's reasoning needs no further elaboration. Indeed, our social nature is so transparent that, other than execution and outright torture, solitary confinement is considered the most punishing and deleterious sentence for a human being. Just like physical sciences, our social and political sciences would benefit from a willingness to evolve and to accommodate fresh ways of thinking. This is important because recent developments in fields such as anthropology and sociology already tell us that "we have exposed the mythical substructure of our 'social science'—what once appeared unassailable axioms, the *stable points* around which our self-knowledge is organized, are scattering like mice."[295]

The dimensions of human psyche this chapter discusses impede our spiritual growth, forming formidable hurdles in our pursuit of meaning, purpose, and even joy. We can refer to these weaknesses as the tyrannies of: Fear, Want, Victory, and Identity. It would also be entirely reasonable to consider them as mental and psychological diseases created by the Hobbesian system.

In human life, there is a necessary place for all of the four human frailties under discussion here. The distinction this chapter makes is that, instead of meeting the genuine individual and collective human needs, these fragilities are often exploited by our institutional structures. And that distinction, between genuine need and exploitable vulnerability, is of pivotal significance.

It is also important to evaluate all these in an interactive dynamic to appreciate the full impact on human psyche and our society. The current exploitation of these ego-self vulnerabilities reflects a severe and unprecedented societal phenomenon, both in terms of intensity and scope. According to the *Dhammapada*, which is a collection of the Buddha's sayings, self-mastery (or subduing one's base-ego) shields us from being exploited through these doorways of human susceptibility.

> Excellent are tamed mules,
> Thoroughbreds and horses of Sindh,
> also tuskers, great elephants.
> But better than them
> is one who has subdued oneself.[296]

Tyranny of Fear

As twentieth century's preeminent philosopher Bertrand Russell explained, "fear is the main source of superstition and one of the main sources of cruelty."[297] As Russell goes on to say, to conquer fear is the beginning of wisdom towards the pursuit of truth and a worthy life.

The instinct and emotion of fear has been critical to the survival of the human race. When the context is not manipulated, fear is usually a useful emotion in human life. But, in today's world, that is usually not the case. Fear has been historically used for exploitation. Those who leverage fear understand that, in the human mind, survival emotions take precedence over reason and truth. While the capacity for fear is innate to human psyche, the nature and intensity of the emotion can be—and frequently are—externally created and manipulated. As an example, we'll use the famous murder scene in Alfred Hitchcock's 1960 psychological horror movie *Psycho*.[298]

The shower scene is rather terrifying. However, we must understand the minor and major causality in this case. What creates the terror is not just the facts of what happened—that's the smaller component. The real driver is in the accouterments: the extreme closeups and other visual effects, the short duration of the scenes, the music and other audio effects, the anticipation created, etc. The seconds-long scene took a whole week to film, involved fifty cuts and seventy-seven camera angles. It wasn't just the audience that was riveted on the scene, Hitchcock himself invested a lot of effort into it, which indicates his grasp of human psychology and how to influence it. One film critic pointed out that Hitchcock had described his technique's objective as "transferring the menace from the screen into the mind of the audience."[299]

In other words, the terror this scene induces may have more to do with all the sensual embellishments than just with the facts of the scene. Surprisingly, real life may not be so different from the techniques used in Tinseltown. And perhaps Shakespeare's metaphor of the world being a stage may be, in some ways, reflective of reality. We just have to keep in mind that "transferring the menace from the screen into the mind of the audience" is accomplishable only with some level of cooperation from, or receptivity by, the subject.

The exploitation of fear is found in every domain of life, from advertising to electoral politics. Many still remember the Willie Horton ads—circa 1988 in the Bush-Dukakis presidential contest—that exploited racial stereotypes and fears. That should come as no surprise since "irrational fears" is the first of the three elements in Dr. King's theory of racism. Clearly, those running the Willie-Horton ad in the campaign understood that very well. The arousal of the common person's fearful imagination offers immense utility in shaping political contexts, partisan perceptions, and for the mobilization of blind passions.

Tyranny of Want[300]

For us to be able to live, certain physical needs have to be met. Air and water come to mind. This category is really not fungible. What this means is that any meaningful change in the quality of air or water, or any pollution of them, would pose a serious detriment to us. Then there is the need for necessities such as food, clothing, and housing. There is some level of fungibility there, in that there are almost an infinite number of options in terms of the nature, the quality, the quantity/amount, etc., that would be sufficient to meet the human need. Then there are needs such as transportation, source of livelihood, etc. There are also various other types of non-material needs, including emotional, familial, psychological, moral, and social. Those are not the focus of our discussion here. (In fact, those crucial needs often are sidelined in creating the more "physical" cravings of consumption, possession, and acquisition.)

Societies have historically met their members' needs in different ways. When the sole purpose of so many institutional entities is to focus on profit, the concept of genuine need very quickly morphs into needless craving that is detached from authentic need. Success in meeting that objective also creates unquenchable acquisitiveness within a society's members, and the drive to imitate what others have, and the cycle goes on. With this conditioning, the concept of contentment, which every religion promotes, is ejected from our psyche.

As alluded to by James Baldwin, an American writer and orator, within such a structure-based system, there may still be an implicit understanding to fulfill human spiritual needs through the material route, thus bringing us "much closer to being metaphysical because nobody has ever expected from *things* the miracles that we expect."[301] As an example, note the category labeled *Inner Beauty* included within the cosmetics section on the website of a big-box retailer (image in Figure 4). Thus, the very concept of "inner beauty" is now a cosmetic notion, because it can sell whatever makeup a corporation wants to sell. Psychologically, this obsession with image "creates an image of the self ... that is utterly lacking in natural generosity."[302]

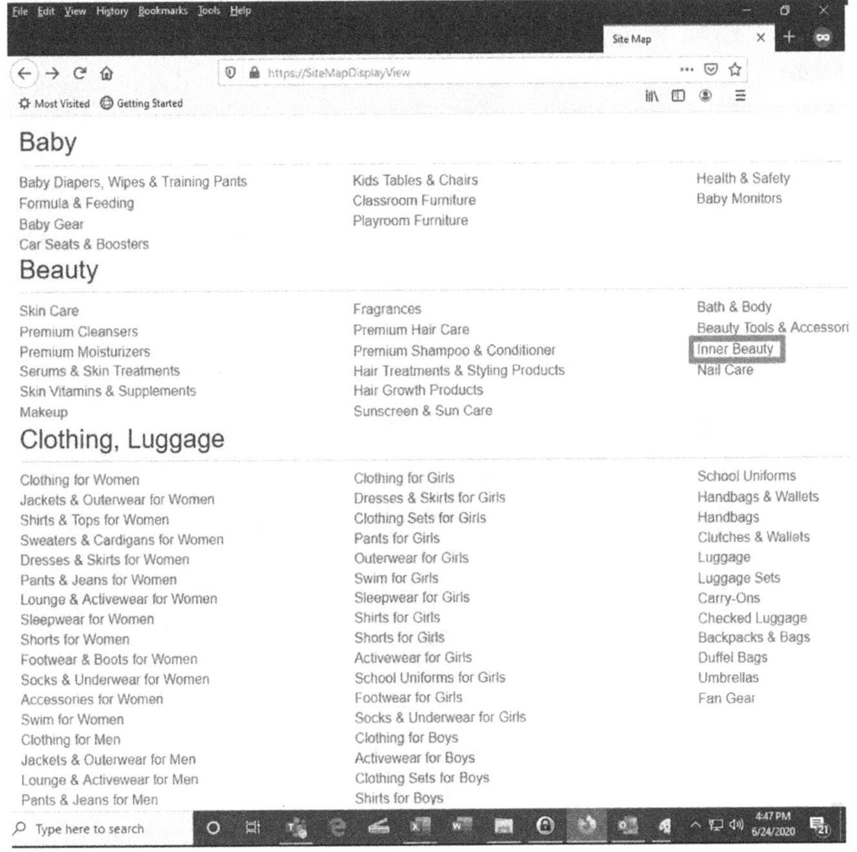

Figure 4

Another example of a "society where 'respect' for personal status has become a leading value,"[303] is the positive light given by the media to the egregious excesses of billionaires and celebrities in showing their success. But the same media give negligible space to the countless millions who are homeless or hungry. Clearly, keeping them faceless keeps their plight meritless.

We would be told that such is the self-correcting mechanism of the "free market." Yet the patent contradictions of these mechanisms stay far away from the public consciousness. Why, for example, is it that in the United States—a society where the military is considered sacrosanct by so many—some 15-20 percent of active-duty military families are food insecure?[304] And how do we justify the millions of children who chronically face hunger and food insecurity in the richest society ever in human history? Is it consistent with Jesus's message in a country with the largest Christian population in the world? Indeed, the system has successfully obfuscated that thought and deliberation at both the collective and the individual level. The side effects of this need-want inversion are highly informative and instructive. And yet, as eminent British psychologist Adam Phillips says, "agreeing to talk about winners and losers is part and parcel of the phobic avoidance, the contemporary terror, of kindness."[305] He points out that kindness—"not sexuality, not violence, not money—has become our forbidden pleasure."[306]

PUBLIC AS INFORMED DECISION-MAKER: QUESTIONS FOR A DEMOCRACY

- When did our media and government actually begin actively informing the public about climate change and its impact? Did Exxon conduct a study decades ago whose conclusions showed the potential implications of climate change?[307] Did Exxon immediately inform the public about that study? Was the public ever informed about that study? Will the public ever know the truth about that study?
- Why is it that a significant portion of the US municipal water supply does not meet national safety standards?[308] Was it equally polluted fifty years ago? Was bottled water all the rage fifty years ago? Does the average citizen realize that two-thirds of bottled water is filtered tap water?[309] How is it that large beverage companies can purchase municipal water at low prices and then sell at high profits? In 2018, it was estimated that $31 billion were spent[310] on bottled water in the United States.

Wouldn't the billions be better spent on fixing the municipal water system?

- Why are commercials aimed toward children created using child psychology? Are psychologists involved in the preparation of such commercials? Would a healthy and spiritually purposeful society target young and impressionable children to sell goods, especially with the help of psychological manipulation techniques such as neuromarketing?[311]

Insert 4:1

What we are witnessing is that meeting the needs of our economic systems can become hazardous to us in an individual as well as a collective sense. The profit need necessitates that more and more wants are created so that the demand and supply capacities keep nudging each other up and up "forever." Most human societies in the past would have considered it to be a rather odd outlook on life given the common spiritual theme in most religions that "the matters of Torah do not endure except in one who considers himself as one who does not exist."[312]

Because human nature avoids the dissonance that any contradiction creates, the hazard—even when clearly visible—would have to be overlooked. And yet the contradiction is in our face. To paraphrase James Baldwin, the failure to look reality in the face diminishes the nation as it diminishes the individual. Our current systems of living meet the wants of a small minority to the extreme, and yet they ruthlessly ignore the genuine needs for a meaningful survival of a very large percentage of its population—the very populations that keep the systems breathing.

Not just a vivacious but a simply functional society should be able to notice the moral and existential dilemmas such problems present. Societies that ignore the reality of injustice may one day have to pay even a bigger price than their evolutionary decay. In his poem titled "Harlem," Langston Hughes went on to say that a "dream deferred" festers and then explodes.

Let's close this section with an excerpt from Lord Byron's poem titled the "Age of Bronze":

> And will they not repay the treasures lent?
> No: down with everything, and up with rent!
> Their good, ill, health, wealth, joy, or discontent,
> Being, end, aim, religion—rent, rent, rent![313]

Tyranny of Victory

Setting and achieving goals is a praiseworthy attitude and achievement. It facilitates our ability to live a life with clear meaning and purpose. Such an attitude is necessary for an individual to live a life that is meaningful for their own self and for the society. This chapter highlights that the current state of human societies projects a different picture than the pursuit of these desirable attributes of success. And if we are willing to question the status quo, the picture begins to clear up.

In accordance with the Hobbesian model of extreme individualism, some of the traits and attributes that our politico-economic systems promote include avarice, envy, exclusivity, power, etc. Life itself seems to be treated as a zero-sum game. We cannot "win" unless someone "loses," as if the validation of our being is a function of this Hobbesian paradigm. The manifestations of this can be found everywhere, from the legal systems making life and death decisions to the most mundane everyday activity. When carefully evaluated, we see that the two sports-related examples below are two sides of the same coin.

A large percentage of people in Connecticut are staunch fans of either the New York Yankees or the Boston Red Sox. The fanaticism can be real and bigger than life. I know of at least one religious individual in Connecticut who literally prays to God for the victory of their team. To add to the irony, neither of these teams is from Connecticut, so there is no ostensible basis for such a connection. In Europe, deadly violence among spectators at football games (called soccer in the USA) is not that uncommon, all in the name of sports! These two examples may present different results, yet they share a common root to the phenomena.

The need to be in this adversarial mode all the time tends to remove compassion from the individual's mindset, and perhaps may even increase sadistic tendencies as the ideological stance of such belief. The system-imposed, win-lose model creates winners and losers in a rather deterministic fashion.[314] In a binary frame of reference, even ostensible cooperation becomes competition from some angle. The collaboration needed for a society to be functional is thus not perceived to be an essential ingredient of the mental models that govern attitudes. Competitive instinct, while part of human nature, has been a lesser theme to the main motif of collaboration and caring. Explaining evolutionary human history, cultural anthropologist Mary Clark points out, "Social bonding to one's group was a biological necessity—for adults as well as infants."[315]

Very clearly, nature—which man is part of—does not follow the Hobbesian formula. It is innately collaborative and self-managed, where every component works in synch with each other—just like the human body and its trillions of cells.

Dr. Mae-Wan Ho was a biochemist who specialized in organisms. In her study of sustainable living systems based upon quantum cohesion, she concluded that "coherent state thus maximizes *both* global cohesion and also local freedom."[316] She further emphasized that "by following to logical conclusions the development of western scientific ideas since the beginning of the [twentieth] century, we come full circle to validating the participatory framework that is universal to all traditional indigenous knowledge systems all over the world."[317]

Interpreting this in a sociological context, Dr. Ho is saying that individual freedom and societal cohesion (and functionality) can be simultaneously maximized only if we use non-Hobbesian (i.e., collaborative) paradigms in the way we function and interact. Nature evidences this axiom again and again.

In explaining the "group cooperation" behavior of highly evolved flower species, botanist Michal Yakir explains: "As opposed to the strategy of 'every flower for itself,' the more advanced ones developed a compound ... of many crowded, tiny flowers [that] ... collaborate ...

but each one gets to produce its own fruit and seed separately. The collaboration preserves individuality. But combines resources."[318]

The Hobbesian pivot, in the past three centuries, towards adversarial human conduct has been a drastic step back in human progress. That determination is in synch with this Jain teaching: "Those whose minds are at peace and who are free from passions do not desire to live at the expense of others."[319] It is important to realize that even within the context of a democratic nation-state, the domestic implications of "victory" at any cost can have grim expressions.

A case in point is the 2011 nuclear disaster at Fukushima, Japan, and its aftermath. As noted by the *Scientific American*, the commission named by the then Prime Minister Naoto Kan reported that the "potential evacuation ... affected 50 million people."[320] This would have meant, as Kan later recounted, "the end of Japan as a functioning state."[321] He stated that "the information supplied to him by the nuclear power industry in the aftermath of the meltdowns proved false"[322] and "announced a commitment to end nuclear power in Japan by 2040."[323]

Timothy Mousseau of the University of South Carolina has spent years studying the environmental impact of the nuclear disaster at Chernobyl. His research around the Fukushima accident showed results similar to Chernobyl in Ukraine, which was, at that time, part of the Soviet Union. And the Japanese authorities did not seem to have been pleased by the researcher's work. As Mousseau explained to *Harper's*: "One reason we do not know as much about Fukushima as we should is that the Japanese—*the government, academia, the corporation, it's all the same thing*—really discouraged research. I was certainly pressured not to publish my findings."[324]

Desirable results are easy to attain under such conditions. For example a campaign ("*the right not to know*") by the local Japanese authorities to discourage the screening of children for thyroid cancer had, by 2016, delivered declining numbers of thyroid cancer in children.[325] Prime Minister Shinzo Abe's 2014 energy plan stated that "Japan will push to restart the dozens of reactors closed after the disaster, and potentially even build new ones in the future."[326] In

2021, Prime Minister Fumio Kishida further endorsed Abe's policy.[327] A January 10, 2022, journalistic piece, however, gives the lie to such sanguine official posture:

> TEPCO [Tokyo Electric Power Company] is suffering some very serious setbacks that have '*impossible to deal with*' written all over the issues.... TEPCO still does not know how to handle the enormously radioactive nuclear fuel debris, or corium, sizzling hot radioactive lumps of melted fuel rods and container material in [reactors] No. 1, No 2, and No.3. They're not even 100% sure where all of the corium is and whether it's getting into underground water resources. What a disaster that would be, what if it is already? Never mind.
>
> The newest wrinkle at TEPCO involves the continuous flow of water necessary to keep the destroyed reactors' hot stuff from exposure to air, thus spreading explosively red-hot radioactivity across the countryside. That constant flow of water is an absolute necessity to prevent an explosion of all explosions, likely emptying the streets of Tokyo in a ... 'mass evacuation.'[328]

Understanding some of these concerns in more detail leads one to realize the real "impossibility" of the task at hand. Given this information and Mousseau's testimony above, we'll never know what has been—and is being—hidden from the Japanese people. No conspiracy here; these Japanese entities simply seem to be acting to protect their own interest. And yet the need for "victory" in their interests has propelled the leaders of various institutions to possibly work against the interests of the society whose interest they claim to serve.

Tyranny of Identity

A sense of belonging, a primeval human sentiment, has helped us with our survival, and has brought us together in mutual respect and harmonious living. The human tendency, however, to attach to tribalistic identity has been historically exploited by political interests to diminish human agency.[329] Recognizing and ameliorating this vulnerability is all the more important today because our collective human well-being (and perhaps survival) depends upon it.

The argument in this book is not that one should give up one's identity. Instead, the case being made is that such an identity should not be allowed to overcome one's independent discernment capacity within any sociopolitical system. Unquestioning loyalty to one's identity can offer no emancipatory benefit: political, psychological, collective, or individual. Instead, it becomes a vehicle of exploitation by those with agendas. As elaborated below, the exploitability of identity resides in how it can be used to take away the capability of objective judgment from us. We all fall victim to it in one place or the other, to one degree or the other. The nationalistic and religiopolitical identities especially are almost always built upon histories that are simultaneously mangled and embellished. How a person perceives their identity is often influenced by such distortions of history. Besides, by "attaching" to our identity, we "become" our identity—losing part of who we really are.

The term "identity" in this book is used mostly in the sense of social, group, and collective affiliation[330] based upon such classifications as national, religious, gender, racial, ethnic, etc. By leveraging and stoking narrow tribal passions, it is this social identity that is often used to accentuate in-group and out-group mentality, prejudice, stereotyping, and even hatred.

In the politico-ideological context, such affiliation (and loyalty, perceived or promoted) is abused in ways we are not always aware of. The harmful impacts of this exploitation, though, show up in ways totally outside such an identity. To understand the detrimental and exploitable aspect of identity, we would need to understand how we humans become attached to identities and how such attachment depletes, if not paralyzes, our capacity for agency.

For example, a sizable percentage of my fellow US citizens think and function in a way showing congruence with the nationalistic exclamation "my country, right or wrong!" There seems to be no realization that this habit diminishes a citizen's ability to rationally form political opinions and enhances their vulnerability to emotional exploitation by political agendas. Indeed, such attachment to national identity is highly detrimental to the national interest itself.

This point was captured well by G.K. Chesterton, a British philosopher: "'My country, right or wrong' is a thing that no patriot would think of saying except in a desperate case. It is like saying 'My mother, drunk or sober.'"[331] English novelist Patrick O'Brian similarly expressed that nationalism "generally comes to mean either my country, right or wrong, which is infamous, or my country is always right, which is imbecile."[332]

It should be clear that using—or worse, believing in—this expression is so much against the interests of US society that the expression should be deemed unpatriotic. Yet, the reality is quite the opposite; and that reality is feasible only because of our tendency not to challenge the prevalent narratives promoted by socio-political systems.

Application of the exploitation of these vulnerabilities can be commonly seen not just in geopolitics but also at the national political scene. In the United States, a citizen is supposedly either a liberal or a conservative; a Republican or a Democrat.[333] One may have some other options available, but they practically are—or have been made—essentially meaningless or, at least, irrelevant in terms of governance.

The unquestioned adoration and boundless enthusiasm for one's candidate of choice in the US politics is also rather instructive. There is no harm in supporting the policies of a specific party. What is being underlined here, however, is the phenomenon wherein a large percentage of a democratic society has effectively been converted into janissaries of one or the other political party, making mindless cheerleaders out of citizens expected to be critically responsible towards governance of the country. Governance, we know, is a serious responsibility for a democratic society. And yet, based upon the identity parade, the campaign process in the United States has been turned into some fusion of professional wrestling and Hollywood celebrity.

Ironically, those savvy enough to understand and openly resist this game are often punished by the political system. A good example is that of J Edgar Hoover's FBI, trying to strip Einstein of his US citizenship by classifying him as an undesirable immigrant. Einstein's crime? He spoke up against racism and militarism! The irony of this situation is that Einstein's behavior was entirely a reflection of the values (freedom of speech, human rights, etc.) that the US identity ostensibly stands for. Who was being true to American values and identity, Einstein or the US government?

The need for belonging is innately human. Its manipulation into the current notions of identity, however, may come from our inability to see or accept the internal conflict between right and wrong on the one hand and identity-based affiliation on the other. Choosing the latter is often at the expense of connecting with our inner truth, creativity, and passion. (Attribution and confirmation biases in psychology explained in chapters 1 and 6 respectively.)

As individuals and as a society, redefining our "group-connections" helps us retain our belonging while we transcend the undue limitations of a mere tribal identity. At the least, we should be able to find "identities" that do not unduly bind us in sectarian and parochial straitjackets. Even better would be the propensity to discard the *idol* of "unity in identity" and pursue the *ideal* of "solidarity in principle." It is easy to see how our unity in identity nullifies our solidarity with the humanity within us.

The stereotypes that classify us and thus create judgments—because that's what an identity-based system gravitates towards—do not define us. It is only the independence and integrity with which we practice our beliefs and principles that truly define us. Therein lies our true freedom—the fire that can burn away our illusions.[334]

If one is not attached to one's identities, one can still be proud of them without clouding one's independent discernment capacity in exercising one's agency. And that's why non-attachment to identity is perhaps the best vehicle to be genuinely true, and of service, to all our identities—because that path enhances human agency.

As the four "tyrannies" show, it is easy to think that we are simply "victims" of whatever wrong happens in the society. The reality may be different. Humans are spiritual beings, and the seemingly unsolvable problems of the material world can be solved by the spiritual route—and perhaps the spiritual route alone. The exploitation of our instinctual nature becomes possible only in the absence of a clearly defined moral and ethical framework, and the nonrecognition of our human vulnerabilities. And that's what allows various external forces to make us work against our own interests.

CHAPTER 5:

EDUCATION—MAKING OR BREAKING A SOCIETY

"The emancipation of the mind and the soul is a necessary preliminary for the political expansion of the people."

—Bhimrao Ramji "Babasahib" Ambedkar[335]

My maternal grandfather taught me how to read before I started elementary school. My memory says that he did this not by using books but by newspapers instead. My interest in reading newspapers, therefore, began at an early age. He was a remarkable man, recognized by the British Empire with the highest titles short of knighthood awarded to its Indian subjects. He handed those medals and citations to me when I was barely twelve. What I still possess, more importantly, are the memories of our discussions about topics such as poetry, religion, and the history of India. These laid the foundation of my "education."

The British philosopher Lorna Finlayson left school when she was thirteen. Referring to the way the current system is now ingrained in the collective social psyche, she says: "My convictions about schooling ... invariably meet with incredulity.... Any serious departure from politics as usual is liable to be derided as infantile. But it's possible both to imagine and to identify historical and contemporary instances of things being done differently. There were not always police, prisons and schools."[336]

For a philosopher to feel intimidated that any departure not only from the concept of education but rather from "politics as usual is ... derided as infantile" is quite instructive. The last sentence in that excerpt signifies that even the commune of philosophers has bound itself not just in a single mode of thinking, but rather in the modes enforcing that way of thinking. Philosopher Roberto Calasso's musing expresses a like concern: "But where can that which doesn't accommodate thought be accommodated? No longer in the University."[337]

My personal experience from several decades ago points to the preconceptions and misconceptions about education.

In the mid-80s, an acquaintance from the University of Washington in Seattle approached me requesting that I volunteer for the adult literacy program that was being sponsored by the local universities and community colleges. The next evening, I attended an orientation at Everett Community College. The presenter highlighted information that seemed somewhat sensational. I remember the statistics, which indicated that almost a third of the US population was completely or functionally illiterate. (In those days, that number was around 60 million.) Certainly, a large percentage of that group had a high-school diploma. When the presenter finished, I raised my hand and pointed out that this was unbelievable and couldn't possibly be true. "Why don't you volunteer as a tutor and see for yourself?" was the response. So, I did.

I still remember the full name of my student, though here I will call him Harley. He had a high school diploma from a local school whose name I recognized. He was also completely illiterate—to the extent of not even being able to adequately recognize the letters of the alphabet or knowing the sounds of those letters. He had memorized how to sign his name. He was fond of various sports, especially football. Even though I had no interest in sports, I used it as a vehicle of instruction.

This experience was rather revelatory. Harley, a white man, was not only my age; he also possessed the same level of intelligence and inquisitiveness. How then had Harley remained entirely illiterate after twelve years of full-time schooling?

This brings up several other questions. Why is it that such a large percentage of people in the United States with high school diploma are in the same boat as Harley? Can we really rely upon a system to impart learnedness if it cannot even be depended on to consistently impart the ability to read the letters of the alphabet? Any quick answers are apt to misguide us into myopic ideas and Band-Aid solutions. Questioning the quality and motivation of our teachers is certainly the wrong answer. If anything, it is sad that we are in this situation despite the spirit and motivation of our teachers at all levels. Information in this chapter, as well as elsewhere in this book, will help the reader locate the forces that adversely impact the US education system.

Over a half century ago, after describing the poor state of "Negro schools in the South," James Baldwin went on to comment on the state of education in general—even for white children: "It is hard enough, God knows, under the best of circumstances, to get an education in this country. White children are graduated yearly who can neither read, write, nor think, and who are in a state of the most abysmal ignorance concerning the world around them."[338]

That my observation of schooling in the United States was similar to Baldwin's decades earlier is remarkable. One of my clear learnings has been to separate the concept of education from schooling including at the university level. It is reasonable to conclude that there may be no direct correlation between schooling and what ought to be considered education.

William Deresiewicz, who taught humanities at Yale, has written specifically about the state of education in the United States: "As for the moral purpose, the notion that college might prepare you for life by inciting contemplation and reflection, it is typically dismissed in my experience ..."[339] As for the cognitive function of education, Deresiewicz sounds equally emphatic: "It is not the humanities per se that are under attack. It is learning: learning for its own sake, curiosity for its own sake, ideas for their own sake."[340] If valid, this conclusion immediately leads to another question: Why would a society's system of schooling not be primarily geared towards developing the cognitive and moral dimensions of its children?

Before moving on, it would be helpful to review an example that shows the embodiment of education and cultivation in an "uneducated" individual.

A quarter of a century ago, in connection with my job, my wife and I moved to Italy and lived just outside of Milan. After a few weeks, I needed a haircut, and a couple of people in the office recommended a close-by barber.

Giovanni was a gregarious man, quite a few years older than me. By then I was able to speak some Italian; and I discussed all kinds of things with him. He surprised me by guessing a few things about me from my demeanor. I enjoyed his company and was also happy with the haircut. To my chagrin, though, I realized upon reaching home that I had not paid Giovanni. I was so preoccupied in my conversation with him that I just said goodbye and walked out. I felt embarrassed.

I returned to the barbershop the following day. I asked him how it was that he also forgot to ask for payment. Lo and behold, he did not forget to ask—he chose not to. He realized I had simply forgotten, and he decided not to embarrass me by stopping me when I was on my way out. I was dumbstruck. This was the first time I had met Giovanni; I was not an Italian. And he knew I was leaving without paying him his dues. He still forwent his fees so as not to embarrass a stranger.

Would it be fair to say that Giovanni, who did not have a college diploma, was still more educated than a lot of people with them? If so, then it might be reasonable to say that our concepts of and assumptions about what it means to be educated may need rethinking.

Democracy—A Product of Education

The quality of freedom and democracy is directly dependent upon the quality of education in a society. Complacency in this regard threatens not just the effect but the very meaning of the concept of democracy.

In their 2014 study, "Testing Theories of American Politics: Elites, Interest Groups, and Average Citizens," political scientists Martin

Gilens and Benjamin Page posed the question: "Who governs? Who really rules? To what extent is the broad body of U.S. citizens sovereign, semi-sovereign, or largely powerless?"[341] Their conclusion: economic elites and groups representing businesses have "substantial independent" impact on government policy, whereas average citizens or mass-based interest groups have "little or no independent influence."[342]

The rationale is not that a democratic republic should follow some simple formula where policy is decided by the desire of the majority in a raw poll of some kind. There are many reasons why such an approach might sometimes result in bad policy decisions ("tyranny of majority" is an apt aphorism to validate this understanding). The point, however, is the overall effect in which the political system consistently and visibly works against the interests of the society as a whole—and yet most people are kept completely unmindful of the reality. As the current political climate indicates, a large percentage of Americans, based upon their experience, have developed the belief that the government and the political system all but ignore them and work against their, and possibly the society's, interests. Evidence shows that they may have reached the correct conclusion. Yet, if our society is able to get out of the current inertia of our political system—and actually became informed about the reality—we may be able to completely turn things around.

This section simply highlights the sheer dependence of the quality of democracy on the quality of education in society. To that end, it would be important to clearly, though broadly, conceptualize[343] our notions of education as well as democracy.

Education entails nurturing and tutelage that develops the faculty to examine, consider, evaluate, and synthesize information, to use logic, to process information to reach clear-headed conclusions, to reflect, to separate truth from falsehood, to possess insight, wisdom, compassion, sense of responsibility, and other related skills and competencies. In a nutshell, education is that which lifts our intellect and spirit to a higher plane.

A democratic system of governance or a republic is that which derives its principal power from the people, and whose objective is to serve the needs of the society as a whole. Decisions in a democratic system sometimes do favor a small minority, yet the impetus would be the overall benefit of the society. The ordinary citizen would have the ability to influence the process and the outcome on a somewhat equal footing with others. Small segments or interests would not be able to exert undue influence on the decision-making process. The ordinary citizen would be relatively informed about important affairs, and about how decisions are being influenced. Information in this regard would be openly available and accessible. Significantly, a citizen's "right to truth" in a democratic system would be honored and implemented by the system.

It is the direct connection between education and democracy that underscores why the very concept of education is far too "sacred" to be under the thumb of political and economic structures and interests. That responsibility has to be shouldered by the institutions of culture and education in a society—without undue influence from the religious, political, or economic establishments.[344]

Literacy and Education in the United States

History tells us that there was no hyperbole in Thomas Jefferson's famous words in his letter to J. Hector St. John de Crèvcoeur in 1787: "... ours are the only farmers who can read Homer."[345] Two hundred years later, educator Paul Russell Anderson echoed the same sentiment in his book *Platonism in the Midwest*: "It is no mere figure of speech to say that farm boys followed the plow with book in hand, be it Shakespeare, Emerson, or Thoreau."[346]

Charles Dickens was taken aback by the reception he received in 1842 when he visited the United States: "I can give you no conception of my welcome. There never was a King or Emperor upon earth so cheered and followed by the crowds, and entertained at splendid balls and dinners and waited upon public bodies of all kinds... If I go out in a carriage, the crowd surrounds it and escorts me home."[347] Would another internationally recognized author receive a similar treatment today? Would even the media notice such a visit?

Thomas Paine's *Common Sense*, published in 1776, is estimated to have sold around 500,000 copies within a short period.[348]

The country's population at that time was around 3 million. Proportionally, that booklet would have to sell some 40 million copies today to match the per capita purchase rate! Is it even conceivable today that a socio-political treatise with a philosophical bent would receive much reception beyond the academic world?

It is easy to see how the above examples could be considered evidence of a relatively informed and engaged public, a prerequisite to democracy in a society. It may be worth pausing here to point out that Thomas Paine did not have formal schooling beyond age twelve. Shakespeare's schooling was similar. Could either of them be called uneducated? What gave them the writing skill, the thinking prowess, and the imagination they are known for? It would not be far-fetched to say that both these Englishmen received their education in a culturally-conducive societal environment, and that such an environment was not utterly controlled by political and economic institutions. (The list of such luminaries without formal schooling would be endless, though not in today's world.)

What then has diluted and corrupted our concept of education? The answers connect us to the same causes ailing other elements of society and can be traced back to the systems of economic and political power all over the globe. The price of not facing that reality becomes steeper with time. The sections below highlight some unconventional facets of the problem and equally unconventional ways in which we can think of solutions. As we bring information together in one whole, patterns and connections do begin to emerge.

Ignorance & Arrogance: A Wicked Combination in Education

In the present-day environment, a myriad of drivers negatively influence our systems of education. There is an interesting and complementary set that does not get much attention: the combination of arrogance and ignorance that can be infused in our educational systems. This is especially applicable to those considered exemplary. The antidote would be to bring genuine humility and boldness, qualities consistently promoted by our spiritual teachings.

Niall Ferguson[349] is a well-known scholar of history and a prolific writer. He has been affiliated with Harvard, Stanford, and the London School of Economics (LSE). LSE's website identified the professor as "one of the world's most eminent scholars."[350] In 2004, *Time* magazine named him one of the one hundred most influential people in the world.[351]

In an interview he gave to the *Guardian* some years ago, Ferguson reportedly said, "The rulers of western Africa prior to the European empires showed zero sign of developing the country's resources."[352]

Never mind the usual excuse-making of empire, the logic seems to justify not just theft of African resources but also slavery and genocide of Africans related to the European empires. Their crime? The Africans of yesteryear "showed zero sign" meeting the expectations of a self-described "fully paid-up member of the neo-imperialist gang."[353] And the same interview shines even more light on this thought pattern:

> I think it's hard to make the case, which implicitly the left makes, that somehow the world would have been better off if the Europeans had stayed home. It certainly doesn't work for north America, that's for sure. I mean, I'm sure the Apache and the Navajo had all sorts of admirable traits. In the absence of literacy we don't know what they were because they didn't write them down. We do know they killed a hell of a lot of bison. But had they been left to their own devices, I don't think we'd have anything remotely resembling the civilisation we've had in north America.[354]

For "one of the world's most eminent scholars," and "one of the 100 most influential people in the world" to be so blithely ignorant and dismissive of the rich heritage and history of the indigenous people in North America should be a concern to a worthy educational system. Documented Western scholarship shows that indigenous North Americans were as cerebral as, if not more than, their Western counterparts:

> Anthropologists who spend years talking to indigenous people in their own languages, and watching

> them argue with one another, tend to be well aware that even those who make their living hunting elephants or gathering lotus buds are just as sceptical, imaginative, thoughtful and capable of critical analysis as those who make their living by operating tractors, managing restaurants or chairing university departments. A few, such as the early-twentieth-century scholar Paul Radin ... ended up concluding that at least those he knew best—Winnebago and other Native North Americans—were actually, on the average, rather more thoughtful.[355]

Indeed, quite a few "scholars and professional researchers ... have to actually make a considerable effort to remain so ignorant."[356] If the very concept of education remains anchored in the agenda of chauvinism, the result can only be further disharmony. It is also worth remembering that casting an image of the "other" as inferior is how not just slavery but genocides have been promoted and justified.

Such proclivity by an educational system to remain historically innocent, and perhaps "exceptional," comes with a heavy price. The reflexive contempt for other civilizational beliefs and practices of living—and the outright refusal to acknowledge the intellectual complexity and spiritual beauty of our human heritage—keeps all of the human race deprived of the benefit of respectfully-shared knowledge and wisdom.

Ultimately, though, the concern is not simply about the delusional supremacy that dwells within such mindset, individual or institutional. Rather, the concern is that the problems the human race currently faces are being exacerbated by it. The problems created by the criminality, violence, and evil of the past cannot be solved by the hypocrisy, sophistry, and propaganda of the present. Enlightenment grounded in cultural humility and spirituality is what we need. We now, more than ever, need the wisdom and leadership of those who still understand and practice their cultures: the indigenous peoples of Africa, America, and Australasia. Individuals and institutions who still promote the geopolitical game of the last few centuries are doing grave disservice to the human race.

Shaking Academe's Absolute Faith in Science as God

Science and technology have become virtually unassailable disciplines and domains within society. Such a phenomenon comes with its own peril and decay that our education system ought to be aware of.

First, however, it is important to clarify a pivotal point. Unlike nature, science is not self-actualizing, it is not self-regulating, it is not self-restoring, and it is not self-expressing. What we call science is simply the human discovery, knowledge, interpretation, enunciation, application, manipulation, and subversion[357] of the laws of nature. (Besides, there really is no "science" as we know it outside the laws of nature.)

As the human grasp of the laws of nature changes, our concept of science also shifts. Nature is independent of human discovery; it exists whether or not science understands how it works. Science, however, is entirely human-contingent, in addition to being entirely nature-contingent. What we call science exists because we humans have gained some knowledge based upon our observation of nature. Unlike nature, therefore, science exists with the human as the principal and the agent. Humanity is the subject that shows, determines, and ordains the validity of science.

Science, unlike nature, therefore, has no independent voice, expression, projection, or agency of its own. Its voice and projection flow through human institutions and individuals, highly influenced by financial, political, and ideological motives[358] and highly prone to corruption and self-dealing. Concentration of power and profit can be antithetical towards the expansion of information and knowledge. The sole focus on growing power and profit distorts the moral compass. Such an impetus can even make some entities pursue paths against the collective human goals of liberty and survival. Science, just like religion, could become a means to serve power. Science, when misused, can also become a grave menace to our collective wellbeing and existence. And this is a message that every high-school graduate should understand.

While the subject is beyond the scope of this book, we should remember that absolute faith in science could be as blinding as that in religion. The risk of being misled becomes all the more significant when the "public consciousness has not yet assimilated the point that technology is ideology."[359] As this section shows, the concern would be well beyond Henry David Thoreau's misgivings about "improved means to an unimproved end."

For example, digital technology and artificial intelligence (AI) have recently been emerging as largely unquestioned phenomenon with singularly perilous risks and threats to human freedom and the future. This technology is becoming another "religion" given absolute unquestioned acceptance by all; it is thus forced upon even those who are not interested. This threat is an important consideration deserving our deliberation. The force of AI and digital technology, when combined with the loci of profit and power, presents a menace whose implications are not adequately understood. And therein lies the greatest concern—in terms of the human future, we may be walking into a "prison" whose confines and controls we do not understand.

The basic inevitability of the future of digital technology can be observed in an interview with a software developer in *The Age of Surveillance Capital* by Shoshana Zuboff. The software developer envisions a world where "we can know if you shouldn't be driving, and we can just shut your car down ... we tell the TV to shut off and make you get some sleep, or the chair to start shaking because you shouldn't be sitting so long."[360] These eventualities may be more innocuous than disturbing when compared to other perils technology has in store for us.

General Omar Bradley, last of the generals promoted to the five-star rank within the US military, was the first-ever Chairman of the Joint Chiefs of Staff in the early 1950s. In the Armistice Day Address delivered before the Boston Chamber of Commerce on November 10, 1948, Bradley described some of the challenges humankind faced at that time:

> With the monstrous weapons man already has, humanity is in danger of being trapped in this world by its moral adolescents. Our knowledge of science has clearly outstripped our capacity to control it. We

> have many men of science; too few men of God. We have grasped the mystery of the atom and rejected the Sermon on the Mount. Man is stumbling blindly through a spiritual darkness while toying with the precarious secrets of life and death. The world has achieved brilliance without wisdom, power without conscience. Ours is a world of nuclear giants and ethical infants. We know more about war than we know about peace, more about killing than we know about living.[361]

For a serving Chief of the Army Staff to convey this message deserves special attention. Over the last several decades since Bradley used those words, the challenges the human race faces have only grown exponentially and indeed, even Bradley could not have fathomed the scale and scope of the risk packed in his prescient forewarning. The systems and structures, national and international, we humans created over the last century have plainly failed to deliver on their ostensible objectives. Not only that, the perils our scientific discoveries and institutional structures have jointly created are uniquely existential for the human race.

Oxford philosopher Toby Ord, in his book *The Precipice: Existential Risk and the Future of Humanity*, reveals his calculation that the risk of human extinction over the next century is around 15 to 20 percent.[362] He divides the risk between "natural" and "anthropogenic" (human-made) causes or determinants. Ord allocates climate change and nuclear war in the "natural" category, whereas "unaligned artificial intelligence" and "engineered pandemics"[363] are in the anthropogenic category. Two points are of significant importance in his conclusion.

First, almost all of this risk is from "anthropogenic" drivers. Virtually all of the extinction risk comes from "unaligned artificial intelligence and engineered pandemics."[364] In his analysis, therefore, the risk from climate change and nuclear war is minimal.[365]

Second, and even more importantly, the 15 to 20 percent risk as allocated by Ord applies only to 100 percent human extinction. For example, per Ord's reasoning, a nuclear winter would still leave quite a bit of New Zealand livable. Therefore, the risk of 100 percent human extinction is virtually zero from nuclear warfare. Using the same logic, the risk of complete extinction the human race faces from climate change is almost zero. That's why threats from climate change and nuclear catastrophe are virtually irrelevant in Ord's analysis.

Contrary to this academic analysis, these threats are clearly relevant to human survival and suffering; they simply cannot be ignored. Ord's analysis, however, may explain why a lot of billionaires find New Zealand[366] their "favored refuge in the event of a cataclysm."[367] This modern enlightenment was termed "apocalypse insurance" by a tech billionaire.[368]

Two important points not clarified by Ord need special attention. First, as we lower the bar from complete to partial extinction, the percentage dramatically shoots up. For example, the likelihood of a 50 percent wipeout of the human race within the next century would be remarkably larger than Ord's estimate. Second, practically speaking, all four human-extinction threats[369] mentioned above—climate change, nuclear Armageddon, unaligned artificial intelligence, and engineered pandemics—are creations of scientific advancement, whether we classify them as natural or anthropogenic. They all are equally grave and ought to be taken equally seriously. It would thus be fair to say that a healthy skepticism regarding human enlightenment, especially when it comes to science and technology, would be well-founded.

There is something curious about the nature of science that was captured by Richard Feynman in his characteristic fashion: It is impossible to find an answer that someday will not be found to be wrong. In other words, even the "truth" coming from science today has a variable nature and is certain to change tomorrow. Remember, science is not self-actualizing, self-regulating, or self-expressing. The "voice" of science flows through institutions and individuals driven by financial, political, and ideological motives. It is, therefore, as susceptible to abuse and propaganda[370] as other socio-political domains. This aspect of science's weakness cannot be overstated. It should be the academe's responsibility to make "education" open to such realities.

The Intellectual Industry

Several years ago, I was a little jolted to read the expression "education industry" in *The Economist*. I don't remember the exact prescription being offered by the famed periodical to solve the education industry's problems. Perhaps I should not have been so surprised at the use of that phrase. To me, though, it was a strange realization that nothing—not even what we call education—can be free from commercial imperatives.

Change in the ethos of the education industry was also evident to me from an article in the *Guardian* many years ago, where a journalist interviewed a well-known professor. The journalist begins his piece by commenting: "My first thought, on meeting [the professor], is that he looks too smart to be an academic."[371] So, an academic can be too smart today to follow in the footsteps of Plato, Maimonides, and Avicenna!

The intelligentsia of a society is generally believed to be comprised primarily of its poets, writers, scholars, and journalists. Given the current state of ideological, partisan, and commercial loyalties of most journalists (and even many academics), it should be no surprise that even those inside these fields view their role somewhat differently. The ideological and commercial alignment and activity have reached a level where many within the intelligentsia cannot really be considered independent. It is only logical that the media is now openly, even if sometimes unwittingly, lowering the expectations[372] one should have of the intelligentsia of society.

Bound by structure and constrained by institutional pressures, even the otherwise unaligned could face hurdles in performing their function. Then we have the burgeoning industry of think tanks (mostly special-interest outlets serving ideological agendas). The net result, it would perhaps be fair to say, is the creation of an "intellectual industry" whose job now is to prepare briefings and talking points[373] palatable enough to serve the psychology of the client and the political needs of the wind that blows. As long as the activity is in line with the expectations of the client, there is virtually no intellectual failure, lack of due diligence, or moral degradation that produces any consequences for the institution or its agent.

Consequences, of course, befall the agent who rebels against the system, such as a whistleblower, regardless of the high ethical, moral, and professional nature of their stance.

Understanding Propaganda in Our Information Environment

"How easy it is to make people believe a lie, and how hard it is to undo that work again!"[374]

—Mark Twain (Samuel Clemens)

The socio-political landscape globally presents a disconcerting fusion of nationalism and propaganda. About recent conditions in Eurasia, Pankaj Mishra says:

> Hyper-patriotic media have emerged in India, China and Russia over the last decade, together with pseudo-thinkers who have upgraded national self-images by hailing the glories of Hindu civilisation, Russian empire, and Confucian harmony... Today, the news and analysis received by the vast majority of people in India and China as well as Russia is—in the words of the head of the Levada Centre, Russia's independent public research organization—a compendium of 'lies and hatred on a fantastical scale.'[375]

The fanning of these societal trends can usually be traced to the highest echelons of the political system. Xi Jinping's July 2021 words at the Chinese Communist Party (CCP) centenary celebration provide an example. As he declared, the CCP would "unite all the sons and daughters of the Chinese nation, both at home and abroad, behind the goal of national rejuvenation."[376] At a November 2021 meeting of senior party leaders, this "Xi Jinping Thought" was officially endorsed as "the essence of the Chinese culture and China's spirit."[377] Needless to say, the condition in much of the rest of the world varies only in degree from the descriptions above.

In the United States, the word "propaganda"[378] is not frequently used to point to a prevalent internal condition. Perhaps it would be fair to say that, to save one's sanity, the word is best avoided domestically.[379] The image seems to be that propaganda mostly happens in other parts of the world. The vacuum, however, is filled by the coinage and usage of phrases such as fake news, alternative facts, infodemic, conspiracy theories, and even "truthiness." Whether or not there is any propaganda in the United States, the need to more fully understand the concept remains—at least the most common modalities in which propaganda is conducted:

1. by repetition/coverage—for example, when the least important of ten truths is repeated and emphasized time and again, it is likely to assume a higher and more instrumental validity or value in the mind of the recipient of such communication.
2. by commission—presenting substantially false information as authentic and true.
3. by elision (or omission, suppression, selection, obfuscation, interpretation, censoring, sophistry, or clever argumentation)—the safest and the most versatile of all modes.

Another way to think about the propaganda paradigm would be through the two categories of *suggestio falsi* (suggestion of an untruth) and *suppressio veri* (suppression of the truth). In the model above, suggestio falsi would roughly cover commission (and repetition), whereas suppressio veri would overlap elision and omission.

It is important to be mindful that the more sophisticated propaganda models rely mostly upon elision and omission rather than commission. Suppressio veri is much more effective as a vehicle of persuasion and mental conditioning. Besides, it is censorship (suppressio veri) that creates the environment where selective suggestio falsi becomes potent and decisive. Censorship, therefore, deserves particular attention in understanding propaganda.

And censorship is not just implicit or voluntary as commonly perceived in the West; it is explicitly and actively enforced by our institutions, sometimes blatantly. History provides many examples, such as the excision of non-conformist language used by Dr. King in his collection of sermons published with the title *Strength to Love*. Phrases such as "the ugly practice of our nation," "a deep-seated change," "evil because it is based on a contempt of life" were expunged by the publisher.[380] Why? Because they explicitly referred to segregation, capitalism, and colonialism respectively.[381] Talking about the early Christian church, Dr. King commented: "Its views on war were clearly known because of the refusal of every Christian to take up arms."[382] That had to be taken out too.[383]

Legendary war correspondent Martha Gellhorn began to write in the 1930s. Despite her illustrious background, she was not given the opportunity to cover the Vietnam War. In 1966, she did manage to get to Vietnam on her own and wrote a series of pieces, but no US newspaper[384] would touch them: "Everywhere I was told," she would later recall, "that they were too tough for American readers."[385] Subsequently, Gellhorn's attempts to return to Vietnam were officially thwarted through visa refusals and bureaucracy.

And journalist Glenn Greenwald's recent departure from *Intercept*, which he co-founded, could be classified as enforced censorship. That, reportedly, has to do with *Intercept's* desired outcome of a presidential election. Within the week before the 2020 elections, Greenwald wrote an article that threw negative factual light on then-candidate Biden. Reportedly, *Intercept* would not allow him to do that, and Greenwald would not water down his writing to the management's satisfaction.[386] Even *Intercept's* co-founder, whose contract reportedly stipulated that he would not be censored, could not write what he considered necessary for the voting public to know.

While it is relatively easier to find and "prove" examples of censorship (compared to the more elusive "commissioned" propaganda), it is important to realize that the two are just different sides of the same coin. In fact, censorship is just a subset of propaganda because it falls within the third category: "elision." In other words, where there is censorship, there is propaganda.

The product of the intellectual industry is an implicit censorship paradigm that may be subtle and is usually denied, yet it is not so hidden. If we simply factor in what some former insiders have to say, that conclusion is truly irrefutable. The undeniable consequence is that reality is always constricted, yet the threat to freedom of speech and intellect is not widely acknowledged. The societal consequences are perturbing.

Colonized Imagination Undermining Education

The cultural milieu within which one grows up has historically provided context and contribution towards educating the citizen. Also, until fairly recently—let's say until the industrial revolution—the relationship of human cultures with nature and surroundings was that of dependence and interdependence. Historically, this understanding, directly influenced by our spiritual belief systems, drove the societal paradigms of education. The concept of human "mastery" over nature is rather new. Even though nature itself reminds us again and again that it cannot be mastered by humans, yet, in seemingly irredeemable human hubris, we keep pursuing the mirage. Remedying the current disconnect in that regard, however, may not be as out of reach even within the present systems of education.

Dr. Martin Shaw of the Schumacher College in Devon, England reminds us of the Gaelic tradition where educational stories were called the "swan-feather cloak ... every moment of your life should have you clothed in story... What I see around me [now] is children with colonised imaginations. They don't suffer a deficit of attention, but a deficit of images that arrest the soul. Once you provide them [stories], you are in the business of real education—to lead out."[387]

It would be important to clarify two significant points that Shaw underscores. First, the notion of understanding our existence through stories and fables deserves a lot of attention. Not just a Gaelic notion, it's a human one. Its manifestation and application become abundantly clear when we take a respectful glance at the indigenous cultures in America or elsewhere in the world. In her poem titled "The Speed of Darkness," Muriel Rukeyser may be referring to a similar understanding when she says, "The universe is made of stories, not of atoms."

Second, Shaw's expression of "colonised imaginations" is not just for societies that have literally faced colonization in the past. It applies equally to societies that have called themselves "free" during the recent past. We can see the applications of the concept in the various types of "conditioning" that we see today through numerous mechanisms—because it is this conditioning that delimits or defines our imagination. Nobel-laureate Rabindranath Tagore's concern about the insidiousness of this monstrosity was captured as follows by the British writer Jay Griffiths:

> In the early twentieth century, Rabindranath Tagore set up Santiniketan in Bengal to protest at British colonialist schooling. Classes were held outdoors; the natural world was honoured as a teacher. Stories, music and art were integral to learning. Exams were not. Nor was the world of business. Generating art in everything, Tagore's aim was to regenerate the moment with noticed beauty to turn the meanly quotidian into a daily ceremony.[388]

Tagore was protesting the colonialist system of education because he understood that schooling based on learning *about* the world cannot do justice to education. Only a teaching system that is based upon learning *from* the world imparts real education. The difference, seemingly simple, is significant. In the former case, a single lens can be imposed to view everything. In the latter, everything comes with its own lens. Consequently, to provide a simple implication, the "learning about" teaching system gravitates more towards emphasizing "what to think," whereas the "learning from" system focuses on "how to think." These simple-sounding distinctions can make all the difference. And that is why the ability and willingness to observe things from multiple lenses yields a more meaningful education. Tagore obviously understood what the British Empire did not.

Griffiths continues: "It is not just the overtly colonised indigenous cultures that know this; not just the nations that have suffered imperialism or slavery, but any human being who has felt the stress, cruelty, insufficiency or marginalisation of education."[389]

The "stress, cruelty, insufficiency, and marginalization of education" that Griffiths references would likely be felt by all of us who expect our education systems to promote an understanding of our multi-colored cultural heritage and common human bonds.

Resulting Deficiency in "Education" and Its Societal Impact

Educator and author William Deresiewicz makes an insightful observation about the state of education all over the world: "I wrote a book about the problem with elite higher education in America, but what I've learned from the correspondence I've received over the past year is that it's not just *elite* higher education, not just *higher* education, and not just America."[390]

Commenting on the critical reasoning of high school and college students in the United States, a 2016 study by Stanford's History Education Group concluded: "Overall, young people's ability to reason about the information on the Internet can be summed up in one word: bleak."[391]

This is notwithstanding other studies showing that the IQ of the average young adult today, with an increase of about thirty points in the twentieth century, would score in the genius range of several decades ago.[392] And the young adults of a few decades ago, if scored on the current curve, would classify as "intellectually challenged."[393]

As the Stanford study shows above, this high IQ clearly doesn't convert into today's young adult's ability to deal with complex societal problems or to relate better with others. Worse, as pointed out in chapter 1, we may be seeing a global dumbing-down phenomenon caused by our sociopolitical environments. Robert Sternberg, who teaches human development at Cornell University, warns us that "we are creating a society of smart fools."[394]

The message that seems to be lost on us is that smarts, schooling, and even experience are no substitutes for perceptivity, judgment, and wisdom. Capturing the substance of the current phenomenon, Neil Postman's observation in the 1980s was:

> A great metaphor shift has taken place in America, with the result that the content of much of our public discourse has become dangerous nonsense... we do not measure a culture by its output of undisguised trivialities but by what it claims significant. Therein is our problem.[395]

If Postman is correct in his assertion that dangerous nonsense is now considered significant, how would we even be able to tell the difference between education and ignorance? As a democratic society, that may be one of the greatest crises we face.

CHAPTER 6:

REALIZING THE PLACE OF CULTURE IN SOCIETY

And be not conformed to this world: but be ye transformed by the renewing of your mind.

—Romans 12:2

Margaret Thatcher once infamously said: "There is no such thing as society."[396] Even when we are mindful of her logic that individual and family are the only real "units" of a system of governance, we still have to ponder the implication of her words. If we accept her thesis, how does a "non-existent" society become functional, let alone vivacious? Or does the state fully replace the society? Should we really give up on the idea of society altogether and further accentuate the Hobbesian nature of our current existence?

In a 1996 *New Yorker* piece titled "Why I Wrote the Crucible," Arthur Miller showed the hollowness of the "no society" paradigm. Commenting on Fascism and Communism in the middle of the century, Miller suggested: "Few of us can surrender our belief that society must somehow make sense. The thought that the state has lost its mind and is punishing so many innocent people is intolerable. And so the evidence has to be internally denied."[397]

The denial implied by Miller is by the ordinary people who should be able to see what's really going on and yet are unwilling or unable to face that reality. (In her book *The Evil of Banality*, Elizabeth Minnich underscores the current relevance of this same subject.) It is the culture of a society that empowers or takes away from the citizen the will and capacity to tackle such societal realities. In this context, society can be defined as an extended community network creating kinship bonds on various possible dimensions: moral, traditional, spiritual, sartorial, linguistic, artistic, culinary, commercial, etc. The place of culture, therefore, is of instrumental importance in ensuring meaningful functionality of a society.

In recent history, the concept of culture seems to have devolved into a virtually irrelevant phenomenon in a society. It gets identified in a disjointed way with food, art, and ritual. Besides, the word has been turned into a euphemistic cliché by its banal use in defining the ethos of a structured organization—for example, a corporation's "culture"—or how such an entity functions. In fact, such a reference seems to be the primary use of the word these days.

As Appendix A indicates, culture and structure are very different institutions in their outlook and role in a society. While the concept of structure has already been clarified (see chapter 3, subtitle "Structure and Corruption: Defining ... the Concepts), this section considers how to conceptualize culture in a fuller yet graspable way.

What Is and Is Not Culture?

Culture is the lived code, substantially unwritten, that binds together a society's fabric. Culture is that which permeates the living space and is practically ubiquitous in the societal milieu or environment; the norms one learns from mother, "mother" here used as a metaphor for the family as well the society. Culture flows through the poetry and literature of a society. Yet, empty professions of values or slogans do not constitute culture. To be called culture, those values would have to be practiced organically, such that one member of the society can rely upon others to voluntarily follow those values and norms without needing the force of law. In other words, the professed "values" would essentially be congruent with the voluntarily lived practice for the whole to be classified as culture.

Culture is not "experienced" by being a tourist in a foreign country, by visiting a museum or an ethnic restaurant, by live attendance of a Broadway show or an opera performance; nor can it be experienced by reading a book or owning the work of famous artists. Culture, though, can be "observed" by interacting with a group of people from that society or by watching how they conduct themselves.

Social customs, rituals, family structures, relationship protocols, art, clothing, food, and medicine all form the culture of a society. Yet, they have to be looked at in a holistic way to evaluate the way life is lived within the society according to its culture.

In chapter 5, we discussed the Italian barber Giovanni. In that instance, his interaction and judgment were strongly driven by the culture within which he lived. Another excellent example of this was provided by Diego Cordovez, a UN negotiator who was central to the multilateral peace negotiations in Afghanistan after the Soviet invasion of the country in 1979. In his memoir, Cordovez describes an evening in 1986 when he took a taxicab in New York City driven by an Afghan refugee, a former military officer who had defected after the invasion. The driver recognized Cordovez and refused to charge him for the ride. Why? "I cannot take money from a friend of my country," was the cab driver's reason! "Such are the Afghans," writes Cordovez, "wonderful people."[398]

Those familiar with the Afghan culture may recognize that the cab driver did nothing extraordinary. In his action and behavior, we are simply seeing a glimpse of the typical Afghan tradition. He was not being "emotional," he was simply living his culture.

The culture of a society would also contain negative elements. Interestingly, the earliest and clearest indicators of such attributes are exhibited in the commonly known conduct and behavior of the rich and powerful in a society, even if such conduct is not part of the official ethos propagated by the system. This is especially important because the shallowness of a society usually begins at the top; those habits may take some time before widely permeating within the public domain.

Culture is "lived" in a society among its members who are actually practicing the culture the society lays a claim to. It is effectively an expectation of how other members of the society would conduct themselves, an expectation that can be relied upon in one's daily decision-making. Similar to ethics, culture is something we practice consistently, not something we can possess or inherently have.

A society perceives its culture through its historical consciousness (i.e., historical reality or its perceived place in history). As this consciousness changes, it transfigures culture. Yet, at any given time, culture is the present practice and interaction within the society. Culture is thus a lived phenomenon that is defined by society, implicitly or explicitly. Culture is not something that is "implemented" with the use of legal apparatus. A state, or other structured institutions, can stipulate the accepted norms and ethos. They can also influence the culture of a society. But a state cannot unilaterally stipulate or determine the culture of a society.

Language: The River Within Which Culture Flows

The subtitle here is more than just a metaphor. It is an expression of our consciousness of what is important in our lives, the precepts that organize and govern who we are and how we conduct ourselves. It is also a statement of realization that words and language form the very basis of how we understand things—that without some form of a language, our learning and communication are distorted, if not significantly impeded.

And still, another version of distortion in human societies can happen if varieties of language "streams" and their underlying traditions are swallowed up by a dominant "river." The loss is common for all humanity. The institution of empire in all its shapes and forms is well-known in this regard; the Roman Empire alone is said to have extinguished around a thousand languages. And that is why, in understanding the evolution and present form of how human societies are organized globally, "the language already implies an explanation, even a justification ... existing debates almost invariably begin with terms derived from Roman Law, and for a number of reasons this is problematic."[399]

Most obviously, immeasurable human heritage and wisdom is lost without a trace. This includes the loss of theories, practices, concepts, and words that would likely be very different from theories, practices, concepts, and words we are familiar with. That leaves us at a great disadvantage in our understanding of myriad domains of knowledge, even history: "All this achieves ... is to leave us literally at a loss for words when confronted with certain major aspects of human history."[400] And the inability to understand history is bound to impact the shape of the future we are able to even imagine or perceive.

Over millennia, cultures developed languages to preserve their way of life, belief systems, food and medicine, spiritual traditions and practices—their very essence. In that backdrop, the extinction of languages over the past few centuries is tragic and instructive. 90 percent of the world's population today speaks 100 of the most well-known languages. The remaining 6,000 or so languages are spoken by only 10 percent of humanity. Each one of almost 3,000 languages has only 5,000 or fewer speakers.

No wonder, at least half of the world's current languages are expected to be extinct within the next few decades. (Every two weeks, we lose one of them.) The destruction of the carrier of a culture then automatically entails the devastation of the culture.

In traditional cultures, the human connection with nature is captured by the language of myth and ritual. Unfortunately, such richly traditional languages are under threat of extinction. This homogenization may be convenient in terms of commerce and statehood. Analogous to the biodiversity loss afoot, the rapid decline in languages and cultures takes away from us precious value systems, the richness of different philosophies, practices, and ideas. It is these value systems that would function as the vehicles of transformation needed in today's world.

The Place of Language in A Democracy

If we humans are political animals (*zoon politikon*) as Aristotle stated, our capacity to reflect upon, deliberate, and negotiate social direction would be one of the foremost values in a society—especially a democracy. Yet, parallels of what was described in the previous section as the "loss of words" can also be seen in a democratic country with one dominant language when the sophisticated use of that dominant language becomes limited to a small subset of its population. The larger percentage of the society is thus made to disconnect from various sources of knowledge. In effect, most in the society are disempowered from exercising their prerogative and agency in the affairs of the country, even though it would still be called a democracy.

The reasoning here can be looked at as a corollary to the examples, in the previous chapter, of Shakespeare and Paine. Frederick Douglass[401] would be another example of the same phenomenon. They all exhibit that developing command of language was instrumental in the development of their intellectual and communication faculties even though they had little formal schooling. They were thus able to influence the thought process within society. In the case of Shakespeare, he still influences the thought process of much of the English-speaking world. Paine's role in the American Revolution can simply not be overstated. As for Frederick Douglass, we have to realize that there would be no Abe Lincoln as we know him if it weren't for Douglass. The point is this: as indicated by Harley's example in the previous chapter, the effective denial of not only education but even literacy to a large percentage of society is tantamount to disenfranchisement. And that is just one mechanism of subverting democracy.

Most cultures, even in the presence of relevant written material, have traditionally transmitted their principles orally using parable, allegory, song, poetry, etc. The Iliad and the Odyssey were products of an oral tradition, transmitted over several generations of Greek poets to become the epics they are. (This also means that Homer was likely not the original creator of these works!) The texts in the various sacred scriptures were also oral traditions for a long time and are meant to be heard, not merely to be read. Arguably, hearing a text in its original language may have a deeper impact that simply cannot be replicated by reading its translation.

Education through oral transmission is unique in many regards. In that respect, the loss of oral tradition is a loss of culture and religion in one dimension or the other. Such loss in our culture amounts to a loss in our education that cannot be made up by books or diplomas.

Loss of Culture Entails Loss of Key Societal Values

In *On Kindness* (see chapter 4), Phillips and Taylor write: "Most people, as they grow up now, secretly believe that kindness is a virtue of losers."[402] This should come as no surprise given that the prevalent ethos of our modern world seem to follow Nietzsche's master-slave moral binary in which morality and humility are appropriate only for the inferior and the impotent.[403]

The book points to the steady downgrading over the past three hundred years of the concepts of kindness and compassion from "a universal imperative ... to the prerogative of specific social constituencies." As it clarifies, Hobbes's "arguments were slow to gain ground but two centuries later it seems we are all Hobbesian."[404] It also makes evident how this transpired: "with Hobbes, selfishness and aggression were transformed from moral vices into psychological fact."[405] A pivotal remedial dimension to the concern comes from the human need from the society towards nurturing in the art of kinship and places a serious responsibility upon a society's culture and education: "the child who is failed in this regard is robbed of one of the greatest sources of human happiness."[406]

Phillips and Taylor bemoan how Hobbes's Leviathan, "the urtext of the new individualism," dismissed kindness as "a psychological absurdity."[407] This "Enlightened" psychological state is indicative of a low point in education and culture. On the other hand, kindness and compassion are central to our religious teaching. And it goes hand in hand with the concept of humility. When Pope Francis uses the word "meek" for Jesus, it is this combination he is referring to (Matthew 11:29: "Learn from me; for I am meek and lowly in heart ..."). The following excerpt from an apostolic exhortation (*Evangelii Gaudium*) by Pope Francis directly enunciates how kindness is a strength, not a weakness:

> Whenever we look to Mary, we come to believe once again in the revolutionary nature of love and tenderness. In her we see that humility and tenderness are not virtues of the weak but of the strong who need not treat others poorly in order to

> feel important themselves. Contemplating Mary, we realize that she who praised God for "bringing down the mighty from their thrones" and "sending the rich away empty" (Lk 1:52-53) is also the one who brings a homely warmth to our pursuit of justice. She ... sets out from her town "with haste" (Lk 1:39) to be of service to others. This interplay of justice and tenderness, of contemplation and concern for others, is what makes the ecclesial community look to Mary as a model of evangelization.[408]

Yet, the testimony provided by Phillips and Taylor makes clear the attitude that kindness is considered a virtue of losers in today's society. In the United States, the paradox to reconcile is that of a society overwhelmingly populated by people who identify as Christian (and a country with the largest Christian population in the world) to be so far from the spirit of Virgin Mary. The four tyrannies (fear, want, victory, and identity) provided us a good starting point towards solving this puzzle.

Ironically, as religion's exploitation in the socio-political environment and the resulting conditioning go up, it should be no surprise that the overall comprehension of religion and even spirituality goes down. The rigid religious-secular divide in the societal psyche in many parts of the world may also play a part. This is underlined by an excerpt from the writing of Professor James W. Morris, who refers to the attitude of Ibn Arabi[409] (or Ibn al-Arabi, thirteenth century), considered the foremost Sufi master (al-shaykh al-akbar):

> As any teacher of religious studies at the university level still quickly discovers, nothing could be a greater veil to serious understanding and penetration of classical religious texts and spiritual traditions than what beginning students have been socially conditioned to think of as "religious"—and it does not seem to matter much whether the attitude toward those initially unconscious restrictive assumptions happens to be positive or the opposite, or what particular cultural

> forms and content are involved. Not surprisingly, then, one constant theme ... [in Ibn Arabi's writings is to call into question] the unexamined assumptions, implicit beliefs, and guiding attitudes of those ... who naturally tended to consider their own forms of learning as unimpeachable and certain knowledge.[410]

As a remedial approach, Morris then cites Ibn Arabi's precept of keeping an inquisitive and questioning mind. Such comfort with humility and boldness is not only a good rule for theologians and scholars of religion, it's also a desirable rule for the academe to question its own modus operandi. The boldness that Ibn Arabi suggests within a system of learning is not the same thing as arrogance (especially the kind relating to the history professor quoted in chapter 5, subtitle "Ignorance and Arrogance ..."). It may, in fact, be quite the opposite. Ibn Arabi's boldness comes from a realistic assessment of man's place in God's creation. This intellectual and spiritual humility reminds us of our own limitations, constraints, and vulnerabilities. It also allows a fertile ground to emerge where ideas collide and cross-pollinate. Above all, though, this spiritual grounding provides us the self-mastery that keeps us from taking advantage of others, a temptation that ultimately damages our own long-term interest because it is almost always against the interest of the society. Humility, therefore, becomes a vital attribute in our educational, religious, and cultural environments.

Deception and Division as the Basis of Political "Culture"

Propaganda is most influential when it is a rationalization of
the desires, sentiments, prejudices, or interests
of those to whom it is addressed.[411]

—Aldous Huxley

Gradually I came to realize that people
will more readily swallow lies than truth,
as if the taste of lies was homey, appetizing: a habit."[412]

—Martha Gellhorn

In the epigraphs above, Huxley and Gellhorn give us a guiding glimpse into how basic human weaknesses are deceptively exploited to serve various political agendas. The overall result is grossly against the well-being of an overwhelming majority of the human race. What is the impact on a society when the prevailing political ethos place deception above any cultural tenets of the society? The question is critical because the damage to the society caused by the dilution and deterioration of its culture may be irreversible.

We begin this discussion with the curious dichotomy within the opinions of Ted White, the legendary journalist[413] who received the Pulitzer Prize for *The Making of the President 1960*, a book that essentially invented the genre of books about presidential campaigns. National politicians, as he described them in that book, were "men whom I have found over the long years the pleasantest, shrewdest and generally the most honorable of companions." As for his "comrades of the press," the outlook was no less rosy because their "reporting at every level of American politics purifies, protects and refreshes our system from year to year."[414]

In a letter to a friend on August 31, 1960, however, White seems to have a different take on the whole system and its workings:

> [It] is all fraudulent, all of it, everywhere, up and down, East and West. The movies, radio and state and books and TV ... and the foundations and universities and scholars, they are all fraudulent too ... and the Commissars and the Krushchevs and the Mao Tze-tungs, they are fraudulent equally; it is all a great game.... The scenery of politics is ridiculous, absolutely ridiculous. Yet I must report all this as serious.[415]

The important question here is not which of White's takes is more accurate, but rather why, at virtually the same exact moment, he has one opinion for public consumption and an entirely contradictory one in private? We may never have an answer to that question, but surely the same reason applies to many in a position to intimately understand, or perhaps even create, the political landscape.

In that background, we'll examine the falsehoods and deceptions that currently prevail at the highest levels of government all over the world. During President Trump's term in the Oval Office, *Washington Post* started a "Fact Checker" project to keep track of the president's "untruths." As the *Post* reported: "By the time Trump left office, he had accumulated 30,573 untruths during his presidency—averaging about 21 erroneous claims a day. Trump made about six false or misleading claims a day in his first year as president, 16 a day in his second year, 22 a day in his third year—and 39 a day in his final year."[416]

It would be erroneous to think that President Trump was an exception to the rule. It may well be his clear-eyed understanding of the "rule" assisting him in the communication strategy he adopted. *Washington Post* ran a similar "Fact Checker" for President Biden's first-hundred days to show that he also has a long list of falsehoods to his credit.[417] Besides, President Biden has a sufficient history of other falsehoods during his time in public service[418] for us to conclude that such craftiness just comes with the territory. And the United States is no exception either. Citizens of another country who believe that their leaders do not engage in such guilefulness and mendacity may be residing in an illusory bubble.

The business of deceit and lies to the public, it should come as no surprise, is really part and parcel of the modern-day system of governing the nation-state. And the lies propagated mostly for self-promotion pale when compared to the lies used to facilitate or hide high crimes, inhumanity, corruption, or sheer incompetence. Insert 6:1 provides an excerpt from an interview of Candidate Biden by the *New York Times* Editorial Board in December 2019.[419]

LIES? YES. RESPONSIBILITY? NO.

NYT: Reporting out from The Washington Post about **years and years and years of generals in Afghanistan essentially lying about the conduct of the war.**[420] Eight years as vice president, you know this issue very intimately. **Have the American people been lied to about what we're doing there?**

Biden: **Yes. Yeah.**

NYT: What do we do about it? And why **should they trust you again?**

Biden: They should trust me because ... **I was the vice president of the United States of America. I was not president** of the United States of America, number one.

NYT: **Do you have a responsibility** to say that [the people have been lied to] in public, though?

Biden: **No** ...

—*New York Times*, January 17, 2020;
(emphasis added)

Insert 6:1

This, by any standard, is a gravely depressing statement on the state of affairs. The man who had been the vice president of the country for eight years accepts that he was aware of high crimes yet was not responsible to do anything about it. This also makes clear that the whole administration was aware of these crimes and not a peep was heard from any corner. (If there were a peep, it must have been silenced effectively.) That the paper of record practically kept this information under wraps is also an instructive example of how such affairs are managed.[421]

As the partisan power tussles intensify, the nation pays the price. Instead of emphasizing the uniform prevalence of chicanery in the political system, the public is bombarded more and more with rhetoric of division and partisanship. In a 2021 post-election article in *Harper's*, a prominent political commentator said: "It's true enough that most white conservatives are not monsters, and that some of them are not bigots[422] ... Red America is responsible for most of their own problems—and ours—thanks to the policies and the candidates they have supported for decades. But rather than acknowledge any of that they have simply doubled down ..."[423]

This piece discussed the disenchantment of the white working class with the Democratic establishment, and their pull towards President Trump's message. The writer first evaluated and factually debunked many of the prevalent theories by some other media pundits. In conclusion he says: "Something must have been done to them, the people, to make them so desperate that they would empower a president as puerile, unqualified, and openly venal as this one."[424]

A careful evaluation may show that the "something [that] must have been done to ... the people" of this country has to do with the necessary ideological divides that have been created by the Hobbesian struggles for more and more power, and the resulting environment of news, entertainment, media, information, education, etc.[425] If so, why is this political commentator so unwilling to accept (or so amazingly unaware of) the role of the domains or systems he himself represents and serves?

In another piece regarding the ostensible Russian meddling in the 2016 US elections, a liberal British journalist concludes: "A democracy such as the United States will always be divided—of course it will ... because Americans are too quick to turn viciously against one another. The culture war has made the country vulnerable in the disinformation wars."[426]

Why does a democracy such as the United States have to be "divided ... [and] viciously against one another"? Contrary to what this political commentator posits, it may be the internal "disinformation wars" that have created the "culture war." And, embedded in their culture wars, the intellectual rigidity among media commentators keeps widening the artificial divide. Another journalist confirms this conclusion in *Harper's*: "bad information is a weapon wielded in an occasionally violent domestic political conflict rather than a cold war between super powers."[427]

The irony of all this is the underlying superficiality and hollowness of these divisions—and the political system's non-acceptance of what the public feels. Even in the 1990s, this popular sentiment was captured by a scholar with the following words: "Everywhere I travel, I find an almost universal sense among ordinary people that the institutions on which they depend are failing them[428] ... this fear is creating a growing sense of political frustration and alienation ... Yet the real issues go far deeper than a simple rejection of big government."[429]

Not surprisingly, the principles and interests of the ordinary conservative and the average liberal may not be that different. For that matter, the concerns and misgivings of the everyday people who want to "drain the swamp" may be very close to the concerns of those who want to "occupy Wall Street." And that reality simply cannot be waived away by the media pundits.

Creation of A Culture of "Reality Crisis" and "Information Disorder"

Many countries, especially the United States, enjoy the collective perception and belief that propaganda and censorship happen "elsewhere" (but not "here"). Yet, in the subconscious mind, even Americans seem to have an inkling that things may not be so exceptional in the US. A September 2021 Gallup Poll indicates that only 7 percent of the US population have a "great deal" of trust in "the mass media—such as newspapers, T.V. and radio—when it comes to reporting the news fully, accurately, and fairly."[430] Another 29 percent have a "fair amount" of trust. In 1974, those numbers were 21 percent and 48 percent respectively. (The overall level of trust thus has gone from 69 percent in 1974 to 36 percent in 2021, indicating a drastic drop in public confidence.) Looking from another angle, 64 percent of Americans do not trust the mass media today. And there is more to this phenomenon. According to other recent polls:

- Thirty-six percent of Americans believe that CNN is "sometimes or very often a source of disinformation."[431] And 36 percent of Americans also believe that the

Chinese government is sometimes or very often a source of disinformation.[432] (This poll was conducted around January 2021.)

- Five percent of regular viewers of Fox News believe that "white nationalism is a very serious threat." Among Americans who do not watch Fox News, that number is 72 percent.[433]

The poll results may carry educational implications. In the United States, for the Chinese government to enjoy the same level of mistrust as CNN is an interesting scenario. For Fox News viewers to have a perception so far off from the average American citizen is rather instructive too. (It is likely a similar scenario would emerge if the poll involved regular watchers of CNN or MSNBC.)[434]

Two factors also have to be kept in mind. First, part of the public consciousness (or the causative imagery) for such observations comes from partisan bickering and labeling that remain limited to reflexively blaming the other party and its satellite media for being partisan. Such partisan "awareness" though becomes just another narrow version of exceptionalism and may not open a window into grasping the fuller reality.

Second, confirmation bias—tendency to select information that confirms our beliefs and filters out information that invalidates our beliefs—makes people gravitate to the media channel that affirms their outlook. Here, then, it is not that people are looking for truth and finding a channel that is more reliable in truth-telling. They may instead be looking for whoever conforms to their outlook and may abandon it if the channel dilutes its promotion of that ideology.

As the interparty fissures translate into public schisms, information management becomes more of an imperative, and even more divisive narratives emerge. What also seems to be consistently promoted is the belief that the state of disinformation is almost entirely caused by the relatively open information distribution ushered in by the internet. In the United States, at least, the 2016 presidential election is often presented to be the watershed when deception and falsehood began to be deployed in earnest within the political system.

According to a 2019 Pew survey, some 50 percent of the US population believes that "made-up news" has become "a very big problem in the country today"—a figure weighty enough to rank along with "violent crime."[435] Even more interesting is the recent public perception that makes much of this awareness to have suddenly condensed into common consciousness after the 2016 presidential elections.

As the "unified vision ... produced by twentieth-century television"[436] dilutes away, no longer having the traditional gatekeepers of information ascends in projection as the crux of the trouble. Newspapers, radio, and television—in addition to universities and think tanks—no longer provide all the information, and, in that process, also no longer perform the verification function. Voices in the media are goading us to reminisce about that time. Also visible is the evolving need to control and reverse the unraveling image of a system that was fully trusted for so long. All this commotion deprives attention and thus plausibility from the rationale that the problem being faced may be that of truth and trust—not ambiguity and control.

The new metaphor of the "information ecosystem" is often used to imply pollution spreading in the system. And the solution being offered ubiquitously would mend the problem by fixing Big Tech's[437] algorithm as well as the introduction of some "necessary" regulation. Ironically, as a media insider points out, this undertaking is "simply an unofficial partnership between Big Tech, corporate media, elite universities, and cash-rich foundations."[438]

Aspen Institute's announcement about the formation of the "nonpartisan" Commission on Information Disorder, whose commissioners include Katie Couric and Prince Harry, may be one such step. The "About the Commission" page on its website indicates that the project is meant to "help government, the private sector, and civil society" in the effort to "engage disaffected populations who have lost faith in evidence-based reality." The objective is to "respond to this modern-day crisis of faith in key institutions."[439]

So, we are supposed to believe that the Commission and its funders are fully in possession of the "evidence-based reality"—and that the population is entirely ignorant of it. This is a flagrant denial of the validity of the real-life evidence the population is witness to and what is causing the "crisis of faith in key institutions." If, as implied by the Commission's statements, the population under discussion has been misled with disinformation or propaganda by players that are mostly institutional, the "crisis of faith in key institutions" may be entirely reasonable. Should the public be required to believe only MSNBC and not FOX, or vice versa? Perhaps it would be too much to expect the royalty-studded commission to acknowledge this Catch-22 logic that justifies its existence.

The Commission states that its purpose is to create "lawful and ethical means by which the federal government can promote fact-based information."[440] The Orwellian language aside, this goal "comes as governments around the world have started using emergency 'fake news' and 'disinformation' laws to harass and arrest dissidents and reporters."[441] It is not clear how the Commission will deliver its help to the government, but what it is going after seems to be a good recipe for the promotion of an authoritarian system. The very people the Commission wants to "engage" may well be justified in their concern about the implications of its agenda.

In December 2019, University of Washington (UW) launched its Center for an Informed Public (UWCIP), which shares its goals with the Aspen Institute's Commission on Information Disorder. According to a UW publication, being "perfectly equipped to make sense of the myriad conspiracy theories," CIP will be the "response to the rise in disinformation and the erosion of trust in our democratic institutions."[442]

An academic researcher at UWCIP comments on the information available at the Centers for Disease Control and Prevention's Vaccine Adverse Event Reporting System (VAERS). In explaining why VAERS is reporting an inordinately high number of adverse events from COVID-19 vaccines, the researcher implies that the CDC data is untrustworthy because "these unverified reports can be filed by anyone."[443] UWCIP, unfortunately, does not seem to realize that its statement to "debunk" a certain narrative is resoundingly debunking UWCIP's own raison d'être. Two points:

First, there is no valid information available to suggest that CDC's VAERS data system is compromised.[444] (The vaccine skeptics, on the other hand, verifiably claim that the CDC—in violation of its traditional practice—is hiding massive amounts of data.[445]) UWCIP's suggestion could thus be reasonably looked upon as a conspiracy theory.

Second, VAERS (jointly administered by the CDC and the FDA) has been around for a long time and is extensively relied upon by the medical community and researchers. For UWCIP to insist that this federal system is corrupted and untrustworthy simply proves that the erosion of faith in public institutions is entirely justified.[446] To promote its stated agenda, UWCIP itself seems to be engaging in conspiracy theories and erosion of trust in public institutions.[447]

Not to be left behind, the New York Times advocated in February 2021 for the office of a "reality czar" which "could become the tip of the spear for the federal government's response to the reality crisis."[448] To his credit, the author himself shyly accepts that the idea "sounds a little dystopian."[449] One can only wonder what Orwell would say in that regard!

As another journalist points out in *Harper's*: "Indeed, it is possible that the Establishment needs the theater of social media persuasion to build a political world that will make sense, to explain Brexit and Trump and the loss of faith in the decaying institutions ..."[450] Yet it seems that strict social media management by Big Tech was after all not the desired ideal.

On April 21, 2022, Hillary Clinton tweeted, "For too long, tech platforms have amplified disinformation and extremism with no accountability."[451] That same exact day, in a speech at Stanford University, Barack Obama stated, "while content moderation can limit the distribution of clearly dangerous content, it doesn't go far enough... A regulatory structure, a smart one, needs to be in place."[452] (Ironically, in the same speech, Obama also labeled himself "pretty close to a First Amendment absolutist.")[453]

Following all this, the Department of Homeland Security (DHS) announced in May 2022 the creation[454] of an entity named the Disinformation Governance Board ("DGB"). Even the favorable coverage by *Politico.com* could not dispose of the newspeak.

> 'The irony is that this board is really kind of boring,' said a DHS official who was not authorized to address the topic on the record. 'It was designed to protect against the very thing that we're being accused of doing—that is, it was designed to protect the free speech, privacy, civil rights and civil liberties of all Americans.'[455]

Politico's Jack Schafer upends DHS's "designed to protect" claim with these words: "Who among us thinks the government should add to its work list the job of determining what is true and what is disinformation? And who thinks the government is capable of telling the truth? Our government produces lies and disinformation at industrial scale and always has."[456]

Shortly after the DHS announcement, attorney generals from twenty states—expressing a concern about the "chilling effect on free speech"—called to disband the group.[457] Even the Wall Street Journal railed against a "one-way ticket to ostracism," and demanded that the DHS "pull the plug" on the DGB.[458] Glenn Greenwald, a non-establishment leftist progressive commentator, declared that "the concept of 'anti-disinformation expert' is itself completely fraudulent... There is no conceivable circumstance in which a domestic law enforcement agency like DHS should be claiming the power to decree truth and falsity."[459]

We began the previous section with the words of journalist Theodore White. As he stated in 1960, "the scenery of politics is ridiculous." That scenery seems to have further deteriorated. The risk for the society is that the prevailing ethos of the political system would completely overcome the culture and the systems of the society with irreversibly deleterious effects.

Countering the Trend of Thought Pattern Dominance

Under certain circumstances, the prevalent Hobbesian conditioning promoting dominance over the other has been a grave detriment to the human race. The built-in "tyrannies" make the ground fertile for this human proclivity to do great damage.

How this works can be viewed solely from the dominance of one culture or system of education. As stated earlier, the Roman Empire is estimated to have been responsible for the loss of over a thousand languages. It is, however, not just the field of anthropology where we notice the implications. They exist in our daily lives. Domingo Francisco Velasco is a traditional healer in Mexico. His words, referring to the historical injustice in his region and to his people, are instructive: "The worst thing you can do is impose. This is the main problem with humanity."[460]

That simple statement carries an ocean of meanings. Velasco's point is important because, in the context of agency, such imposition has deleterious consequences for a society. The means of imposition, however, can be different. An analogy can be drawn from the Orwellian and Huxleyan models. In the Orwellian model, imposition is often by some mechanism of coercion. In the Huxleyan model, however, it happens through conditioning. This is a vital point to understand as the results delivered by both these means are equally pernicious. In the Huxleyan scenario especially, the victim is an equal—and often willing—participant in the imposition. Our present-day acceptance and use of "technology"[461] may be seen in just this Huxleyan context.

A counter-intuitive application of how conditioning works can be seen in the following mundane and personal example. I do not use a smartphone. There is a complex amalgam of well-thought-through reasons—sociological,[462] philosophical, scientific, personal[463]—that drive this decision. Frequently enough, people try to convince me that I should at least use a smartphone in a limited fashion. I am given all kinds of reasons why it would be beneficial to me, and I have been the object of affectionate and well-meaning jokes and commentary from friends.

Yet, in so many years, virtually no one has seriously tried to find out my reasons for resisting the smartphone. Perhaps there is no need to ask. What reason could there possibly be beyond stubborn eccentricity? The vehicles of conditioning, when unquestioningly accepted, become so strong and inescapable as to make us lose all inquisitiveness in our day-to-day life.

Yet again, this loss has to be through some degree of choice. It is an act of volition that allows our own imprisoned possibilities—that the mind possesses but does not discover—to remain chained beyond realization. Modern humans are more likely to allow external notions to shape our thinking and feeling, instead of tapping into our inner wisdom. This habit becomes an add-on to the conditioning by the prevalent systems—against our personal and societal interests. As Thich Nhat Hanh, a Buddhist monk, says, "... we may assume that we are a peaceful person, a representative of peace, but this might not be the case. If we look deeply, we will observe that the roots of war are in the unmindful ways we have been living."[464]

Let's focus on the word "unmindful" here as a big source of our current human dilemma. James Baldwin, half a century ago in his book *Nobody Knows My Name*, presciently observed that when we give up freedom in our thought process, our choices then get made for us by those who control our societal structures: "Freedom is not something that anybody can be given; freedom is something people take and people are as free as they want to be. One hasn't got to have an enormous military machine in order to be un-free when it's simpler to be asleep, when it's simpler to be apathetic, when it's simpler, in fact, not to want to be free, to think that something else is more important."[465]

What makes Baldwin's observation poignant is that an individual's thought processes are reflective of the societal way of thinking. That is because the system we live in teaches us how to identify value in word, action, thought, conduct, interaction, connection—indeed, in one's state of being.[466] As the individual is constituted, however, so is the collective (because the individual influences the collective). Thus, the individual and the collective, on some dimension, become mirrors of each other.[467] The "unfreedom" of the individual Baldwin refers to is reflective of the unfreedom of the collective, and vice versa.

If the culture of a society forms an individual, then its absence is to be compensated for. In such a case, the vacuum is filled by the ethos of societal structures—university, political party, place of employment, etc.—in the current law-driven societal configuration. The ethos and subconscious thought habits inculcated in the individual by such structures are different from those of a non-legal culture. As Appendix A shows, the influence of fundamentally Hobbesian nature of structures then dominates.

Going back to Baldwin, our unquestioning acceptance of the imposition of assumptions mindlessly surrender us to external ideologies in an act of voluntary weakening of the self. (Part three will show how these human weaknesses can also dilute the spiritual message.) For a democratic society, such an attitude by its members is not just a symptom of the prevalent "imaginicide." It can also be seen as a harbinger of times ahead as Baldwin, Orwell, and Huxley all feared. Unless, of course, the human will and agency are commensurate with the challenge.

PART THREE:

RELIGION'S EXPLOITATION TO SERVE AGENDAS

Found that we were still where
we had begun the journey,
the shore had been travelling
along with the boat.[468]
—Saifuddin Saif

CHAPTER 7:

THE MONEY MACHINE

No one can serve two masters ...
God and mammon [money].

—Matthew 6:24

The love of money is the root of all evil.

—Timothy 6:10

Several years ago, I was in China on business. One day, I was riding in a brand-new Audi driven by the owner of a factory. Our company's representative in China was in the front passenger seat. (The rep spoke English, whereas the factory owner did not.) A figurine in gold was attached to the car's dashboard. While I recognized whose image the figurine depicted, I still asked our company's rep what that image represented.

"Buddha," replied the rep, "Mr. [so and so] is a Buddhist."

"What is the purpose of this figure on the dashboard?" I asked.

"Money," he said, "Buddha will bring money [to the factory owner]."

A couple of years later I was back in China and, coincidentally, one day I found myself in the same car with the same co-occupants. This time, though, things were different. There was another figurine on the dashboard sitting close to the original Buddha statuette. I could not place this new figurine. It looked rather bizarre and was highly motion-sensitive by design. As the car moved, the image shook in a dizzying fashion. "What is this new figure?" I asked the rep.

"This is also Buddha," he said.

"Why does he need two Buddhas on the dashboard?" I asked.

"More money," he said, "Buddha will now bring even more money."

The point here is not to judge anyone's religious belief, but rather to be able to see how something absolutely antithetical to a teaching can be an object of sincere belief. Within his understanding of his religion, the believer is getting attached to the very source of *dukkha* that his religion—in the very first of the Four Noble Truths—advises to stay away from. Even otherwise, the message in the actual teaching is unambiguous: "This is peace, this is exquisite—the resolution of all fabrications, the relinquishment of all acquisitions, the ending of craving; dispassion; cessation; Nibbana."[469]

Hobbesian Hedonism as a Religious Tenet?

We have already discussed the role played by Thomas Hobbes's doctrine in shaping the various facets of present-day society. *On Kindness* by Phillips and Taylor clarifies that even those Enlightenment thinkers who disliked Hobbes's misanthropy did accept his hedonistic premises.[470] The resulting consequences on the ethos, thought patterns, and priorities of a society are far-reaching. The reader is likely to be quite familiar with the abuse of religion for financial gain. The goal of this chapter, therefore, is to create the mental connection for the reader between the in-tandem evolution of personal greed within the institution of religion and social ethos under Enlightenment philosophy.

Religion has historically been exploited for personal and institutional power. Now we see its abuse for profanely commercial purposes and enhancement of personal wealth. The most effective way to this end is to take whatever an audience is looking for—driven by societal values—and repackage it as sanctioned or preferred by scripture. Reverend Terry Cole-Whittaker is an Emmy Award-winning evangelist who was described by the *LA Times* as "the bubbly minister whose 'you-can-have-it-all' philosophy has made her the darling of the Me Generation."[471] With the use of her "principles of prosperity," she would exhort her congregants and TV audience to change their ways by finding Jesus Christ. She would further facilitate the process by offering her prosperity "Campaign Kit" which "appears to have a dual purpose. As it brings one nearer to Jesus, it also provides advice on how to increase one's bank account. This makes her followers extremely happy and confirms their predisposition to believe that prosperity is the true aim of religion."[472]

As the *LA Times* pointed out in 1985, "Her most popular slogan and the heart of her gospel—'Pro$perity: Your Divine Right'—is commonly seen on buttons and bumper stickers."[473]

Reverend Terry later also established an ashram in India to offer further enlightenment to Westerners via Indic religions.[474] Appreciably, Lakshmi had to be pulled into the bankers' syndicate when God alone wouldn't provide all the "mammon" for the reverend's venture.

Compared to such focus on wealth and self-promotion, there's the example of Michael Faraday, who declined a knighthood (offered by the British government in recognition of his service to science) on religious grounds—he believed that accumulation of wealth and pursuit of worldly reward would be against the word of the Bible. Who comes across as more faithful to the message, spirit, and principles evoked and inspired by the Bible? This also leads to the inference that the potential of exploitation is commensurate with a society's culture, values, and ethos.

On 20 September 2013, Pope Francis warned us against this exploitation in a meditation themed "Power of Money" using these words:

> We must guard ourselves against the temptation to idolize money, for this may weaken our faith and accustom us to the deception of meaningless and hurtful desires that lead people to destruction and perdition ... There is something about the attitude of love towards money that takes us away from God ... Greed is the root of all evil. Overtaken by this desire, some have wandered away from the faith and are

> grabbed by many torments. It is the power of money that makes you deviate from authentic faith. It cuts you off from the faith, and weakens you so that you lose it ... instead strive for righteousness, faith, charity, and patience, in opposition to vanity, and against pride ... It is the road of humility in Jesus Christ, who being rich became poor to enrich us with his own poverty. This is the way to serve God. May the Lord help us all to not fall into the trap of the idolatry of money.[475]

The message is essentially the same in all religions. Teachings generally exhort a religion's adherents to look after the welfare of the needy, the hungry, the homeless, the orphan, the sick, etc. Many religious organizations take steps and provide platforms to achieve this objective. Like any other human institution, however, this too is prone to the same corruption and abuse that forms a society's cultural fabric.

Monopolizing Power and Profit?

Concerns have been raised in the past also about people's ability and will to exploit religion for their financial gain. Such concerns, however, are often expressed in a way that smears the very concept of religion, polarizing such conversation and taking attention away from the real sources of the problem. When such expression is polemical, we often find that the base of information being used to draw a disagreeable conclusion is rather limited.

Rather inflammatory, a comment by Thomas Paine comes to mind: "All national institutions of churches whether Jewish, Christian or Turkish, appear to me no other than human inventions, set up to terrify and enslave mankind and monopolize power and profit."[476]

Regardless of the style of such expression, openness in acknowledging others' right to raise such concerns accepts the existence of a common problem, thus adding to our ability in finding solutions at a broader level. True, religion may be used to "terrify" and "enslave" people. Paine's statement though is full of fallacies that are worth considering. First, even if we accept that religion is purely a "human invention" without any spiritual force that leads into such a belief system, it does not render it inferior to other human thought, including Enlightenment philosophy. Second, did the "inventors," such as the Buddha or Jesus, become rich by monetizing these "inventions?" If not, Paine's conclusion is baseless.

Third, even what we call science is a human construct. Following Paine's logic, would it be fair to jump to the conclusion that science was "set up to terrify and enslave mankind?" That would clearly be the wrong answer. Yet this book has clearly pointed out the threats humanity faces at the hands of science—emphasizing that science, when used in the pursuit of power and profit, can be corrupted (see chapter 5, subtitle "Shaking Academe's Absolute Faith in Science as God"). The institution of religion is no different. The exploitation of human nature within the prevalent Hobbesian paradigm effectively uses religion to serve various agendas by capitalizing on human weakness such as selfishness and greed—the very attributes our religions warn us about.

Blaming religion for materialism is not just simplistic, it is disingenuous. When evaluated carefully, naked greed in the name of religion shares the same sources that bedevil human society today. Various parts of this book highlight those sources. When we focus on the real causes of the problem, we are in a better position to find a solution.

CHAPTER 8:

THE SOURCE OF DISCORD OR COMMUNION?

O brother, Wisdom pours into you
from the beloved saint of God.
You've only borrowed it.
Although the house of your heart is lit from inside,
that light is lent by a luminous neighbor.
Give thanks; don't be arrogant or vain;
pay attention without self importance.
It's sad that this borrowed state has put religious communities
far from communion.

—Rumi, Jalal ad-Din Muhammad Balkhi, *Masnavi*, 1:3268-71

I was a teenager and traveling alone to North America and Europe. In the United States, I realized that I would need a visa to enter France. I went to the French consulate. The person who attended to me was the consul general himself. He listened to my situation; then went into the private area of his office. When he came back, he had a thick collection of documents with him. He requested that I read the relevant section for myself so I could understand that his hands were tied. The document made clear in unambiguous terms that the visa I needed could only be issued by the French Embassy in Islamabad, Pakistan. Tough luck!

I mentioned to him the needless complication of this rule and then I said something to the effect: "So you want me to travel back ten thousand kilometers to get this visa?"

He looked at me again, thought for a moment, and then I witnessed a miracle. He took my passport, quickly took care of the visa requirements, and then said something like: "Here it is, enjoy your travels ... what can they do to me?"

It is remarkable how the very definition of "us" and "them" changed in his mind, even if momentarily. Assuredly, this French consul general was fully aware of all the differences—religious, national, racial, ethnic, linguistic—that existed between us. Yet, in that moment at least, something switched, and the human connection transcended the divides created by various identities. The two of us were on one side, whereas his government (which was also his employer) was on the other.

What we see here is the human spirit overcoming the external constructs created by our socio-political systems—this spiritual connection to one's essence provides the opportunity to overcome "otherness" and actualize one's agency. As spiritual beings, we are all in some ways connected to one another. And even in today's world, things can happen when that innate human connection overcomes the artificial and divisive barriers and boundaries.

Challenging Ignorance and Hate

Platforms such as the media and the church can be immensely instrumental in challenging modern ignorance and hate, the interdependent twins that threaten our very existence. Unfortunately, these platforms often perform the reverse function, almost knowingly even if not always intentionally. Something similar to the false dichotomy fallacy advancing preconceptions and misconceptions is often deployed in promoting images of the other; hence an indifference and hostility towards the "other" is created. Frequently enough, this is done in the name of religion, creating a chasm that is antithetical to the basic tenets of that religion. The gulf thus becomes unbridgeable even in everyday circumstances. What then would shatter the biases and misconceptions we scarcely know we hold—barring, of course, a miraculous turn of heart or an epiphany? Such epiphanies are frequently provided by our scriptures, if we keep our hearts and minds open to a deeper understanding. *Taittirīya Upanishad* (1.11.2) grants us such a message:

> Be one to whom a mother is as a god, be one to whom a father is as a god,
>
> Be one to whom an *Acharya* [teacher] is as a god, be one to whom a guest[477] is as a god.
>
> Those acts which are irreproachable should be practiced, and no others.
>
> Those things which among us are good deeds should be revered by you, and no others.

Everyone who comes into our life being a "guest" does seem to be such an epiphany in this scriptural teaching. And the inspiration grows manifold when we ponder the deeper implication of "guest" in this teaching—finding a resonance with Jesus's definition of "neighbor" in the well-known good Samaritan verse (*Luke* 10:25-37). And yet, that's far from the prevalent understanding of the concept of guest or neighbor. In Dr. King's summation, "one of the great tragedies of men's long trek along the highway of history has been the limiting of neighborly concern to tribe, race, class, or nation."[478]

In that regard, instead of blaming secular science or philosophy, Rabbi Heschel placed the responsibility at religion's own door for having become "irrelevant, dull, oppressive, insipid."[479] The reality goes even further than that because there is no denying the grievously detrimental role various establishments have historically played in the name of their religion. Indeed, as Dr. King points out, the religious establishment has "often been an active participant in shaping and crystallizing the patterns of the race-caste system."[480] Referring to the Christian Church, Dr. King said: "We must face the shameful fact that the church is the most segregated institution in American society ... The church has a schism in its own soul that it must close."[481] Despite this reality, it would be unwise to deny the potential role of religion in our lives which, according to King, are bound "in an inescapable network of mutuality, tied in a single garment of destiny."[482]

Claiming True Selfhood

Ted Hakey, a former US Marine who lived in Meriden, Connecticut, provides a good example from both sides of the picture. Hakey likes to shoot guns (federal agents found twenty-four in his house). In 2017, incited by what he had been seeing on the media, Hakey decided to "do something about it." He did not need to go far—there was a mosque next door to his house. Some of the thirty shots he fired at it could have killed people had it not been the middle of the night. Hakey's life changed when he sat down with the mosque leaders to apologize.[483] Hakey now considers himself a changed man, especially because of the relationship he developed with Zahir Mannan, one of the leaders. "We talk about things I don't even discuss with some of my best friends," Hakey told NBC Connecticut. "It just became a relationship that's really, very tight."[484]

This example goes to show how a shallower understanding of our faith can sometimes have a misguiding effect on us because it allows our ego to take over. As an antidote, *Sri Guru Granth Sahib* (M.1, p 657) provides an opportunity for reflection: "When I am in my ego, then You are not with me. Now that You are with me, there is no egotism within me."

Hakey pointed out the key that opened his mind and heart: "I just realized all the misconceptions I had about Islam were wrong, because I didn't know any actual Muslims... I just want to tell people to *think for themselves*."[485]

This last sentence deserves a lot of attention because it presents one of the greatest challenges in the current socio-political environment. Reclaiming our right and responsibility to feel and think on our own, using our own heart and mind, is an important part of the solution we need to solve the problems we face as a society, and as members of the human race.

There is another irony worth mentioning here. The mosque Hakey shot at belongs to the Ahmadi school. Some Muslims, especially in Pakistan, go out of their way in excoriating and persecuting the followers of this school.[486] The story thus presents layer over layer of self-righteousness, intolerance, bigotry, and pain; perhaps one could say it paints a rather accurate picture of what is currently the overall human condition. This story's crux, though, has to do with the tender conduct of the actors involved, especially Hakey and Mannan who, in claiming their true selfhood—even in difficult circumstances—have shown how to manifest and sprout the seed we all carry. Hakey's insightful awakening was aptly captured in a verse by Ghalib:

> The perplexity emanating from
> my suspicion of the "other,"
> Mirrors the degree of my distance
> from my own true reality.[487]

The Conscious Antidote

The lesson Hakey teaches us is that the antidote has to be conscious: to respect and honor the other in the spirit of mutual affirmation and discovery. This is a responsibility we all carry; its manifestation is not an optional luxury or subject to happenstance. As a guide, we can use Rabbi Heschel's counsel that we "cannot remain aloof or indifferent. We, too, are either ministers of the sacred or slaves of evil."[488]

> By oneself is wrong done,
> By oneself is one defiled,
> By oneself wrong is not done,
> By oneself, surely, is one cleansed.
> One cannot purify another;
> Purity and impurity are in oneself (alone).
>
> —Dhammapada 12.9

The clergy within various religions shoulder a heavy responsibility to monitor parochialism in their messages. It certainly would help if the clergy were able to transcend narrow identities and develop a basic understanding of the drivers of global affairs and the place of religion in these affairs. Doubtless, it is difficult to claim or reclaim our selfhood in a vacuum of pivotal information and the understanding it can generate.

As we saw in Hakey's case, when the heart takes over, the greatest beneficiary is the one who allows oneself to engage in such a process. Finding sacredness in the other does not just create societal harmony, it may also be an essential milestone in the path to a more meaningful self-discovery. Our religious traditions provide us the roadmap for such self-exploration.

CHAPTER 9:

THE REALM OF SELF-RIGHTEOUS EXCLUSIVITY

The lightning of Theophany was meant for me,
not the Sinai Mount;
Wine gets poured into the cup
in accord with the drinker's fount.[489]

—Ghalib, Mirza Asadullah Baig Khan

In the couplet above, Ghalib displays his usual sleight of hand, in this case by beginning with an arrogant statement, and then immediately turning it around to show his humility. What a splendid way to convey his message. (Compared to the translation, the original wording is much more beautiful and enigmatic, requiring going beyond the literal.) Numerous centuries prior, Rumi also advised against such arrogance, though much more explicitly:

> Please don't request what you can't tolerate:
> A blade of straw can't hold a mountain's weight.[490]

Because the truth is infinitely more than what humans can endure or contain, any notion of exclusive "ownership" of the truth can only be a sign of ignorance and usually also indicates insecurity wrapped in arrogance. That's the way we can interpret Rumi's words, in addition to the apparent literal meaning.

Sincerity Is Not Enough

On two occasions in the year 2020, two different acquaintances invited me to convert to another religion for my salvation. It didn't offend me at all. I can clearly see not just their sincerity and concern for me, but also a sense of purpose in this effort. I do, however, find an important lesson in this tendency, making it clear to me that the ostensible "firmness" of their faith had taken away their ability to observe and realize that I might already have a strong faith within my own religion. It also took away from them the capacity to see that I might be well informed about their scriptures and that—as part of my existing faith—I already held their religion in high esteem. In effect, the self-righteousness of their belief seemed to have taken away the capacity to reflect upon and appreciate all this. Their sincerity in wanting to help me to salvation cited in these instances should neither be denied nor denounced. It must be understood—because its application within the field of religion is far and wide (even in the comprehension of violence in the name of religion).

In his *Sincerity Is Not Enough* sermon, Dr. King stressed that sincerity is to be balanced with intellect in matters of faith: "But to say to a man that he must be sincere and conscientious, important though they be, does not cover the ground. Sincerity is not enough. If sincerity is not buttressed by intelligence, it can become the most ruinous force in human nature."[491] Exploiters of religion, not just the agents of proselytization, would find it easy to recruit the sincere "believer" who does not learn to balance sincerity with intelligent reflection.

About a decade ago, a Jewish friend mentioned to me that a certain clergy member (from another religion), who was their friend had earnestly shared his belief that he would go to hell in the hereafter because he did not believe in a certain component of that person's religion. This was just a conversation between two friends and caused no friction in the relationship. Yet, the societal implication of such self-righteous dogma must be considered. The religious establishments promoting such ideologies may be serving their own selves, but would it not be fair to consider them as sources of division within the human race?

Religion: The Means or the End?

People of faith becoming confused about what we worship or serve is a fairly common tendency. To paraphrase Wilfred Cantwell Smith, a preeminent theologian of the twentieth century, original (initial) Muslims believed in God; modern Muslims believe in Islam. And the message would apply equally to other "brands" of religion too. "Religion is a means, not an end," declared Heschel. "It becomes idolatrous when regarded as an end in itself... To equate religion and God is idolatry."[492] The validity and implication of this message deserve to be considered. The deification of symbols in a monotheistic context especially, as Karen Armstrong further points out below, is a grave error, not merely an innocuous vogue:

> This type of religiosity is actually a retreat from God. To make such human, historical phenomena as Christian "Family Values," "Islam" or "the Holy Land" the focus of religious devotion is a new form of idolatry. This type of belligerent righteousness has been a constant temptation to monotheists throughout the long history of God. It must be rejected as inauthentic.[493]

I have even heard some followers of "monotheism" in high places (political as well as religious) talk about "our" God vs. "their" God. Dwelling in such exclusiveness simply exacerbates the existing fractionalization. And, ironically, such an attitude displays to us the blueprint for the irrelevance of religion. It behooves us to realize that the effort to invalidate the other may ultimately be a decision to invalidate our own faith.

And when the claim of uniqueness doesn't work, then it's originality—that others have just copied our message. Besides basic human weaknesses that have played their part throughout history, human conditioning in a hyper-competitive, modern world seems to make us want to be the only ones whom God favors, turning our spiritual pursuit into a zero-sum football game.

A God Who Is Mine Only

A proprietary claim upon the Truth and divine guidance is commonly promoted by various religious establishments. In this thought pattern, any consideration given to accepting the validity of other scriptures becomes heresy and blasphemy. As if God could be so narrow-minded as to merely follow man's capricious impulses. The desire to be in such secure possession of the Truth—an objective truth that is all ours and only ours—takes away our ability to lose ourselves in the mystery of that truth and all the other truth that is all around us. Our often-misplaced certainty thus becomes the cardinal hurdle to our quest and discovery.

The question then is: Does the Creative Power that brought us into existence really care who possesses a superior brand of religion? The answer coming from the *Bhagavad Gita* (9.29) may be quite the opposite:

> I am impartial to all creatures,
> and no one is hateful or dear to me;
> but men devoted to me are in me,
> and I am within them.

While some mutual influence and inspiration cannot be denied, our religions are independent moral philosophies and spiritual paths. While we see similarities, there simultaneously are differences that any theologian can parse to no end. Regardless, we do have to keep in mind that, even in the area of theology and not just in ethical and moral attitudes, the differences sometimes have more to do with form than substance. The theologically irreconcilable differences among the various religions may simply prove the basic teaching they all share: "understanding" the Ultimate Truth is beyond human faculties.

French anthropologist Marcel Mauss pointed out that "societies live by borrowing from each other, but they define themselves rather by the refusal of borrowing rather than by its acceptance."[494] Different religions being independent pathways to our spiritual quest cannot be denied. Yet we see similarities in their teachings. A claim to monopoly or uniqueness may reflect one's ignorance of historical realities. Comprehending the past three thousand years alone tells us that human civilizations, cultures, languages, customs, and rituals have evolved in an interactive fashion, along with those of their neighbors, near or far. (The old Persian and the Vedic Sanskrit languages, for example, emerged from the same source language.)

We may find similarities among different religions because of such influences and also because they may be inspired by a Single Source. In that regard, the *Qur'an* (16:36) points out, "And indeed, within every community have We raised up an apostle [entrusted with this message]: 'Worship God, and shun the powers of evil!' And among those [past generations] were people whom God graced with His guidance ..."

Paul Kriwaczek was a British historian and author. In his book *In Search of Zarathustra*, he calls Zoroaster (Zardosht, Zarathushtra) the First Prophet. Kriwaczek added: "A belief in good and evil, angels, the Devil, heaven and hell, the coming of a Messiah, and an eventual end of the world... Every one of those ideas first appeared in Zarathustra's teaching long before the start of recorded history, a message as influential today as it ever was."[495]

He goes on to describe an encounter with the minder of a Zoroastrian temple close to Yazd, Iran. In answering Kriwaczek's question to express the core of the Zoroastrian teaching, the minder responded: "Easily. Our basic beliefs are very simple. Choose truth and oppose lies. And always strive for good words, good thoughts and good deeds."[496]

During my childhood, my mother introduced me to the Parsee religion (the Zoroastrianism practiced by a small minority in South Asia) and explained that their adherents followed the teachings of Zardosht. I believe she knew virtually nothing about the man or his message.

Surprisingly, though, if I had to make a statement about the core Islamic teaching my mother imparted to me, it would not be much different from the statement of the Zoroastrian temple's minder. If, as the *Qur'an* says, God has sent prophets to all communities, then Zardosht would indeed be one of those prophets.

The Buddha explained to his disciples that his teachings are not the destination, but rather a means of traveling. In other words, the destination is not exclusive—those following different "means of traveling" may get there too. Following that advice would enable us to benefit from the teachings of our own religion while we recognize the validity of the other's belief system.

Seeing Our Common Humanity

If an eternal divine message produces no luminous resonance within our limited human consciousness, maybe our own mirror needs polishing. Ego-driven human constructs can cloud human consciousness, thus hindering reflection in one's thought process. Religious doctrines (created by humans) that place inordinate emphasis on the afterlife at the expense of human conduct in this life provide such an example.

When the pursuit of the afterlife becomes an all-consuming obsession, we entirely forget that the Power that will reward us in the hereafter may measure our qualification based upon our "performance" in this life. Rabi'a al-Adawiyya (also called Rabi'a of Basra, eighth century) is considered one of the cardinal saints in Islam. Her message highlights that a blind pursuit of the afterlife is not the purpose of our spiritual quest in this life:

> I carry a torch in one hand
> And a bucket of water in the other:
> With these things I am going to set fire to Heaven
> And put out the flames of Hell
> So that voyagers to God can rip the veils
> And see the real goal.[497]

ONE COMMUNITY, MANY TITLES

"To what is One, sages give many a title ..."

—Rig Veda 1.164.46.

"As they seek refuge in me, I devote myself to them; Arjuna, men retrace my path in every way."

—Bhagavad Gita 4.11.

"VERILY, this community of yours is one single community, since I am the Sustainer of you all …"

—Qur'an 21:92.

NOW every community has had an apostle; and only after their apostle has appeared [and delivered his message] is judgment passed on them, in all equity; and never are they wronged.

—Qur'an 10:47.

"And, indeed, [O Muhammad,] We sent forth apostles before thy time, some of them We have mentioned to thee, and some of them We have not mentioned to thee. And it was not given to any apostle to bring forth a miracle other than by God's leave."

—Qur'an 40:78.

Insert 9:1

This book accepts the validity of paths provided by various spiritual traditions. Even the teachings converge in many ways among the various paths. But its objective is not an effort in ideological relativism or congruency. There is no intent to show whether or not these different paths lead to the same "destination." The reader must make up their own mind in such matters.

According to Ramakrishna, a nineteenth-century Hindu mystic and guru, God alone is and all spiritual paths lead to the same goal. Realization of Unity may lead to similarly ecstatic insights. Perhaps Ramakrishna and others of high spiritual attainment can make such a statement. For the rest of us, it would be advisable to simply accept the validity of the different spiritual belief systems followed by the rest of humanity. This book aims to highlight how wisdom coming from different traditions can convey a similar message, which can then be used to treat our common human concerns.

Part of our spiritual quest is to be able to see our common humanity, probably through the lens of the belief system or faith we follow. That may be the best way to counter our own prejudices, as well as the effect of the exploitative political systems globally—wherein the "other" is sometimes so decontextualized or demonized by the political system that we are unable to fully see and connect with their humanity. And our scriptures keep providing us the guidelines that enhance our capacity to achieve that goal.

A clear understanding can be derived from the *Qur'an* (51:56): "I created the jinn [invisible beings] and humankind only that they might serve Me." The clearest implication of serving God in this context would be to sincerely serve His creation in this world without the expectation of a remuneration or reward in return. Leigh Hunt's poem alludes to the beneficent reward to one who approaches the divine through the divine creation.

Abou Ben Adhem

Abou Ben Adhem (may his tribe increase!)
Awoke one night from a deep dream of peace,
And saw, within the moonlight in his room,
Making it rich, and like a lily in bloom,
An angel writing in a book of gold:—
Exceeding peace had made Ben Adhem bold,
And to the presence in the room he said,
"What writest thou?"—The vision raised its head,
And with a look made of all sweet accord,
Answered, "The names of those who love the Lord."
"And is mine one?" said Abou. "Nay, not so,"
Replied the angel. Abou spoke more low,
But cheerly still; and said, "I pray thee, then,
Write me as one that loves his fellow men."

The angel wrote, and vanished. The next night
It came again with a great wakening light,
And showed the names whom love of God had blest,
And lo! Ben Adhem's name led all the rest.

—Leigh Hunt

A New Narrative of Righteousness

Rabi'a al-Adawiyya was asked if she hated the Devil. "No," she responded, "because my love for God leaves me no time to hate [the Devil]."[498] This message stands out not just in its simplicity and beauty, but also in its capacity to ground our concept of faith in the positive and productive—not in the negative and destructive. This attitude helps us move towards love, compassion, service, and kindness—messages that are central to all our religions.

The following Jain teaching (Tattvarthaslokavartika of Vidyanandi 116) alludes to how a human being is simultaneously a small container as well as the infinite ocean: "The water from ocean contained in a pot can neither be called an ocean nor non-ocean, but it can be called only part of the ocean. Similarly, a doctrine, though arising from the Absolute Truth is neither the Truth nor not the Truth."[499]

In the Spirit of Jesus, a book[500] released in 2020, describes its purpose as follows: "We need a new narrative, one that acknowledges there is more to the story of Jesus ... than what we profess and proclaim."[501] As suggested by this new book, to "need a new narrative" is to accept the vastness of the ocean, not to change the nature of the ocean. It is an expression of, and an exercise in, humility. It says that we realize our own imperfection, and that our responsibility to continue the journey never really ends. Indeed, that we acknowledge the divine to be beyond human grasp and comprehension—that sincere interpretations are to be validated yet not worshipped.

The fertile and pluralistic nature of one's own thought is a function of the willingness to respect other traditions and to accept their validity. There is bound to be deeper understanding of the spiritual teachings within one's own faith when one becomes familiar with the thought tools and "modes of being" used by the followers of another faith. Then, and perhaps only then, whenever we come to think that we've understood the message, we know there's more. When we are convinced that we've understood the message, there's still more. The light never stops enlightening—for those who remain open and receptive to it.

Several years ago, a church in Western Connecticut asked me to give a talk to the congregation. It was attended by quite a few people. At the end of the talk, some individuals walked up to me and discussed various topics of interest. Then someone introduced herself to me as Sister Beth from another church in the area. Sister Beth asked me if I had read a certain book by Thich Nhat Hanh. I candidly told her that I had heard the name but had never read any books by the Vietnamese monk. We discussed a few things of mutual interest before parting ways.

About ten days later, I received a package in the mail. Inside was a book by Thich Nhat Hanh with a note from Sister Beth. She had no way of knowing my address so she must have approached the event organizers to get it. What we see is a situation in which a Catholic nun sent Muslim layperson a book written by a Buddhist monk.

Through Sufi teachings, I have known about and understood the concept of non-attachment for quite some time. According to a narration of Prophet Muhammad's teaching, we are just wayfarers in this world. In the tradition of Tasawwuf (Sufism), the world is consistently compared to an inn where the traveler can spend a few days. It was, however, not until several years ago when I read about Lord Mahavira's teachings that the concept of non-attachment (Aparigraha in Sanskrit) actually crystalized into the depth of my conscience, giving me not just an intellectual comprehension but rather a sensory feel for it.

Another example of such enrichment for me occurred some two decades ago when a friend Rabbi Andrea Cohen-Kiener introduced me to the concepts of Teshuva and Tikkun. (Tikkun, in fact, is one of the central concepts that form the theme of this book.) Later, I studied them on my own. I was able to find the similarity and complementarity between Tikkun and the Islamic notion of Ihsan (beauty in action). Moreover, this experience allowed me to deepen my understanding of Ihsan, discussed so much in the Qur'an.

One's ability to deepen and broaden one's understanding in their faith with the help of wisdom from other faiths shows the value of openness in such matters. The spiritual wisdom we possess should not be considered the sole domain of a single religion, culture, or ethnicity. This is a collective treasure with shared "ownership" illuminating us all, limited only by our openness or capacity to absorb the light.

In a sermon titled "The Drum Major Instinct" (inspired by Mark 10:35-45), Dr. King defined the righteousness for which he wanted to be remembered: "If any of you are around when I have to meet my day... I'd like somebody to mention that day, that Martin Luther King, Jr., tried to give his life serving others... tried to love somebody ... tried to be right on the war question ... [tried] to feed the hungry ... [tried] to clothe those who were naked ... tried to visit those who were in prison ... tried to love and serve humanity. Yes, if you want to say that I was a drum major, say that I was a drum major for justice ... for peace ... for righteousness."[502]

The righteousness King wanted to be remembered for is rooted in unconditional service and humility, not the self-righteousness that we sometimes come across in the name of religion. In that thought, King's words lead to those of Rabi'a al-Adawiyya: "God has separated from you every cause of separation which has separated you from Him."[503]

Spirituality conveyed by our religious traditions may not be about a particular rigid belief, especially not one that blinds us from the humanity of others, however unlike that other may be. (Part four of this book shows that the various barriers to a harmonious mutual existence are human made.) Indeed, being spiritual may really be about self-discovery and self-transcendence, the willingness to inquire as Ramana Maharshi, a twentieth-century Hindu sage, famously suggested: "Who Am I?"[504] When sincerely pursued, wherever this question leads is spirituality. When followed with humility, our religions may provide us paths conducive to the journey. As evidenced by the scriptural quotations in this book, we see similarities in the spiritual message of our scriptures, especially when it comes to moral imperatives: concerns about justice in society, human to human relations, the prescriptions and proscriptions to reach one's human and spiritual potential.

These are no mean objectives. These concerns, in fact, lie at the core of our global problems today. Indeed, the problems we face have virtually nothing to do with the presence or absence of a religious belief. And all our spiritual paths also offer us simple "tools" to achieve these goals. It is this understanding and acceptance that provides us the very ground of hope that we humans can find the harmony needed for survival. Ultimately, this hope lies in our willingness and ability to discover and accept the validity of the other. Religion must lead the way—not allow itself to be set up as an impediment to that harmony.

PART FOUR:

BARRIERS TO ACHIEVING HARMONY THROUGH RELIGION

From wisdom's ocean divers emerge
with pearls in hand;
Alas, I still wander the seashore
in search of pebbles.[505]

—Muhammad Iqbal

CHAPTER 10:
LANGUAGE AND TRANSLATION

O Lord, the beloved hasn't understood,
and will never understand my pleas;
Bestow on her another heart,
if You don't bestow upon me another tongue.[506]
—Ghalib, Mirza Asadullah Baig Khan

There is validity to the Italian adage "*traduttore, traditore*" (translator is traitor). We also know that translation of poetry is much more difficult compared to prose. That's because the differences in "ease of conversion" between these two literary forms manifest in terms of words, meanings, coherency, intentions, depth, subtlety, music, and beauty. The nature of this difficulty can be gleaned from Robert Frost's statement, "Poetry is what gets lost in translation."

Not just poetry as Frost highlights, but also poetry's meaning can be substantially lost in the translation. In chapter 2, I quoted a verse in the Urdu language from one of my teachers, a published poet. I'll repeat here my translation of the verse:

> No fork is to be found in the road to gnosis,
> the path leading to bliss also goes to the abyss.

For this same verse, my wife has a completely different interpretation. Thus, if she translated it, you would get a significantly different message. A friend of mine, who is the student of the same teacher, has an entirely different take on the meaning of the same verse. My friend's translation would be miles away from my wife's or mine. The mutual differences have nothing to do with the meanings of the words, but rather how to grasp the whole idea given how the words are used. Thus, if the three of us explained the same verse even in the language of the poetry, the three explanations would be mutually different. Clearly, a translation cannot capture those multiple interpretations embedded in the original construction.

Bernard Knox was the preeminent scholar of classical literature in the twentieth century. Writing about Alexandrian Greek poetry, he elaborates how the connection between the poet and the reader influences the poet's expression: "These poets are men of letters, scholars, and librarians, writing for an audience that will catch allusions, will appreciate imitations, parodies, or implicit repudiations of the classical models. In translation this intertextual depth is inevitably lost ..."[507]

A similar point as Knox's was raised by J. W. Morris, a theologian and professor of religious studies. Talking about the scholarly difficulty of working with Sufi poetry, he writes:

> The masterpieces of Islamic mystical poetry in Persian and other eastern Islamicate languages, [use] very different literary forms ... of expression and scriptural allusiveness, and the same effective power of transformation ... any attempt at a continuous, adequate translation for modern audiences is almost inevitably overwhelmed by the massive annotation needed to detail the underlying context of allusions and the web of symbolic interconnections and resonances originally presupposed by this kind of writing.[508]

The words of Frost, Knox, and Morris abundantly clarify the challenges associated with effective translation. In some ways, the slipup begins with the very concept that translation is conveying the essence of the original. So many facets of our life are built around that entirely faulty assumption. (One can come across instances of translation-induced confusions, even in the field of international diplomacy.)

Words don't just have a meaning; they often also have a sensation that cannot be touched in a different language. While it usually does not pose a problem in conveying the literal meaning, conveying the true feeling of the expression can sometimes become a predicament. This phenomenon can cause significant misunderstandings in the translation of scriptures to be understood by one who may have no background in that specific faith or, worse, who may be coming from a rather narrow outlook on how to interpret these texts. For example, in explaining the word "*svabhava*," the *Stanford Encyclopedia of Philosophy* says:

> The central concept around which all of [seminal Buddhist philosopher] Nāgārjuna's philosophy is built is the notion of emptiness (*śūnyatā*). Emptiness is of course always the emptiness of something, and the something Nāgārjuna has in mind here is *svabhāva*. Different terms have been used to translate this word into English: "inherent existence" and "intrinsic nature" appear to be the more popular choices, but "substance" and "essence" have also been proposed. None of these cover the full complexity of the term, however. We therefore have to give some more detailed account of the way *svabhāva* is characterized in Nāgārjuna's thought.[509]

In translating a spiritual scripture especially, the meaning and message can be lost or distorted, more specifically for any content that needs to be understood in an esoteric sense. The rest of this chapter covers certain other areas where translation or interpretation causes distortions, intended or unintended

Shifting Meanings of Words

In various languages, the meanings of a word can become rather fluid, sometimes even divergently. In Semitic languages especially, a word may offer a range of meanings depending upon the context. Because languages such as Arabic and Hebrew generally do not use vowels in writing, a word or sentence may render itself to various interpretations.

Torah, in Hebrew, has been written without vowels. This opens it up for variations in pronunciation and meaning. Most Hebrew words have triconsonantal roots, and words with the same root consonants are usually related. The situation with the *Qur'an* is the same: "... each Arabic consonant has seven different possible pronunciations depending upon the vowel mark that is put on it. The original transcribed *Qur'an*, like the Hebrew *Torah*, was written without any vowel marks at all."[510] This ambiguity allows multiple meanings to be derived from the same text. Subjectivity is thus unavoidable.

And then, the same exact word may be used in very different languages, with different meanings. For example, the word "*aziz*" means "strong" in Arabic, but "dear" in Farsi (Persian). "Sensible" implies "thoughtful" or "practical" in English, but "sensitive" in Italian. (Though let's also point out that the word "*veda*" means knowledge in both Sanskrit and modern Slovak.)

I remember an instance of perceived hilarity described to me by my colleagues in Italy about my predecessor's assumption of the meaning of the word "pepperoni" when ordering pizza. (In Italy, peperone is simply pepper and not some dried or cured meat.) It's remarkable this individual was a Cuban American and, in addition to English, spoke fluent Spanish. Even having another Romance language as his mother tongue was of no avail to him in his choice of pizza topping that day! It is easy to see how a word may carry a totally different meaning as used by the same ethnic community in another country.

And then there's the legal situation where even a law clearly defining a word does not settle the meaning of that word. The case in point is the United States' 1871 Dictionary Act (1 U.S. Code § 1) which says that, in federal law (unless the context indicates otherwise), words importing the masculine gender include the feminine as well. Activists working for women's right to vote were certain that the law was on their side—which it was. Despite the suffragists' persistent effort to clarify this,[511] lawmakers of the time were determined not to let women have the right to vote. By simply refusing to correctly interpret the law as it was explicitly written, lawmakers denied voting rights to women. It would be another half a century of untiring struggle before the Nineteenth Amendment would be ratified to give women the right to vote. This example makes clear the ease with which those in power can refuse to accept clear meaning of a word if it does not suit them—a Hobbesian situation in which, to fit the prevalent agendas, those in power are purposefully disregarding even crisp language in a law.

Coming back to religious texts, there is an interesting example in the translation of *Ihya ulum al-deen* (*The Revival of the Religious Sciences*, Book 21, Chapter 4) of Abu Hamid al-Ghazali, the eleventh-century Persian polymath. Two qualified translators, Murtada al-Zabidi and Walter James Skellie, have translated the same word as "horse" and "individual" respectively. Despite all the context available within the text, the two translators went in such divergent directions. And these two translations are only about half a century apart! Later, we'll consider the differences that emerge over time in the same language, such that the word meant something entirely different in the distant past than it does now.

Sometimes, even given a single context, multiple translations of a word or sentence would make perfect sense. In Hebrew, for example, an important word, *ayin*, which translates to "where" could also translate to "nothingness," significantly changing the meaning of a verse. For example, interpreting *ayin* as where, Job 28:12 is usually translated: "Where is wisdom to be found." In Kabbalah, *ayin* may be interpreted as nothingness, yielding the translation to: "Divine wisdom comes into being out of nothingness."

As the example above shows, the problem assumes another dimension of immense complexity when we take a sacred and ancient language and try to translate it into another language. Victor Mair is one of the world's foremost scholars of ancient Chinese. As shown in Insert 10:1, the effort he had to invest in translating a single word in *Tao Te Ching* is instructive. (Next to the *Bible* and the *Bhagavad Gita*, *Tao Te Ching* is the world's most translated book.)

TRANSLATING "TE" IN TAO TE CHING

Once I assumed the task of creating an entirely fresh translation of the Tao Te Ching, I became preoccupied with endless details, such as how to convey the meaning of the second word in the title. I spent two full months trying to arrive at a satisfactory translation of *te*.[512] Walking through the woods, riding on the train, buying groceries, chopping wood—the elusive notion of *te* was always on my mind. The final choice of "integrity" is based on a thorough etymological study of the word, together with a careful consideration of each of its forty-four occurrences in the text. In certain instances perhaps another word such as "self," "character," "personality," "virtue," "charisma," or "power" might have been more befitting. But "integrity" is the only word that seems plausible throughout. By "integrity," I mean the totality of an individual including his or her moral stance, whether good or bad.[513]

Insert 10:1

Another such situation is highlighted by the writings of Ibn Arabi. J. W. Morris makes a rather complicated point about the difficulty of translating the text in Ibn Arabi's books, and then overlays the point vis-à-vis understanding the *Qur'an*. It thus requires no stretch of imagination to see how all this would create potential translation problems, not to mention the impact on esoteric interpretations.

"FORCED OR ARTIFICIAL FORMS"

One has only to align [Ibn Arabi's] own underlying Arabic expressions with their normal English translated equivalents to perceive the phenomenologically far richer and more fitting resources of the Qur'anic language—a persistent contrast that constantly bedevils all translators and serious students of [Ibn Arabi's] writing. Thus in English, we frequently [use] painfully forced or artificial, gerundive forms... Even more frustratingly, the richly evocative and multi-faceted Qur'anic language applied to all these common dimensions of spiritual intelligence ... are often expressed in distinctive "reflexive" Arabic verbal forms that manage to convey explicitly with a single word, in ways that would properly require whole sentences in English.[514]

Insert 10:2

Structural Linguistic Limitations and Notional Dissimilitude

All languages have some peculiarities in their structures that may sometimes create a problem when translating from another language. English, for example, has no established gender-neutral, singular, third-person pronoun. Many languages do not face this limitation, except, of course, when it comes to translation into English.

For example, the question is often asked why God (Allah) is expressed as a masculine entity or concept in Islam. This problem has everything to do with the absence of a gender-neutral third person pronoun in English, and nothing to do with Allah having a gender. Because the English language has historically used masculine words (e.g. "he," "man", or "mankind") to represent both genders, it just makes sense to keep following the same convention. ("It" is perhaps too lifeless to refer to God, the very source of life.)

Notional dissimilarities among concepts should also be kept in mind. For example, the way the word "religion" is understood (especially within the secular-religious binary framework) may not adequately encompass the concepts of dharma/*dhamma*, *deen*, etc. The equality of these concepts with our understanding of "religion" may, therefore, not always be so meaningful.[515]

And then we have interpretive changes that accrue to words over time. The centrally important Sanskrit word a*tman*, for example, has evolved significantly.[516] In the Rig Veda, it conveyed the meaning of vital essence or breath. Over time, however, it acquired the meaning of soul or self—and that's the meaning the word still signifies.

The evolution of the Arabic word *shari'ah* is even more interesting.[517] First of all, the word does not stand for any kind of law. Also, only a minuscule part of the *Qur'an* can even be interpreted as signifying "law" (the Book is all about human conduct, not "the law" as we understand the concept now). The word shari'ah (or shar), used two or three times in the *Qur'an*, literally means "the way," or the way leading to water. In its religious sense, it meant a path to the good life[518] (via spiritual values).

The subject of shari'ah, which shows or ordains the way and is the source of spiritual values is, unequivocally, God and God alone. Deen (literally submission or following) would be the following of the shari'ah, and the subject for deen would be the human being. Thus, technically, a human may claim to know or understand the deen. To make such a claim about shari'ah, however, becomes an entirely different enterprise.

Promoted by some well-funded sources for reasons of ideology and power, the present-day view of shari'ah—equated with Islam—to be a fixed body of codified law prescribing the Divine Will is a far cry from the treatment of the concept in the *Qur'an*, and even from the classical Islamic tradition.[519]

The complex subjects covered in this section have rather complicated dimensions to them. The intent here is not to explain the concepts, but simply to highlight that translations and interpretations of such words and notions can create problems in our understanding of scriptures.

Sociological Context

In the languages of South Asia (Urdu, Punjabi, etc.), it is common to use oxymoronic metaphors such as murderer, liar, tormentor/ oppressor (*qaatil, kaafir, zaalim*) to refer to a beloved (the human beloved, not the Divine Beloved). If such language were used in that context in English poetry, it would, at the least, be considered odd. It is also important to realize that the metaphor does not really point to the attributes of the beloved; it is merely an expression of the intensity of the attraction the lover feels. The more vociferous the "blame" thrown at the beloved, the deeper the condition of the lover's pull towards the beloved. The very meaning of the word, thus, gets turned on its head—and every reader of such poetry understands that. While a verse containing such expressions can be translated, it is always difficult to convey the real feelings of the poet or writer. (Literal translations and understanding of such expressions can certainly create havoc in our understanding of what the poet is saying.)

Some things are just much easier to understand within the context of a specific society, past or present. Their meaning in a different time or space may not be as significant or even intelligible. For example, the collection of the material in the *Talmud* took over a millennium to fully collect. One can only imagine the changes in human societies during such a long time period. Another important twist is that Muslims consider the *Qur'an* to be a direct revelation to Prophet Muhammad. Thus, for rationale out of the scope of this book,[520] most Muslim scholars would agree that any presentation in another language can only be an interpretation or rendition, but not a "translation" of the *Qur'an*. In this case, what may sound semantic to many carries substantive importance to Muslims.

While it always helps to be aware of the above-described sociological contexts in our comprehension, the goal of comprehending a scriptural translation, however, should be to grasp the intended effect of the message on the psyche of the society, not to get mired in the sociological surroundings.

Subtlety of Expression and Appeal to Imagination

A little bit of the Punjabi and Urdu poetry I am familiar with is full of subtlety that, to be comprehended, requires an attentive engagement of one's intellectual, emotional, and psychological faculties. Using linguistic methods, such poetry could force one to imagine and interpret at every step. A single couplet could sometimes consume hours of discussion. This point has to be experienced; it simply cannot be understood otherwise. The message in our sacred scripture can be similarly subtle and esoteric; even more so because it is divinely inspired and because it is directed simultaneously towards the soul, the heart, and the intellect.

Sir Muhammad Iqbal, the preeminent Indian philosopher who wrote his own prose and poetry in Persian, made the following piercing observation about Rumi's *Masnavi*:

> People have explained the *Masnavi*, but have not been able to grasp its meaning that, like gazelle, runs away from us [i.e. none has been able to touch the passion, the exhilaration, the implication, the secret that it contains]. People have learnt from Rumi just the dance of the body, yet have closed their eyes to the dance of the soul! Dance of the body causes tumult in dust, whereas dance of the soul causes turmoil in the heavens![521]

It would be unwise to disregard Iqbal in that the *Masnavi's* meaning does run away from us like a gazelle. If none can even fully grasp the *Masnavi's* meaning in its original tongue, how can that meaning be translated into another language?

CHAPTER 11:

PREJUDICES AND AGENDAS

"Remember, then, God's blessings, and do not act wickedly on earth by spreading corruption."

—Qur'an 7:74

"With all this, [remember that] those who are bent on denying the truth are allies of one another; and unless you act likewise[522] *[in solidarity among yourselves], oppression will reign on earth, and great corruption."*

—Qur'an 8:73

In the foreword he wrote for Sarvepalli Radhakrishnan's *Philosophy of the upaniShads*, Nobel-laureate Rabindranath Tagore referred to the then prevalent discourse related to *Upanishads* in the English language:

> It is not enough that one should know the meaning of the words and the grammar of the Sanskrit texts in order to realize the deeper significance of the utterances that have come to us across centuries of vast changes, both of the inner as well as the external conditions of life.
>
> The lack of sympathy and respect displayed in [philosophical writings by Orientalists of the time] for some of the most sacred words [the *upaniShads*] that

> have ever issued from the human mind, is amazing. Though many of the symbolical expressions used in the *upaniShads* can hardly be understood today, or are sure to be wrongly interpreted, yet the messages contained in these, like some eternal source of light, still illumine and vitalize the religious minds of India.[523]

Let's divide this discussion into three distinct segments and approach them one by one.

Bigoted Inclinations of the Translator, His Sponsor, or His Audience

As historians Ariel and Will Durant observed, "Most history is guessing, and the rest is prejudice."[524] Sometimes, the prejudice becomes so dominant in major human decisions that it becomes impossible to imagine what the human condition would be without such manifestations of it. Historical epochs such as slavery and colonization provide instructive examples. We'll go back to India of the nineteenth century during the British Raj.

"Minute on Education" (1835) by Hon'ble Thomas Babington Macaulay is not a scriptural document, but it is directly relevant to our understanding of our common historical spiritual heritage in this context. Macaulay, a member of the Supreme Council of India, addresses Lord William Bentinck, Governor General of the then British-occupied India.

MINUTE ON "EDUCATION"

I have no knowledge of either Sanscrit [*sic*] or Arabic. But I have done what I could to form a correct estimate of their value... I have never found one among [Orientalists] who could deny that a single shelf of a good European library was worth the whole native literature of India and Arabia. The intrinsic superiority of

> the Western literature is indeed fully admitted by those members of the committee who support the oriental plan of education...
>
> I certainly never met with any orientalist who ventured to maintain that the Arabic and Sanscrit poetry could be compared to that of the great European nations... It is, I believe, no exaggeration to say that all the historical information which has been collected from all the books written in the Sanscrit language is less valuable than what may be found in the most paltry abridgments used at preparatory schools in England. In every branch of physical or moral philosophy, the relative position of the two nations is nearly the same.
>
> How then stands the case? *We have to educate a people who cannot at present be educated by means of their mother-tongue.*[525]
>
> —Thomas Babington Macaulay
>
> Insert II:I

Governor General Bentinck approved (and implemented) this "education reform" plan with the following words: "I give my entire concurrence to the sentiments expressed in this Minute." (While what happened in India was by no means as brutal as was "civilizing" the indigenous Americans or Australians, colonialism has to work in a specific format to fulfill its objective, and that format will always have local culture and language as its target.)

Let's now go back to Tagore's subtle comment about "lack of sympathy and respect." The comment would find more resonance now that *Minute on Education* clarifies for the reader the historical background informing Tagore's remarks.

As regards the translations and interpretations of the *Qur'an*, the late Fazlur Rahman, Distinguished Professor of Islamic Thought at the University of Chicago, chose to be much less subtle than Tagore:

> The immediate impression from the cursory reading of the *Qur'an* is that of the infinite majesty of God and His equally infinite mercy, although many a Western scholar (through a combination of ignorance and prejudice) has depicted the *Qur'anic* God as a concentrate of pure power, even as brute power—indeed, as a capricious tyrant. The *Qur'an*, of course, speaks of God in so many different contexts and so frequently that unless all the statements are interiorized into a total mental picture, without as far as possible, the interference of any subjective and wishful thinking—it would be extremely difficult, if not outright impossible, to do justice to the *Qur'anic* concept of God.[526]

It would be appropriate here to point out how things changed in this regard beginning in the twentieth century. Substantially, the work being done by current Western academic scholars (not affiliated with think tanks or funding from religio-ideologue sources) in the field of religion seems to be of high quality, sincerity, and integrity.[527]

Ideological Inclinations & Influences: Individual and Institutional

Prejudices aside, other inclinations or interests of the entities involved in translations can also influence the work. Such agendas may be doctrinal, sectarian, ideological, or political. This translation of John *8:3-11* is from a law-and-ethics textbook produced by the Chinese Communist Party.

> Once upon a time, Jesus spoke to an angry crowd that wanted to kill a guilty woman. 'Of all of you, he who can say he has never done anything wrong can come forward and kill her.' After they heard this, the

> crowd stopped. When the crowd retreated, Jesus raised a stone and killed the woman, and said, 'I am also a sinner, but if the law can only be executed by a spotless person, then the law will die.'[528]

In the scripture, Jesus simply tells the woman, "Go now and leave your life of sin." Most cases of textual manipulation are not so blatant. Even if they seem minor, though, such biases can have a significant impact on the translation—because the objective would be to make a substantive change in an inconspicuous way.

1. The Globally Spread Fraudulent Qur'anic Translation

A scenario in which religio-political and ideological agendas drive translations of scriptures would pose sinister and dreadful implications. And that is the case of the Qur'anic "translations" that have been spread all over the world, often at minimal cost—if not absolutely free—to the recipient. (Here I am referring to concerns outside of honest and sincere scholarly differences in linguistic interpretation.)

Early English translations of the *Qur'an*, until the twentieth century, were essentially driven by the goal of debunking Islam and facilitating the Christian proselytization process. Marmaduke Pickthall's was arguably the first (1930) that was sincere and honest in its effort. It would perhaps be fair to say that the tide began to turn around that time.

The gravest phenomenon to watch for in the present times, since the middle of the last century, is the ideological translations of the *Qur'an* and other religious literature funded and sponsored by the Saudi government. These interpretations of the *Qur'an* promote the official Saudi ideology (historically known as Wahhabism by a large percentage of Muslims). These translations are highly dodgy and twist the message of the *Qur'an*, often blatantly. Because they are printed in millions and disseminated worldwide, these books would be available at a lower cost, even free of charge frequently enough. We are thus more likely to find these ideology-driven Qur'anic translations at libraries and other institutions.

Khaled Abou El Fadl is Distinguished Professor of Law at UCLA. He is also a classically trained Islamic jurist (*shaykh*) and a leading authority on the subjects of shari'ah and Islamic jurisprudence (*fiqh*).

The following is an excerpt from *The Search for Beauty in Islam* (2001), Abou El Fadl's well-known book, shedding light on the extent to which the Saudi system has used its influence to even corrupt the message of the *Qur'an* by deceptive translation.

THE WORD OF GOD: ALTERED AND CORRUPTED

We live in an age and place where the word of God can be altered and corrupted, and all the fancy Islamic centers and bombastic leaders and preachers could not be bothered to care. We live in an age and place where the so-called protectors of the Holy Sites, Mecca and Medina, have become the corrupters of God's Word... Even the commentaries on the *Qur'an* have been cleansed, and Muslims remain largely oblivious to the grave sin.

Beyond editing the work of jurists, now the corruptions have been extended to the translations of the *Qur'an* in English and even the hadith of the companions.

For five years or more now, a beautifully printed English translation of the *Qur'an* has been distributed for free in nearly every Islamic center in the United States...

But the liberties taken with the so-called interpretation of the Arabic is nothing short of *frightening*.[529]

Insert 11:2

It is no stretch to say that this Saudi-Wahhabi project of Qur'anic "translation" / interpretation is utterly fraudulent and lacks even the basic ethics and decency expected of scholarly works, let alone work with religious scriptures. This project does not end with publishing corrupted texts. The concern in this regard is not just Wahhabism's obsession with textual distortions. As Abou El Fadl points out, it is also their "denigration of morality, which the Wahhabis argue shouldn't affect the implementation of Koranic law."[530]

The highly selective and narrow Wahhabi interpretation of Islamic scripture by detaching "law" from the moral aspects of religious teachings is in contradiction with centuries of traditional Islamic juris scholarship. This ideology is globally creating not just a caricature of Islam but a ruthless dystopia in the name of Islam. Ziauddin Sardar, a British polymath who, in the 1970s, lived and worked in the Kingdom of Saudi Arabia, referring to the innate intolerance of reason and intellect within the Saudi-Wahhabi ideology, says: "I met students from the universities of Mecca and Medina and was astonished to learn that they are trained to shun critical thinking and inculcated in an aggressive ideology that demonises all others."[531]

And it is this ideological strain that, over the last few decades, has been promoted all over the world in a rather systematic effort—geared towards the systemic effacement of the essence and spiritual core of the Islamic religion. By leveraging its financial strength, political power, and network of "charitable" foundations, Saudi Arabia is estimated to have poured over $100 billion into this project,[532] including the construction of thousands of mosques, schools, and Islamic centers all over the world.[533] The "largest worldwide propaganda campaign ever mounted"[534] in human history has done wonders for Wahhabism by outright purchasing the affiliations of well-known scholars, as well as acquiring immense institutional influence by endowments to some of the world's leading universities—including those in Europe and North America. The repercussions are far-reaching.

What's more, as a 2013 European Union intelligence report estimates, "15 to 20 percent" of this charitable and educational largesse has been diverted to al-Qaeda and other extremists—and, in some countries, such as the Philippines, "such percentage could reach even 60 percent."[535] A 2009 (leaked) secret cable by US Secretary of State Hillary Clinton acknowledged that the Saudis "constitute the most significant source of funding to Sunni terrorist groups worldwide" and that the country "remains a critical financial support base for al-Qaida, the Taliban, LeT [Lashkar-e Tayyiba in Pakistan], and other terrorist groups, including Hamas."[536]

Doubtless, as the report by the European Parliament concludes, "Saudi Arabia has been a major source of financing to rebel and terrorist organizations since the 1970s."[537] Nevertheless, at a "UK-Saudi Arabia Conference" in 2005, the then British Foreign Secretary Jack Straw clarified that "our two kingdoms are working together to spread security in the Middle East."[538] As the chapter on global terrorism has already shown, there is a strong element of truth to Straw's statement—as soon as we are able to interpret the meaning of "security" in that sentence.

The impact of the prolonged Saudi propaganda blitz on sincere and unsuspecting Muslims, even in North America, cannot be overstated. Professor Abou El Fadl,[539] expressing his experience with Muslims in the United States, says, "As I move from mosque to mosque, I encounter Muslims who seem to think that the harsher and the more perverse the law, the more it's Islamic."[540]

As one can imagine, the implications of this phenomenon are grave, wide-ranging, and, indeed, frightening.

2. Jihad: The Fabricated Holy War

The word "jihad" also provides a good example of warmongering run amok on both sides of the frenzied notion known as the clash of civilizations. The triconsonantal root of the word is J-H-D, which would literally translate to endeavor, effort, or struggle. Karen Armstrong's *The Battle for God*, which was published before 9/11, should dispel any doubts in this regard: "[jihad is] a word that should be translated as 'struggle' or 'effort' rather than as 'holy war,' as Westerners often assume."[541]

In the Islamic context, the teachings, as well as the historical applications of the word, are truly multifarious and can even be polar opposites of each other—implementing inner improvement in the self as well as engagement in a battle. Jihad, thus, could be that of pen, tongue, mind, heart, and of sword. (Could my writing this book be considered jihad?) Stripped of all nuance and filled with distortions by the Islamic extremists and the Western ideological think-tankers alike, this word has been turned into a weapon of mass deception. This excerpt from Abou El Fadl clarifies some of the confusion:

> Jihad, especially as portrayed in the Western media, is often associated with the idea of a holy war that is propagated in the name of God against the unbelievers. Therefore, jihad is often equated with the most vulgar images of religious intolerance.... Interestingly, Islamic tradition does not have a notion of holy war... Holy war (al-harb al-muqaddasah) is not an expression used by the Qur'anic text or Muslim theologians. In Islamic theology, war is never holy; it is either justified or not.[542]

Muhammad Abdel Haleem of the University of London (SOAS), clarifies further with the help of Qur'anic verses:

'HOLY WAR' DOES NOT EXIST AS A TERM IN ARABIC

The *Qur'an* gives a clear instruction that there is no compulsion in religion (2:256). It states that people will remain different (11:118), they will always have different religions and ways and this is an unalterable fact (5:48). God tells the Prophet that most people will not believe 'even if you are eager that they should' (12:103).

All the battles that took place during the Prophet's lifetime, under the guidance of the

> *Qur'an* and the Prophet, have been surveyed[543] and shown to have been waged only in self-defence or to pre-empt an imminent attack...
>
> 'Holy War' does not exist as a term in Arabic, and its translation into Arabic sounds quite alien. The term which is officially used in the *Qur'an* for fighting is qital. Jihad can be by argumentation (25:52), financial help or actual fighting. Jihad is always described in the *Qur'an* as *fi sabil illah* [in the path of Allah; for the sake of Allah].[544]
>
> Insert 11:3

To falsely project inherent violence in the *Qur'an*, some Orientalists have given the name "the Sword Verse" to *Qur'an* 9:5. Referring to "scholars" who engage in selective truncation and use, Abdel Haleem says: "This is pure fantasy, isolating and decontextualizing a small part of a sentence ... to build their theory of war in Islam on what is termed 'The Sword Verse' even when the word 'sword' does not occur anywhere in the *Qur'an*."[545]

The professor tells us that the word "sword" does not appear in the *Qur'an*. Yet some Orientalist champions of war are imaginative enough to invent the "Sword Verse."

The *Qur'an* clearly enunciates the limited just causes for jihad requiring force: "... for defending religious freedom (22:39-41), for self-defence (2:190) and for defending those who are oppressed: men, women and children who cry for help (4:75)... These are the only valid justifications for war we find in the *Qur'an*. Even when war becomes necessary, we find that there is no 'conscription' in the *Qur'an*."[546]

It is easy to see how, with twisted interpretive reasoning, the militant extremists on both sides mold to their purpose teachings that were meant to promote justice and reduce oppression. Commenting on the evolution of the current extremism phenomenon within Islam, Tariq Ali, a British historian, makes the following points:

> Muhammad was not in favor of a clergy on the Christian model. The Caliph was both the temporal and the spiritual ruler. A clergy did develop, in part because the rapid growth of Islam necessitated a religious bureaucracy that could pronounce the verdict of Islam on new problems each week. The *Qur'an* was used as reference, but traditions [hadith, sayings of Prophet Muhammad] had to be invented[547] to facilitate Muslim rule in different parts of the world. As with the Talmud, rival Muslim scholars in the pay of rival rulers or factions could interpret a Qur'anic verse in different ways...
>
> If, as [Francis] Fukuyama has argued, the members of al-Qaeda are 'Islamo-fascists' then one has to ask: when did they become Islamo-fascists? Their religious views have not altered since the time they were recruited by the United States, Saudi Arabia, and Egypt for the 'jihad' against the Soviets in Afghanistan... The basic fact is that radical Islam was brought into being by the needs of the Cold War.[548]

It would also be helpful to realize that the use of the "jihad" concept as inherently violent became more prevalent, pernicious, and intensely vicious—especially in an internecine sense—in the eighteenth century upon the dawn of Wahhabism. Then the twentieth century saw a rapid climb up in this concept and its deployment for ideological and political reasons. Still, during the twentieth century, the word was used primarily "in a national, secular, and political context until, that is, the advent of the anti-Soviet war in Afghanistan."[549]

As for translation, the Muslim militants are aligned with the Western militants to promote jihad as a "Holy War." It is important to keep in mind that "Holy War" comes clearly packaged with an agenda of warfare. The shared stance towards jihad by the warmongers and the sententious ideologues on both sides—using inciteful tactics of hate—is no accident. It is simply that the results desired by the two groups cohere, more frequently than one would think.

Even before 9/11, the wholesale use and propagation of the jihad concept as violent Holy War had already begun, as the example about Operation Cyclone in chapter 1 highlights. In addition, the collapse of the Soviet Union had also necessitated intellectually decrepit concepts such as the Huntingtonian "clash of civilizations" to be erected as real challenges facing the world. After 9/11, of course, the propaganda blitz became truly intense both by the Islamic militant factions as well as the Western forces of conflict.

The problem with translations such as Holy War is that they can only be used for violent purposes on both sides; they cannot become vehicles to solve any problem because even the average Muslim can tell that it is agenda-driven. Such translations, when commonly promoted in the media, come across as belligerent, thus misleading the non-Muslim, and failing to engage the ordinary Muslim. The result is further dissociation of Muslims and non-Muslims in terms of finding a solution.

Rumi the Hippie: Perils of Cultural Appropriation of Islamic Heritage

In addition to bigoted and ideological intentions, there's a third interesting phenomenon that acts as a barrier—not just to the understanding of religious message but, in fact, to human harmony. A trend in the translations of Rumi's work[550] provides a unique phenomenon that may, in some ways, stand on its own. While this section highlights various dimensions of this phenomenon as they relate to Rumi's work, it also explains how such concerns may become applicable to other situations and, in fact, are highly relevant in the current global problems. The need, therefore, exists to discommend this strain of literary plagiarism like all others.

Translations of the *Masnavi*, originally composed in Farsi (Persian), by Jalal ad-Din Muhammad Balkhi (commonly known as Rumi—which means "the denizen of Roman Anatolia"), has been one of the best-sold books of poetry in North America.

Reading some of the commonly available and popular translations, however, may provide no real indication of Rumi's identity, theology, or even the deeper faith-based philosophy that drove him.[551] He may come across as simply a nice universalist mystic, unmoored from the shackles of religion and on a self-ordained mission to spread love in the world. That attitude towards Rumi's work is utterly dubious and unscrupulous. Here's an explanation by the preeminent scholar of Kabbalah, Gershom Scholem of Hebrew University:

> There is no such thing as mysticism in the abstract, that is to say, a phenomenon or experience which has no particular relation to other religious phenomena. There is no mysticism as such, there is only the mysticism of a particular religious system, Christian, Islamic, Jewish mysticism and so on.... [The] prevailing conception of the mystic as a religious anarchist who owes no allegiance to his religion finds little support in fact. History rather shows that the great mystics were faithful adherents of the great religions.[552]

The word "mysticism" is not much used in this book, though we should be clear on what it implies. (Being ill-informed, some people use the word derisively.) As used in these pages, it signifies the spirituality that is aware and accepting of a human relation and connection with God, resulting in an integral and inseparable consciousness of the unceasing Divine Presence. Religion (way of life, state of being) as it emerges from such consciousness is simultaneously passionate, profound, and humble.

The *Masnavi-ye Ma'navi* (meaning "Rhyming Couplets of Spiritual Meaning") was originally written to expedite and enhance the religious understanding of the students at Rumi's *madrassa* (school in Arabic). There is a reason the work is commonly known as an exegesis of the *Qur'an*. Even Rumi's preface defines the *Masnavi* as "the roots of the main tenets of theology ... and the unveiler of the *Qur'an*." (*wa huwa usulu usulu usulu 'd-din ... wa kashshaf al-Qur'an*).

Mulla Hadi Sabzawari, an eminent nineteenth-century Islamic jurist, theologian and philosopher (in his *Literary History of Persia*, E. G. Browne labeled the Mulla "the last great Persian philosopher") says about the *Masnavi*: "It is a commentary on the versified exegesis [of the *Qur'ān*] and its occult mystery, since all of [the *Masnavi*] is, as you will see, an elucidation of the clear verses [of the *Qur'ān*], a clarification of prophetic utterances.... one can find in [the *Masnavi*] all [the *Qur'ān*'s] classic philosophical wisdom."[553]

The best way to describe the Masnavi would be as a complex though fluid and coherent synthesis of theology emanating from direct references, literal or somewhat paraphrased, to the *Qur'an*, the sayings of Prophet Muhammad, and other accepted traditions.[554] That's why Rumi's radical longing to emulate Prophet Muhammad can be seen so frequently in the work. While sometimes subtle, this leitmotif in the six-volume book is ubiquitous and inescapable.

Rumi's immersion in reason, tolerance, love, and inclusive spirituality is not because he parted from authentic Islamic theology but because he fully embraced and lived it. Rumi's dance of the soul follows a beat that is purely Islamic. Indeed, Rumi was simply a Muslim theologian and well-recognized religious teacher all his life. The *Masnavi*, similarly, is just an exegesis of the *Qur'an*, as Rumi himself stated.

It's also important to keep in mind that Rumi is just one of the countless Sufi saints, temporally spread over a millennium, whose poetry represents what came to be known as *Madhhab-i Ishq* (the Religion of Love).[555] The word "*madhhab*" (often translated as "religion") literally means "the way of going."[556] *Madhhab-i Ishq* thus implies a way of being a Muslim in a mode that expresses one's love of the Divine Truth.

This mode of being allows one to experience and identify with values that are true to God's guidance.[557] Love for God's creation, in various formats, including love for human beauty, becomes metaphorical love (*ishq-i majazi*) that could be an experiential vehicle or means that allows one to know Love for the Real Truth. Love, in this context, is so all-encompassing within the Sufi conception as to become the "highest stage to be attained.... From love the adept passes directly to the true knowledge of the Divine mysteries (*ma'rifa*)."[558]

In the Persian language alone, luminaries within the *Madhhab-i Ishq* would include Attar, Bedil, Hafez, Ja'ami, Nizami, Sa'adi, etc., not to mention the same Sufi poetic traditions in so many other languages.[559] These mystic poets represented the religious culture that, for centuries, existed in much of Central and South Asia—more precisely, from the Balkans to the Bengal.[560]

Referring to Sa'adi Shirazi's magnum opus *Gulistan* (The Rose Garden), Thackston Wheeler, the most recent translator of the literary classic, points out, "Sa'adi's *Gulistan* must be one of the most widely read books ever produced. Almost from the time it was written it was the first book studied by school children throughout the entire Persian-speaking and reading world—from Constantinople to Bengal and from Central Asia to East Africa."[561]

And then there is the *Diwan* (Complete Poems) of Hafez of Shiraz (fourteenth century), which was "the most widely-copied, widely-circulated, widely-read, widely-memorized, widely-recited, widely-invoked, and widely-proverbialized book of poetry in Islamic history."[562]

Unfortunately, the treatment of Hafez by western "poets" is even bolder. Some works projected and perceived as translations or renditions of Hafez are not even remotely related to poetry of the great Islamic saint. It is also instructive that such poets may even claim to have seen these Sufi saints in a dream instructing them to engage in such an enterprise. This is a common and curious theme to show as justification for such opportunistic cultural appropriation.

Let's return to Rumi. Similarly to the *Upanishads* or the *Bhagavat Gita*, which can only be understood within the complex evolution of what we know as Hinduism, and just as the Kabbalist *Zohar* cannot be divorced from Judaism, Rumi's *Masnavi* and other such works can only be truly understood in their Islamic light.

Erasmus's humanitarian outlook cannot be separated from his Christian religion, and Shankara's philosophy is not to be understood outside of Hinduism. So too, separating Rumi from Islam and presenting or understanding him as some kind of a mystical freelancer is rather disingenuous, self-deceiving, and even a foolishly harmful enterprise because it extends full cooperation to the extremists who want to keep presenting Islam as the problem.

A translator of any Sufi saint (including Rumi) would need to have an expertise in at least three domains:

1. Poet's language.
2. The Qur'an and Islamic theology.
3. Culture of the saint's time and place.

For that reason, most bona fide translators of religious texts have been academics with a focus in that specialized field covering all three dimensions. A translator who does not have the requisite expertise in such a varied background may produce good poetry of their own, inspired by Rumi; in this case; however, it would be wrong to call it Rumi's translation.

The current vogue in the field of "Ruminticism" includes translations in English by individuals with virtually no knowledge of the Persian language and little background in the intricacies of Islamic mystical poetry. They take other English translations (mostly works of the eminent British scholar R. A. Nicholson's translation which is rather literal), and then throw their own twist on it. Such work can simply not be classified as a translation by any definition. Additionally, one shouldn't be overly surprised to find ideological spin that uses selective omissions, distortions, and even insertions of ideas and thoughts. Even when the result is attractive poetry in its own right, it is not faithful to conveying Rumi's message or even to the very concept of translation.

The first two points above, language and theology, have been covered in this as well as the preceding chapter. As for the third point about culture, we have to be mindful that even familiarity with the language of the poet as well as Islamic theology would not mean one can do justice to translating Sufi poetry. The translator also needs an expertise in the culture and place of the time of poetry.

The already difficult situation of translation is compounded by the amazing complexity of Sufi poetry that comes not just from its full immersion in Islamic theology but also a reliance on an indescribable background of implicit references to a myriad of stories, illustrations, metaphors, and incidents that carry tremendous spiritual import—and that were commonly known by the Muslim audiences of the time (and for centuries later). With the virtually complete loss of inherited culture in much of the Muslim world, this background enjoys little understanding within the sphere of a modern Muslim, let alone a non-Muslim.

While the loss of culture in the Muslim world is relatively recent, the point can also be understood in comparison to the Greek and Latin literature, as mentioned by Bernard Knox in the previous chapter. Not just any Greek or Italian citizen today could do justice to translating such literature. One would have to be a bona fide scholar with solid background in the three disciplines mentioned above.[563]

What is the importance of discussing Rumi's translations in such detail?

It is important to realize that Islamic spiritual heritage (and the vast Sufi literature and other artifacts) constitute common human heritage—just like the Bamiyan Buddha statues and the archaeological treasures in the Levant. This places a tremendous responsibility on us all to preserve and value them in their genuine state. When some "translators" in the West, without any real expertise in Islamic history or theology, go around projecting (even if unwittingly) that Sufi saints were unhinged from the Qur'anic teachings and norms, such an action effectively, without exaggeration, means collaboration with the "Islamic" terrorists[564] and the various other brands of extremists. Whatever the motivations[565]—ideological or personal—the action may or may not be intentional, but non-attention to the consequences would be disquieting.

As this book points out, there are interests (including well-funded and supported inside forces) waging a war against much of Islamic heritage. It can occasionally be gleaned from a rare piece of news in the media, such as the bombing of a Sufi or Shia tomb. It would, perhaps be accurate to say that there is a continuous and widespread "war" going on against the soul of Islam, a war that is happening in most countries in the world, under various guises.[566] As stated earlier, developments in any single religion are not happening in a vacuum; they are part of the geopolitical forces in action. As Dr. King explained, the repercussions will impact everyone—whether or not we understand the phenomenon.

The literati, the poets, and the academics need to play an important role in preserving the integrity of the intellectual tradition in a society. We have to remember that missionaries and academics (especially anthropologists) played a key role in colonialism, sometimes as the foot soldiers of the enterprise. The role these segments of the human race continue to play now has to be the opposite—to highlight our commonality with integrity, to notice the usurpation and destruction of others' cultures, to oppose injustice of any kind—by anyone, even the "poets" engaged in cultural usurpation by pretending to be translators of sacred Islamic poetry.

CHAPTER 12:
PARADOX AND CONTRADICTION

Human kind cannot bear very much reality.
—T. S. Eliot, *Burnt Norton*

The test of a first-rate intelligence is the ability to hold two opposed ideas in the mind at the same time, and still retain the ability to function.
—F. Scott Fitzgerald, *The Crack Up*

In various domains of knowledge, the concept of "truth value," a term used in various academic disciplines, comes from classical logic and entails that a logical proposition can be classified either true or false. In today's world, there is certainly no escaping Aristotle's two notable rules that justify the truth-value notion: the *Principle of Excluded Middle* (PEM), which states that every claim is either true or false, with no other possibility; and the *Principle of Non-Contradiction* (PNC), which states that nothing can be simultaneously both true and false. These Aristotelian axioms seem to mostly work; yet, as we see later in the chapter, a "religious" belief in these principles keeps facing irreconcilabilities in fields of science as well as the humanities.

The message of this chapter is not that one should be ready to reject conventions such as the Aristotelian axioms. Such rejection can become a source of misguidance. Rather, that one should be open to learning new things and, maybe, even find further guidance in the existing sources of knowledge by expanding our framework and perceptivity through reflection. Such cognitive and perceptual agility is necessary to move away from paradigms that cast everything in black and white opposites. (It is also important to realize that such binary reasonings are at the center of the spread of extremist ideologies in the world.) In fact, paradoxes challenge our existing mental models, providing new doorways for intellectual expansion.

The quotes in the epigraph by T. S. Eliot and F. Scott Fitzgerald indicate the essential precondition for sound judgment: one must be able to accept ambiguity and contradiction, and one must realize the vast domain of human ignorance and limitation. Indeed, the price for not realizing that, collectively even if not individually, is rather steep—witnessed generally by the current human condition and the present geopolitical situation in particular.

In that background, it is important to realize that the place of ambiguity, paradox, and contradiction has been accepted within religious traditions, and have been used by them for teaching purposes for a very long time.

Coming to Terms with Contradiction and Paradox in Sacred Texts

True words seem contradictory.

—Tao Te Ching, 78:14

Scriptures are multi-faceted in their message and meaning, and that sometimes introduces further contradictions and paradoxes. Such paradoxes can be found even within the same sacred scripture. For example, Zen Master Dogen Zenji (thirteenth century, founder of the Soto School) points out in his influential *Genjokoan*: "When a person starts to search out the dharma, he separates himself far from the dharma."[567] This is seemingly counterintuitive. One would think that to get to a certain destination, one needs to travel or step towards it and not far from it, though the Buddhist master is advising us to the contrary. In *Tao Te Ching* (24:10-11), Lao Tzu expresses it a little differently: "One who aspires to the Way, does not abide in them."

Whether practical or textual, what's conceptually paradoxical does not necessarily create, in a physical or mental sense, mutual exclusivity one way or the other. Indeed, it is the very acceptance of complexity, nuance, contradiction, and paradox within religion and its teachings that safeguards us from the traps and perils of creedal and moral certainty, which is an essential stepping-stone to extremism.

In chapter 6 (subtitle "Loss of Culture Entails ..."), we asked if Pope Francis's description of Jesus Christ as "meek" should be interpreted literally. What is he trying to convey that needs the use of such evident contradiction?[568] Ma-tsu Tao-i is a famous eighth-century Zen Buddhist master from the Tang Dynasty. A monk posed him this question: "How do you get into harmony with the Tao?" Master Ma-tsu responded, "I am already out of harmony with the Tao."[569] While different interpretations may be drawn here, the contradictory nature of the relationship between the question and the answer is undeniable. And it is this contradiction that is used as a teaching vehicle in spiritual settings.

In Islam, the most fundamental proclamation is: "*la illaha illallah*" (there is no god but God). It can alternatively be interpreted as: "There is no god, only God." In other words, we have to begin with the denial of any form of a deity while we are accepting the existence of God. As the very first statement of faith thus, a Muslim is simultaneously engaging in denial and acceptance of the concept. This is just how religions sometimes approach foundational teachings.

Contradiction, especially when it comes to our understanding of God, really should not be viewed as an incompatibility or incoherence. Driving such judgments are the inadequacy of our conceptual frameworks when we try to understand that which may be beyond language, human senses, logic, and thought. God may even be beyond our concept of belief and unbelief because "the infinite transcends every particular content of faith."[570] Our incapacity to conceptualize is a testament only to the insufficiency of our language, our thought, and perhaps the human mind itself. As the *Guru Granth Sahib* (p 2) points out: "By thinking, He cannot be reduced to thought, even by thinking hundreds of thousands of times."

As this chapter shows, in pursuing science we do sometimes bend the very definition we are using in our logical and evaluative framework. Maybe we should also be able to rethink our concept of truth value (from the rigid Aristotelian binary formula) when pursuing knowledge of God. Perhaps God cannot be fit into that ultra-limited human construct that, in the name of science, has become a thought-habit for us in the modern world.

Most religions make no secret in telling us that God is ineffable, indescribable, unintelligible and unknowable to human faculties, indeed, beyond our comprehension. Yet by writing or reading this book, we are, in some way, in the process of discussing and understanding the same God that is beyond our understanding. The paradox thus begins at the very first step. Also, if God is unknowable, how do we really know that God is unknowable? Such spiritual dilemmas are the paradoxes we have to become comfortable with in our spiritual journey.

Perceptual Paradoxes

A teaching in Jainism (*Uttaradhayana Sutra*[571] 10:31) presents a discussion between Lord Mahavira, the last spiritual teacher of the present time cycle, and Gautama Buddha: "Lord Mahavira said to Gautama,[572] 'When *Dharma* is not seen by the seer directly, it is seen through the wire mesh of words. Conjecture is the wire mesh that covers that window. Multiple sects and systems result from such an indirect observation. The path suggested to you, Gautama, is the direct path of the seer: Be vigilant and a seer of Dharma.'"[573] Mahavira's statement further clarifies that some of the contradictions simply come from "wire meshes," which are the inadequate but the solely existing vehicles of human understanding.

Catuskoti, the Vedic system of logic, is especially central to Buddhist philosophy. It offers four possibilities in a logical scenario. Instead of just the Aristotelian true-false binary, Catuskoti provides two additional options: both true and false and neither true nor false. When added to the truth values we know—either true, or false—this adds to a total of four possibilities. Nagarjuna, the Buddhist philosopher considered the most important after Buddha himself, employed the Catuskoti logic in his teaching. Yet even that model is insufficient in Buddhism. The Buddha is said to have been asked what happens to enlightened people when they die. The expectation was one of the four Catuskoti possibilities. The Buddha remained silent.[574]

Here is a practical example of how the paradox in our perception of religious information could practically impact our decision-making. The August 2019 issue of *Mindful* magazine (p 53) carries a full-page photo of a general in the US Army. In his right hand, the general is holding a book of Rumi's poetry. As part of the message (the goodness of being "mindful"), the photo makes Rumi's book very prominent. Most people, even in the current Muslim world, let alone outside of it, do not realize that Rumi's epic poem the *Masnavi* has historically been called the "*Qur'an* in the Persian tongue."[575]

It is extremely unlikely that the general is aware that the book he holds is a direct interpretation of the *Qur'an*. The question then is: If the general were aware of this direct relationship of Rumi's *Masnavi* to the *Qur'an*, would he still be willing to have that picture published? If yes, would he also be willing to hold the *Qur'an* in his right hand and have the picture published? If yes, how would a large percentage of his compatriots react? What would be the impact on his career?

In order to develop an understanding, the most important question would be this: Why would the inspiration or usefulness of Rumi's work become less so in the minds of some non-Muslims when they realize that to follow Rumi's message is essentially to follow the *Qur'an*?

When we try to answer this question, we can see how paradox and contradiction create a problem in our minds; and yet, in reality, the contradiction creates no incompatibility or incoherence. The image of Rumi's book on its own and its image with the *Qur'an* offer two different presentations of the same reality. Yet the situation would create mutually exclusive behaviors based entirely upon an image, or an illusion. This paradoxical dichotomy emerges not from the truth—that Rumi's poetry is rooted in the *Qur'an*—but rather solely from one's awareness or unawareness of the truth and from one's deeply indoctrinated bias.

It is also important to realize that valuing subjective spiritual experience is not to deny scientific reality, just as valuing imagination and intuition is not to deny reason. We should also not assume that "science" will always be ahead of spirituality in promoting real "scientific" knowledge.[576] It is just that different modes of perceptivity have their unique applicability in various domains of being or living. One's visual acuity cannot help in detecting a smell, and one's auricular prowess cannot help in seeing the bright light. The dimensions of perception are different, and they require distinct perceptive modalities to be sensed. Those at a higher spiritual station may have developed additional perceptive capacities than the ordinary person who has not reached that spiritual state. Thus, if anyone has an "empirical" knowledge of spirituality, it would be those who founded these religions based upon their spiritual perceptivity and those mystics in various traditions who are considered saints and spiritual sages.

The human mind finds it difficult to deal with paradox. Instead, it inclines towards accepting black and white binaries—in part because our Aristotelian rationalism systematically conditions us that way. Such tendencies often lead to rigid interpretations of religious teachings or, at the opposite end, viewing religion as fundamentally irrational.

Paradox and contradiction exist not only in religion; they are very much present in other systems of human knowledge, though not so available or even open for common discussion, sometimes even among scholars of these disciplines. Here, we are talking about fields such as the sciences and the humanities. To comprehend the uncertainty and paradox within various disciplines of scientific knowledge, let's examine a few examples of contradiction in physics, mathematics, and philosophy.

It is clear that the presence of contradictions and imperfect knowledge does not invalidate the knowledge foundation of a discipline. Richard Feynman captured this point rather effectively: "What is not surrounded by uncertainty cannot be the truth."[577]

Accommodating Contradiction in Physics

The discovery of what we call quantum mechanics took place a little over a century ago. The very first thing that disoriented the most brilliant minds of the time was the "wave-particle duality,"[578] which effectively says that physical entities are simultaneously both wave-like and particle-like. The contradiction was ultimately just accepted as is by physicists. And then there was "quantum entanglement."[579] Einstein dismissed it as "spooky" science, although later experiments proved its validity. To be sure, much of quantum physics consists of such seeming absurdities that happen to be real, yet most theoretical physicists don't any longer seem to be concerned about explaining how things actually work in quantum mechanics. The contradictions are taken to be normal and acceptable.

By violating the foundational notions of classical physics, the quantum theory defies our imagination, perceptivity, scientific concepts, and the basic understanding of how things work. Consequently, as the *Stanford Encyclopedia* says, the "aim of any metaphysical interpretation of quantum mechanics is to account for these violations."[580]

Led by Niels Bohr, Werner Heisenberg, Max Born, and some other of the best minds in physics, a concept known as the *Copenhagen interpretation*[581] was introduced to reconcile these violations of the principles of science. Since then, other theories have also been introduced. The "multiverse"[582] concept seems to be the one that has lasted the longest so far. All of these explanations, as the *Stanford Encyclopedia* points out, seem to defy the very foundation of "western common sense."[583]

Many of these constructs, such as multiverse and the Copenhagen Interpretation, seem to be essentially speculative and cannot be empirically verified. Yet, despite all the contradictions, inconsistencies, and speculative explanations, our faith in science and physics remains unshaken. And rightly so. Perhaps, what appears to be paradoxical is so only because it contradicts the existing framework of principles, knowledge, and understanding.

Accommodating Contradiction in Mathematics

Even in the field of mathematics, where we would think that everything is completely logical, contradictions exist.

Set theory, for example, is a branch of mathematics that deals with the properties of objects. This field is important in mathematical logic. The discovery of various paradoxes—Russell's paradox and König's paradox being perhaps the most well-known—has raised questions about the logical consistency of the theory.[584]

Another example in mathematical logic as well as philosophy comes from the Liar paradox, which is really a family of paradoxes that are close to each other in reasoning. Let's create a simple example here:

Statement X: This statement is false.

If Statement X above is true, then it is false. If the statement is false, then it is true. Mathematicians can, of course, make this example much more complicated. Our purpose here is simply to show the inherent contradiction in a semantically correct sentence. This paradox creates real problems in the truth value paradigm. As the *Stanford Encyclopedia of Philosophy* points out, "work on this problem has been an integral part of the development of modern mathematical logic, and it has become a subject of extensive research in its own right.... what's puzzling about [this contradiction] seems to have something to do with truth, or at least, some semantic notion related to truth."[585]

Even Aristotle and Cicero were aware of this dilemma entrenched in philosophy and mathematics. We have thus neither been able to resolve it nor have we been able to get to a consensus. Would it then be fair to say that truth can be contradictory? The understanding and harmonization of what's paradoxical, or even mysterious, today opens new doors to discovery and knowledge. Scott Aaronson of MIT points to such a process in mathematics: "Math, you might say, is a conspiracy theorist's dream: it's the one part of life where, when you see things match up, the odds are excellent that it's not just a coincidence, that there is a deep explanation waiting to be unearthed."[586]

Accommodating the Contradictions of The Enlightenment

The phenomenon we know as the Enlightenment was a revolutionary epoch in European thinking. It impacted the rest of the world because the European colonial empires essentially controlled the rest of the world. The Enlightenment period followed what we call the Renaissance.[587] Today we find several contradictions within our knowledge of Enlightenment philosophy that are poorly understood at a rather wide level. The following excerpt from *The Dawn of Everything*, a book that discusses development and history of the organization and governance of human societies, sheds some basic light on the subject:

> The idea that our current ideals of freedom, equality and democracy are somehow products of the 'Western tradition' would in fact have come as an enormous surprise to someone like Voltaire.... The Enlightenment thinkers who propounded such ideals almost invariably put them in the mouths of foreigners, even 'savages' ... it's almost impossible to find a single European author before the nineteenth century who suggested it would be anything other than a terrible form of government.[588]

Perhaps it would be fair to believe that the thinkers leading the Enlightenment revolution were driven by their sense of human dignity. Yet such assumptions would be misplaced. Most of the Enlightenment philosophers were blatantly racist and left evidence to that effect in their writing.[589] This would include luminaries such as Voltaire, Immanuel Kant,[590] Thomas Hobbes, John Locke, David Hume,[591] and Adam Smith.[592] Here, for instance, is Voltaire:

> [Blacks] "are not men, except in their stature, with the faculty of speech and thought at a degree far distant to ours."[593] [And, as for Jews], "all of them born with raging fanaticism in their hearts, just as the Bretons

> and the Germans are born with blond hair. I would not be in the least bit surprised if these people would not someday become deadly to the human race."[594]

Simply criticizing these philosophers neither points to the real problem nor is the purpose of this chapter. We have to regard them for the revolution they produced in Europe. We also have to acknowledge that many of them actively opposed slavery. That seems to have been a radically bold posture at that time. If there is anything to blame as regards the Enlightenment philosophers, it is the way history is usually described today, without fully presenting the negative aspects within the thought-patterns of these humans. But that's not the purpose of this example either. Because the conceptual guidelines developed during that period still dominate current thought-patterns in all walks of life, the following three lessons are worth our attention.

First, given that this philosophy was so flawed on something so fundamental as human equality and dignity, why do we have to use its doctrines to be the primary guiding light for the human race and its future? Second, these philosophers were part of the environment that brought them up. Even the best of them at the time could not escape how the environment and "education" shaped their minds and hearts. The same applies to us. We are all products of the current politico-socio-economic system and reflect that system to one degree or the other. Our belief and reality, even about our own selves, would thus be a panoply of contradiction and paradox that we may not usually understand.

Third, the moral disposition of these eminent philosophers is not even considered fit to be part of common knowledge today. How then do we know that our moral disposition, individual or collective, is consistent with our positive self-image or even personal and collective interest? Especially so if most of us are making virtually no conscious effort in thought or action to reconcile any of this. The reconciliation of the collision between image and reality—individually and collectively—is sometimes all that stands between our freedom and our illusion.

Accepting Paradox and Contradiction as Valid Realities

Everything we know about our own selves, about others, and about the very nature and quality of human existence contains multitudinous dimensions of contradictions and paradoxes. Everything we know about the structures and institutions that organize our lives also would fall in that category.

When we understand the presence of all these paradoxes and contradictions, we realize the presence of fissures in the thought-processes telling us that science is entirely rational and religion is almost entirely non-rational. The only way to develop a more realistic understanding is by accepting that there are paradoxes in life that are beyond our comprehension (at least through the prevalent ways of thinking that often go unquestioned). Such contradictions exist in every field of knowledge including physics, mathematics, philosophy, and religion. It simply shows the need for humans to be humble about our limitations, instead of the arrogance that is all too often on display.

It would be ironic to ignore a fundamental commonality between religion and science: both these domains share a sense of awe, exploration, fascination, fervency, and wonder when it comes to the mystery we know as existence! Upon an unexpected discovery, there may even be a common sentiment in the expression of wonderment and bewilderment by a scientist and by a person of faith. This bewilderment is expressed by the word *haeyra* or its conjugates in many Asian languages (such as Arabic, Farsi, Hindi, Punjabi, Urdu), and it denotes not just perplexity. Rather, it is also the opening of knowledge that one did not possess before; thus, there is also a strong element of delight in it.

Waheguru is the most common name invoked in Sikhism to refer to God. The word "wah" in this name comes from Persian and is an interjection of awe, admiration, and delightful bewilderment. (The full name thus would literally translate to the sense of "Wondrous Teacher" or "Wondrous Lord" in English, though its spiritual meaning can be interpreted more profoundly.) This type of wonder is a common theme in our spiritual traditions, not just through ritual expressions but more so by perceptual experience. In a poetic verse I have translated below, my grandmother expressed it the following way:

> Bewildered is my heart,
> endless is my bewilderment;
>
> No longer can I discern who I am,
> such is my bewilderment.[595]

By comparing scriptural message, part five of this book will shed some light on the "mutually incompatible" image of our religions. It is important, though, to also realize that the domain of human understanding will keep facing contradictions and paradoxes in our quest for knowledge. It may also be that the human mind may never be able to touch some of these paradoxes, giving rise to conflicts.

As T. S. Eliot and F. Scott Fitzgerald knew, then, the limited human capacity to deal with contradiction and paradox may be part of our human nature. Our current global institutions and structures have historically taken advantage of that limitation, a disconcerting liability we should be cognizant of. To live in a peaceful and just world, we would have to choose and implement the value systems that will spiritually and psychologically anchor us in a sustainable mode of living. Not doing anything would be a hazardous choice.

PART FIVE:

BREAKING THE BARRIERS: "COMPREHENDING" THE DIVINE

When nothing existed, it was God;
had nothing existed, God would've been.

'Tis my existence that degrades me;
had I not been, what might have I been?[596]

—Ghalib, Mirza Asadullah Baig Khan

CHAPTER 13:

DIVINE REALITY IN SPIRITUAL TEACHING

There is one supreme being, the eternal reality (true name),
the creator, without fear, devoid of enmity, immortal,
never incarnated, self-existent,
(known by) the grace of the Guru.
Recite: True at the beginning, true through the ages,
is yet true, O Nanak, and will be true.

—Sri Guru Granth Sahib, Mul Mantar

Eye cannot see him, nor words reveal him;
by the senses, austerity, or works he is not known.
When the mind is cleansed by the grace of wisdom,
he is seen by contemplation—the One without parts.

—Mundaka Upanishad 3.1.8

The Tao that can be told is not the eternal Tao;
The name that can be named is not the eternal Name.
The Nameless is the source of Heaven and Earth;
The named is the Mother of the Ten Thousand Things.

—*Tao Te Ching* 1:1-4

Different names are used in different religions to refer to the Ultimate Truth. It is noteworthy that the expressions Ahura Mazda, Allah, Brahman, Elaha, Elohim, Ein Sof, God, Waheguru, and YHWH share many aspects in how they are described. Even the concept of Tao, which seems to be so different from one of God seems to share some of these attributes. This chapter will thematically specify the teachings from different traditions.

The Impossibility of Understanding God

The human inability to fully understand God is captured by Exodus 3:14 when it says: Ehyeh-Asher-Ehyeh. The full verse is:

> And God said to Moses, 'Ehyeh-Asher-Ehyeh.' He continued, 'Thus shall you say to the Israelites, Ehyeh sent me to you.'

Ehyeh-Asher-Ehyeh is translated variously as I Am that I Am, or I Will Be What I Will Be. This phrase has now become a common refrain, implying that God cannot be defined. And that is a rather common teaching in most religions, implying that God can be known only to God. Rabbi Isaac the Blind (twelfth century), one of the first well-known Kabbalists, even repudiates apophasis by depicting *deus absconditus* (the Hidden God) as "that which is not conceivable by thinking," and not "He who is not, etc."[597] In *Sha'are Orah*, Rabbi Joseph Gikatilla (thirteenth century) elaborates on the difficulty of knowing anything about God:

> The depth of primordial being is called Boundless. Because of its concealment from all creatures, above and below, it is also called Nothingness. If one asks, "What is it!" The answer is 'Nothing,' meaning: no one can understand anything about it. It is negated of every conception. No one can know anything about it—except the belief that it exists. Its existence cannot be grasped by anyone other than it. Therefore its name is 'I am becoming.'[598]

The *Qur'an* (72:26) explicitly debars the possibility of human perceptivity reaching such apprehension: "He (alone) knows that which is beyond the reach of a created being's perception, and to none does He disclose aught of the mysteries of His Own unfathomable knowledge..."

The *Qur'an* (31:27) also points to the impossibility of a human effort yielding any fruit in capturing God's infinite knowledge: "And if all the trees on earth were pens, and the sea (were ink), with seven [more] seas yet added to it, the words of God would not be exhausted: for, verily, God is almighty, wise."

Also frequent are instances where scriptures extend praises to, while acknowledging the unfathomable infinitude of, the Lord. *Sri Guru Granth Sahib* (p 488) provides such an example: "O Lord, Sustainer and Cherisher, You are infinite, unfathomable and endless."

The feeling of wonder and awe is expressed in the *Dead Sea Scrolls* with the following words: "Who can fathom the designs of Your heart? Apart from You nothing has existed, and without Your will nothing will be; yet none can understand Your wisdom nor gaze upon Your secrets."[599]

GOD IN THE UPANISHADS, RIG VEDA, AND BHAGAVAD GITA

He truly knows Brahman who knows Him as beyond knowledge; he who thinks that he knows, knows not. The ignorant think that Brahman is known, but the wise know Him to be beyond knowledge.

—*Kena Upanishad* 2.1-3

Who knows this truly, and who will now declare it, what paths lead together to the gods? Only their lowest aspects of existence are seen, who exist on supreme, mystical planes.

—*Rig Veda* 3.54.5

All this universe, deluded by the qualities inherent in nature, fails to know that I am beyond them and unchanging.

—*Gita* 7.13

Insert 13:1

The Problem with Numeric Classifications

We humans have come up with a lot of classifications to reinforce our imperfect understanding of God. Monism, monotheism, pantheism, and polytheism are just a few of many such phrases. Even within a single religion, it is not uncommon to find theologians wrangling over whose understanding—and whose language—is sound. As stated elsewhere in this book, there may be wisdom in humbly accepting the abundant teaching that the Ultimate Truth is beyond our conceptual frameworks, lexicology, and all other human faculties. In Or Ne'erav, Rabbi Moses Cordovero (sixteenth century) clarifies the constraint of the numbering system in our comprehension of God:

> First, you should know that the Creator, Ein Sof, is the cause of causes, one without a second, one that cannot be counted. Change and mutability, form and multiplicity, do not apply to it. The word 'one' is used metaphorically, since the number one stands on its own and is the beginning of all numbers. Every number is contained in it potentially, while it inheres in every number in actuality.[600]

In the *Zohar*, the transition from duality to unity is expressed in the Wedding Celebration with the following words: "Separate, separated from all, yet not separate. For all is joined to it, and it is joined to all. It is all!"[601]

In a book titled *Being Peace*, Thich Nhat Hanh clarified the significance of the concept of non-duality by separating it from oneness: "Non-duality means 'not two,' but 'not two' also means 'not one.' That is why we say 'non-dual' instead of 'one.' Because if there is one, there are two. If you want to avoid two, you have to avoid one also."[602]

The following insert highlights one of the most important chapters from the *Qur'an*. As the reader will notice, the last verse highlights the difficulty of grasping the essence of God because there is nothing that can be used to "compare with" or grasp the Ultimate Truth.

The English rendering (translation) and the explanatory notes in this excerpt are from Muhammad Asad's *The Message of the Qur'an*.

The explanatory notes have been slightly modified to facilitate the understanding of readers from diverse backgrounds.

QUR'AN: CHAPTER 112 (THE UNITY)

SAY: "He is the One God: God the Eternal, the Uncaused Cause of All That Exists.[v2] He begets not, and neither is He begotten; and there is nothing that could be compared with Him."[v4]

v2: "as-samad" is arguably the most untranslatable word in the *Qur'an*. It occurs in the *Qur'ān* only once (in this chapter), and is applied to God alone. This rendering (interpretation of the word) gives no more than an approximate meaning of the term. It comprises the concepts of Primary Cause and eternal, independent Being, combined with the idea that everything existing or conceivable goes back to Him as its source and is, therefore, dependent on Him for its beginning as well as for its continued existence.

v4: The fact that God is one and unique in every respect, without beginning and without end, has its logical correlate in the statement that "there is nothing that could be compared with Him—thus precluding any possibility of describing or defining Him. Consequently, the quality of His Being is beyond the range of human comprehension or imagination: which also explains why any attempt at "depicting" God by means of figurative representations or even abstract symbols must be qualified as an irreverent denial of the truth.

Insert 13:2

Bawa Muhaiyaddeen, a twentieth-century Sufi mystic, provided his explanation with the following words: "God is One. He has no body, no death, no birth, no beginning, no end, no want, no form, no status. He is not the light as we see it. He is not the sun, the moon, the stars, the fire, or the glitters. He is always pure. He is omnipresent Perfection. He exists as the Atom within the atom, as the Heart within the heart, as Wisdom within wisdom."[603]

No sooner do we step outside of literalism, which keeps contradicting its own self when the task involves the divine, than we realize that the message transmitted by various religious texts—while often foundationally "monadic" (of oneness)—is wrapped in a cryptic shroud. Every definition or categorization in human terms, monotheism or dualism or monism or panentheism, seems overly simplistic.

God is clearly beyond our comprehension. And yet even those who avowedly profess God's grandeur somehow find it difficult to accept the diminutiveness of human faculty and percipience in expressing that grandeur. In this regard, the explanation by Rabbi Abraham Isaac Kook (twentieth century) is succinct and seems to point to the dilemma created by the physical and sensory human existence: "Pure belief in the oneness of God has been blurred by corporeality ... the divine emanates existence and is itself beyond existence... The infinite transcends every particular content of faith."[604]

Comprehensibility of Divine Attributes

Our scriptures from many religions tell us that the essence of the Ultimate Truth is beyond human comprehension. They also tell us that divine attributes are manifest in creation. Not only are they very much within human grasp, scriptures tell us that we are expected to live our lives in accordance with these attributes. We'll briefly touch upon "light" and "compassion" as divine attributes and their common importance in various scriptures.

1. Light:

Scriptures make frequent reference to light in various contexts. This excerpt appears in *Katha Upanishad* (5.15), *Mundaka Upanishad*

(2.2.10), as well as *Svetasvatara Upanishad* (6.14). "Him the sun does not illumine, nor the moon, nor the stars, nor the lightning, nor fires kindled upon the earth. He is the one light that gives light to all. He shines—everything shines."[605]

The following from the *Qur'an* (24:35) and the *Bhagavad Gita* (11.12), respectively, also highlight that light is a divine attribute:

> God is the Light of the heavens and the earth.

> If the light of a thousand suns
> were to rise in the sky at once,
> it would be like the light of that great spirit.

2. Compassion:

Compassion, expressed in various ways, is also an important divine attribute. And our religious teachings, again and again, emphasize its observance and practice.

Being sister languages, the Hebrew Rahamim and Arabic Rahma share their etymology, and also rank among the highest human virtues. RHM, connoting "the womb," is the triconsonantal root of many words in Arabic and Hebrew. The womb thus is the basic abode of compassion, mercy, and love. Insert 13:3 shows that God's most important attributes in the *Qur'an* have a feminine etymology linguistically.

"WOMB"—THE ROOT OF RAHMAN AND RAHIM

In Islam, Rahman and Rahim are perhaps the most important attributes of God. The most frequent sentence in the *Qur'an*, and the one that begins each[606] chapter (surah), translates to: In the name of Allah, the Gracious, the Compassionate (Bismillah ar-Rahman ir-Rahim).

> In the grammar of many languages, certain words have very clear gender quality to them that is reflected in sentence construction. The words Rahman and Rahim are both from the same feminine root: R-H-M—the womb. We should not lose sight of the fact that both these attributes of God (Rahman, Rahim) are feminine in their etymology.[607]
>
> Insert 13:3

Compassion as a virtue is also highly prominent in all the Indic religions. *Maitri* is a Sanskrit word whose counterpart in Pali is *metta*. These words translate to compassion, benevolence, and friendliness. The teachings place this not just as an important concept, but also as an important practice. In Buddhism, Metta meditation as well as the Metta Sutta are commonly known. Texts in Hinduism emphasizing maitri include the *Upanishads* and the *Yoga Sutras* of Patanjali. In Jainism, the concept is also promoted in the *Tattvartha Sutra*.

In Sikhism, three of the Five Virtues are compassion, humility, and love (daya, nimrata, pyar). When we consider the combined effect of the three exhortations, we see how the balance is strongly tilted towards an ethos of interpersonal responsibility—not just to one's kith and kin, but to the "other" as exhibited by the verse below. It's remarkable how the substance of intent (innate kindness) is given preference over form (visiting a shrine or even giving of alms): "Be kind to all beings—this is more meritorious than bathing at the sixty-eight sacred shrines of pilgrimage and the giving of charity." (*Sri Guru Granth Sahib*, M.5, p 136)

Understanding God by Apophasis (Negative Theology)

God, as most religions tell us, is fundamentally and transcendentally different from all that's graspable by human thought, senses, or imagination. God's powers are beyond all comparison, categorization, connotation, or comprehension. God is not what can be described because God is beyond language, beyond description, and beyond comprehension. That is the reason apophasis (negative theology) is often used to describe God. (However, as exhibited earlier by the words of Rabbi Isaac the Blind, even apophasis is no panacea to the limitation of human comprehension in this regard.)

The great Jewish philosopher Maimonides (twelfth century) explains: "The description of God by means of negatives is the correct description—a description that is not affected by an indulgence in facile language... With every increase in the negations regarding God, you come nearer to the apprehension of God."[608]

Meister Eckhart, Christian theologian and mystic of the thirteenth century, condensed it using the following words: "God's *niht* fills the entire world; his something though is nowhere."[609] Gregory Palamas, a Byzantine Christian saint of the fourteenth century, explained the negative relationship in contrast with the creation: "He is not being if that which is not God is being."[610]

Michael Sells, a historian and scholar of religion, highlights the ubiquitous use of apophasis by Jews, Christians, and Muslims during the last millennium: "apophasis lived on after this period in the post-exilic Kabbalah of Isaac Luria, in the Spanish mystics, in Jacob Boehme, and widely throughout the Islamic tradition."[611]

Brihadaranyaka Upanishad (2.3.6) explains why there is the need for the "neti, neti" formulation: "Now therefore the description (of Brahman): 'Not this, not that' [*neti, neti*]. Because there is no other and more appropriate description than this 'Not this'. Now Its name: 'The Truth of truth'. The vital force is truth, and It is the Truth of that."

Unique and Incomparable Divine Nature

Most religions inform us of the unique divine nature that is beyond words or human concepts. In describing God or the Ultimate Truth, the message is about the hidden and incomprehensible essence of that which permeates everything, and yet is beyond anyone's grasp.

In Kabbalah, the Ten *Sefirot*—singular *Sefirah*—are Ein Sof's revealed attributes/emanations that interact with each other and the world. In his Commentary on the Ten Sefirot, Rabbi Azriel of Gerona (thirteenth century) clarifies his understanding of the boundless Ein Sof:

> Infinite. It is absolute undifferentiation in perfect, changeless oneness. Since it is boundless, there is nothing outside of it. Since it transcends and conceals itself, it is the essence of everything hidden and revealed... Emanating from Ein Sof are the ten sefirot. They constitute the process by which all things come into being and pass away. They energize every existent thing that can be quantified. Since all things come into being by means of the sefirot, they differ from one another, yet they all derive from one root. Everything is from Ein Sof, there is nothing outside of it.[612]

Imam Birgivi, a sixteenth-century Islamic scholar and mystic, further explains the sheer incomparability of God to any concept or thing we are familiar with:

> He[613] is other than all we know or can imagine. He has no age. He was before always, and will be after the after, forever. He is self-existent and does not depend on anything. His essence is only His. It is unknown to anyone but He... He created all from nothing and can turn all into nothing. Nothing has the power to resist Him... He is the cause of all and everything. All are in need of Him, while he needs no one and nothing. He said 'Be' and all became. Everything will be gone when he says 'Be gone.' He is the creator, bearing no resemblance to what He created.[614]

In reality, though, we come across an understanding of the Ultimate Truth that is very different from these familiar teachings. To advise against such trends, *Orot ha Qodesh* by Rabbi Kook provides the following message:

> The innermost point of the awareness of God has become so faint that the essence of God is conceived only as a stern power from whom you cannot escape, to whom you must subjugate yourself. If you submit to the service of God on this empty basis, you gradually lose your radiance by constricting your consciousness. The divine splendor is plucked from your soul.[615]

Bahá'u'lláh, the prophet-founder of the Bahai Faith, elucidates the concept of God as follows. Noteworthy is how he qualifies that such knowledge becomes evident to discerning and illuminated hearts.

> To every discerning and illuminated heart it is evident that God, the Unknowable Essence, the Divine Being, is immensely exalted beyond every human attribute, such as corporeal existence, ascent and descent, egress and regress. Far be it from His glory that human tongue should adequately recount His praise, or that human heart comprehend His fathomless mystery. He is, and hath ever been, veiled in the ancient eternity of His Essence, and will remain in His Reality everlastingly hidden from the sight of men.[616]

The words from Kook and Bahá'u'lláh are addressed to a general audience. Nevertheless, even within religions in which God is understood to be beyond human comprehension, some theologians go around pretending they "know" God or, at least, know clearly what God would approve or disapprove of. The quotes from Unayza and Ibn Arabi make that point.

According to Unayza[617] of Baghdad, a tenth-century Sufi saint: "The a'rif (gnostic) is neither one who describes God nor one who passes on information about Him."[618] One wonders what she would say about theologians who expect others to follow their definition of God, or the effrontery of those who go around imposing upon others purely human interpretations as God's Guidance or Shari'ah?[619] Ibn

Arabi's description politely classifies such theologians as "mongers of doctrinal formulations who contradict one another and denounce each other."[620]

We grow and ascend in insight when, in humility, we accept the limits of our intellect and comprehension. Paradoxically, this humility-induced acceptance of our limitation is the source of agency and power that the human race needs today. Over two millennia ago, under the title "The One God of the manifold world," the Svetasvatara Upanishad (4.1) captured the human need and hope for the endowment of wisdom: "He, the One and Undifferentiated, who by the manifold application of His powers produces, in the beginning, different objects for a hidden purpose and, in the end, withdraws the universe into Himself, is indeed the self-luminous. May He endow us with clear intellect!"[621]

CHAPTER 14:

TRANSCENDENT MEANING IN THE TEXT

Demolish the mosque, the temple,
demolish whatever would tumble;
Break never a fellow heart,
for the Beloved Lord does therein dwell."[622]

—Mia'n Muhammad Bukhsh

In the couplet I translated above, why is an Islamic theologian prescribing the demolition of a mosque, or perhaps all of them? But then, is he? Of course, he would neither promote the demolition of any place of worship, nor would he condone violence of any other sort. So then, what is he promoting in the first hemistich of that couplet? For the real message to manifest in meaning, we have to cross the barrier of forms, appearances, and words. Transcending forms and appearances is, in fact, his clear message here. And that is just the beginning of the many teachings in that couplet.

Even when the reading of a religious scripture is rather elementary, it often delivers a consistent result: the initial understanding will be upgraded with a subsequent reading of the same passage. Every new reading, in a state of humility and sincerity, entails a process of continual learning. Thus, our spiritual benefit and growth from the experience is a correlate of our inner sincerity and faith, which determines the light that our heart is "prepared" to receive from the scripture. Our understanding of the message is likely to remain imperfect; it is just a matter of degrees that can be improved within that imperfection. That understanding can open a lot of doors in ascending the tall ladder in improving one's understanding.

The barriers discussed in chapters 10 and 11 are created for us by others, whereas the barriers discussed in this chapter emanate from our habit of, and comfort in, taking the easier route rather than engaging in the struggle to comprehend the scriptural message.

Unfolding Meaning

Even the outwardly visible aspects of various religions (including doctrine, ritual, moral and ethical teachings, etc.) don't get enough coverage to make the average person have some preliminary awareness of such facets of various religions. More reflective or esoteric aspects of even one's own religion are entirely out of the question.

It is easy to see certain similarities in various principles and practices of different religions. This is especially true of the socio-ethical aspects of such teachings. The transcendental meanings of our scriptures, however, are not so commonly brought up—and often stay as an academic subject or something reserved for theologians. However, it does enlighten the lay person to develop some acquaintance with their own scriptures and accept that scriptures in other religions may also have multiple interpretations. It is in our societal interest to develop this understanding—because misconstructions of scriptures, one's own and that of the "other," are usually exploited by religious extremists and political systems.

Chapter 10 clarified the difficulty in dealing with ancient versions of our sacred languages and the difficulty in accurately translating certain parts of the scripture. Well beyond that reality is the phenomenon of certain messages appearing to be meaningless at best, if not outright incomprehensible[623]—even when they can be understood or translated with perfect accuracy. In such cases, whether or not one accepts the validity of such interpretations, one would have to accept that the reflective understanding can shed some light on what's being said, but only when such understanding comes from a bona fide source. This book quotes several such scriptural verses. The exercises below provide some examples.

In most ordinary writing, fiction or otherwise, reading something once or twice usually provides enough understanding of the text, and repeated readings would quickly stop adding any value. More philosophical writings sometimes require more attention or repetition to grasp the meanings of certain points. People of spiritual understanding, however, would say that reading the scripture multiple times keeps opening windows of inner understanding that did not exist before. The experts agree on that point. Victor Mair, referring to the layer upon layer of meaning within Lao Tzu's writing, says: "One can read and reread the Tao Te Ching scores of times without exhausting the insights it offers."[624]

James Winston Morris is an Islamic theologian who has taught at University of Exeter, the Sorbonne, Princeton University, and Boston College, among others. In explaining the process of reading Ibn Arabi's writing—specifically, the *Futuhat al-Makkiyya* in this case—he compares it to the process of reading the *Qur'an* and says that the process of reading Ibn Arabi "is remarkably similar to the ongoing process of reading the *Qur'an*. Most obviously, no one can ever claim to have 'finished' reading any part of that book: in light of the reader's own changing spiritual experiences and learning situations, each chapter continually reveals new facets and new thematic connections and complexities at each encounter."[625]

If Ibn Arabi's writing is so transcendent, then what do we say about the *Qur'an*? And that point cannot be overstated:

> The Qur'an is called the 'ocean of meanings,' in which each verse contains hundreds of thousands of levels of interpretations... the outward levels of meaning are called the *Qur'an*, or the recitation, but when the heart is opened to the inner levels of meaning, it is called *al-furqaan*, discriminating wisdom. The deepest meaning are called *al-nujmaan*, which means the light of a shower of shooting stars... All the names of the absolute, whether in Sanskrit, Pali, Hebrew, Greek, Aramaic, Arabic, or other sacred languages, contain this essential light... 'We make no distinction between any of the books or the messengers who

> bring them'[626] ... they all come from the same source, called the Preserved Tablet (*al-lawh al-mahfoodh*).[627]

Similarly, no one can ever claim to have "finished" reading and understanding the Bible, the *Sri Guru Granth Sahib*, the *Dhammapada*, the *Upanishads*, or any of the scriptures from all the other traditions.

> We understand him [as a wheel]
> with one felly, with a triple tire,
> With sixteen end-parts, fifty spokes,
> twenty counter-spokes,
> With six set of eights,
> whose one rope is manifold,
> Which has three different paths,
> whose one illusion has
> two conditioning causes.[628]

This quatrain is from *Svetasvatara Upanishad* (1.4). Literally, the stanza is quite indecipherable. Yet it contains allusions that become clear upon struggle or guidance. For example, "triple tire" refers to the Three Qualities according to the *Sankhya* Philosophy, whereas the "six sets of eights" include the eight producing causes of *Prakriti* (original conditions), the eight constituents of the body, the eight forms of superhuman power, the eight conditions (*bhava*), the eight gods, and the eights virtues. A full interpretation of this quatrain alone could vary considerably depending upon the follower's depth of scriptural understanding.

Insert 14:1 provides an exercise as an invitation to reflect upon some scriptural verses that demonstrate the need to go beyond the literal meaning.

REFLECTION: AN EXERCISE

Psalms *119:18*: "Open my eyes so I can see wonders out of your Torah."

Question: How can we interpret this statement by King David in a non-literal way?

Psalms 34:9: "Taste and see how good the Lord is."

Question: How would a human taste the Lord?

Deuteronomy 8:3: "One does not live on bread alone, but rather on all that issues from the mouth of God."

Question: Besides bread, what all does one live on that issues from the mouth of God? (Hint: Genesis 1:26, 1:27, 2:7; Qur'an 7:156, 18:65; Gita 10:20, 14:30 and countless other teachings may provide ideas in furthering an understanding of this message.)

Odes of Solomon 11: "and I drank and was drunk with the living water that never dies, and my drunkenness gave me knowledge."

Question: How can drunkenness become a source of knowledge? Why is this language so universal among highly-spiritual people?

Insert 14:1

Differentiating Substance from Form

These verses are from *Haft Awrang* (Seven Thrones of Grace), a Persian literature classic by the famous Sufi poet Nuruddin Abd ar-Rahman Ja'ami (fifteenth century). He exhorts us to swiftly cross the bridge of form so as to be in the terrain of meanings.

> For, without having emptied the wine-cup of the
> Form [*surat*]
> You will not attain to taste the draught of Meaning
> [*ma'ni*]
> Do not, though, tarry overlong with the Figure [*surat*]
> But bring yourself swift across the bridge.[629]

In the religious context especially, the relationship between word and meaning can sometimes be similar to the one between form and substance. If the endeavor in our faith resides in discovering the principles in the scriptures and not just the forms created by words, then a rigidly literal approach may sometimes amount to what in business parlance would be called "the downsizing" of revelation. As we see time and again—the Saudi-Wahhabi ideology is just one example—literalism can often be the mother of obscurantism and extremism. This is achieved by oversimplifying complex religious ideas and presenting them in a simplistic fashion. And this becomes one of the common modes of creating hatred and misunderstandings, thus gaining the ability to use religion for various nefarious purposes.

A reliable rule of thumb: where there's literalism, extremism is lurking nearby (though there would always be exceptions to such a rule). And that's just one reason why some tension between word and meaning, form and substance, is essential to a coherent plurality and healthy development of our beliefs and practices.

It is not just the ordinary people; history tells us that even spiritually accomplished saints have sometimes slipped up in managing that balance. An eighth-century story comes to mind about Sufi saints Rabi'a al-Adawiyya and Ibrahim Ibn Adham, both of whom have been mentioned previously in this book. (While this narrative is hagiographic, the lesson is crucial.)

There are many accounts of how Rabi'a couldn't get to the *Kaaba* for Hajj for a long time. One of them involves Ibrahim who took fourteen years to travel to Mecca for his pilgrimage because he stopped frequently to keep offering his prayers. But when he got to Mecca, he could not see the Kaaba. He complained to his own self asking if he had gone blind. A voice then informed him that the Kaaba had itself gone to meet a woman because she was so dear to

God. He headed out of Mecca to find that woman and soon came across Rabi'a. "What's this craziness you've brought into the world, woman?" he exclaimed. "It's not I who am the author of craziness," she replied, "but you. You were crazy enough to take fourteen years to get to the Kaaba with your ritual prayers, while I, with my inner prayers, am here already."[630]

Rabi'a effectively told Ibrahim that his insistence on being so devout as to offer the ritual prayers at every step of the journey, while ignoring the passion to quickly get to the Kaaba, may have been the reason why the Kaaba became invisible to him.

Another way to understand Rabi'a, especially as it would apply to scriptures, is the following: Form is a vehicle to convey the substance. When the form overrules the substance, however, the meaning may be downgraded, if not utterly lost. Insert 14:2 provides another exercise to invite more reflection.

ENDURING TO FIND THE KINGDOM: AN EXERCISE

Matthew 10:22—[Jesus said] "... but whoever endures to the end will be saved."

Matthew 24:13—[Jesus said] "But whoever endures to the end will be saved."

Question: What are the above two verses in reference to? Do they imply that relation of individual to God has to remain until the end of one's life? Or do they imply that the world will soon come to an end?

Luke 17:21—"Look - the kingdom of God is within you."

1 Corinthians 3:16-17—"For God's temple is holy, and you are that temple."

Question: Can the above guidance in Luke and Corinthians be literally interpreted? If this "kingdom" and "temple" is already manifest in

> everyone who claims to be Christian, then why is that manifestation not so palpable within a large percentage of Christians? How would we respond to a non-Christian who says that the two verses are equally applicable to her?
>
> Matthew 19:24—"It is easier for a camel to go through the eye of a needle, than for a rich man to enter into the kingdom of God."
>
> Question: Is this injunction absolute or is there room for interpretation? What kingdom of God is difficult for a rich man to enter? Is there something a rich man can do to undo this injunction? [Hint: Aparigraha in chapter 18, Luke 10:42, etc.]
>
> Insert 14:2

The message from theologians sometimes also is that what one gets out of the scripture is in accordance with one's stage or station of spiritual attainment, insight, and perceptivity. According to Abu Talib al-Makki, a tenth-century Islamic jurist and scholar, every Qur'anic verse has seven meanings; the most basic being the "external/exoteric" (*zahir*); going all the way up to "reality" (*haqa'iq*) for the prophets.[631] And then we have Rabbi Isaac Luria's intimation that "the Torah at Sinai had 600,000 faces, one for each soul that received it."[632]

Here's a necessary clarification. While the literal can sometimes be inadequate or even misleading in the formation of a fuller comprehension of the scripture, it is the most reliable place to begin to understand the meaning. Language, after all, is an amazing vehicle of communication. That's why it makes sense to always begin with the literal meaning, then allow our faculties to interpret the message. Daniel Matt, one of the world's leading academic authorities on Kabbalah and the Zohar who has taught at the Graduate Theological Union in Berkeley, Stanford University, and the Hebrew University of Jerusalem, puts it this way: "The text of the Torah is simply the starting point, a springboard for the imagination."[633]

The habit of combining inquisitiveness and humility is a potent enabler in our quest for comprehension. Instead of making us stay bound in preconceptions, this habit makes us realize the reimaginative power of new ideas promoting meaningful and reconfigurative engagement within our cognition. The smugness and preconceptions, as Rabbi Abraham Kook points out, can lead to a "darkness" that further takes us towards a "mindless faith."

> The crude complacency of imagining divinity as embodied in words and letters alone puts humanity to shame. Heresy arises as a pained outcry to liberate us from this strange, narrow pit, to raise us from the darkness of letters and platitudes to the light of thought and feeling. Such heresy eventually takes its stand in the center of morality ...for it must consume the filthy froth clinging to mindless faith.[634]

Instead of demanding that the scripture be utterly perspicuous (obvious), the rabbi would likely suggest an expansion of our horizons to become more perspicacious (insightful). If that means realizing the need to develop and going up a notch or two in our perceptive faculties, that can only be a good thing. Accepting the limitations of our language is a necessary step in that journey. The inspirational function of words in our scriptures is to spur our faculties of "thought and feeling" as indicated by Rabbi Kook. Limiting ourselves to only words can become a limitation in our spiritual and intellectual growth. That may be why chapter 26 of *Zhuangzi* (*Chuang Tzu*) ends with:

> The fish trap exists because of the fish; once you have gotten the fish, you can forget the trap.... Words exist because of meaning; once you've gotten the meaning, you can forget the words. But where shall I find a man who has forgotten words so I can have a word with him?[635]

CHAPTER 15:

HUMAN—THE SPIRITUAL BEING WITH AGENCY

You are diffused throughout and permeating all places and interspaces; You are known to be deep within the hearts of all beings.

—Sri Guru Granth Sahib, M.5, p 318[636]

Shrouded in mystery I am,
there's no knowing my appellation or attribute;
I myself know indeed,
but how would it come into the grasp of the multitude?[637]

—Mirza Yas Yagana Changezi

When a person turns from living to lifeless, where does life go? Where did it come from? Is life just another biological "thing?" Medical science reductively understands the human biological body down to the subcellular level. Yet, it seems to have no information to understand the basic questions stated above. The Enlightenment philosopher Georg Wilhelm Friedrich Hegel famously claimed: "The wounds of the spirit heal, and leave no scars behind." Within the parameter of rationalism—without any empirical evidence—how can we rationally talk about "spirit" when we have no acceptance of what it might be, where it resides, or even its very existence?[638] Why does it seem that Enlightenment philosophy is pretending to know what is clearly beyond its domain (and perhaps even antithetical to rationalism)?

We do now have scientific evidence[639] showing the positive impact of spiritual state on our physical and emotional well-being. Experientially, it would make sense: spirituality is what brings a deep sense of meaning and purpose to our lives, and that influences our health. What we would call "spiritual", though, does not fall exclusively within the domain of "religion" alone. There are various avenues to realizing the connection with one's inner truth and essence. It is this spiritual connection to one's essence that allows one to fully actualize one's agency. Religions and scriptures simply provide proven avenues that can be followed to discover and realize one's inner self. As the guidance from *Guru Granth Sahib* (M.5, 48.18) indicates: "He is contained deep within each and every heart. He is always with you, as your Helper and Support."

Even religious people should accept that religion's image as being dogmatic is rather prevalent, and perhaps rightly so. The disparate nature of interpretation and practice yielding this image may simply be indicative of innate human strengths and limitations at play because, clearly, human weakness itself is not caused by the message within the scripture. Understanding this interplay of human strength and limitation, therefore, becomes necessary when we are exploring human spiritual nature and agency.

"Agency" is one of the most complex English words used in this book. Here it means the inherent human capacity of decision-making and action—somewhat independently of other (external) factors, yet in consort with those factors. This chapter explores the concept of agency as an innate expression of human spirituality.

Innate Nature and Agency of Human Being

The link between spirituality and agency becomes easier to explore when we develop an understanding of human nature as promoted by our religions, especially on the social and moral dimensions. It would be highly meaningful to clarify this understanding in the context of, and in comparison to, the stance generally taken by Enlightenment philosophy regarding human nature.

Chapter 4 underlined the role played by Enlightenment philosophers such as Thomas Hobbes in the evolution of today's adversarial social systems and thought patterns.[640] Here, we'll briefly clarify the general concept of innate human nature within Enlightenment philosophy. This would then provide us the context to understanding human agency within our scriptures.

Hobbes famously invoked the notion of human "state of nature." This idea can be interpreted as innate or natural human mindset, psychology, and attitude. In this condition, as understood by Hobbes, an individual's actions are bound only by one's personal need (or desire) and the power one possesses to fulfill that desire vis-à-vis another person. In this state of nature, Hobbes had declared human life to be "nasty" and "brutish,"[641] needing "the terrour of some Power"[642] so that "Justice, Equity" may prevail.

Hobbes, therefore, prescribed the despotic tyranny and arbitrary power of an absolute sovereign.[643] The draconian solution Hobbes ordained was needed to counter the "dissolute condition of masterlesse men, without subjection to Lawes, and a coercive Power to tye their hands from rapine, and revenge."[644]

Clearly, the Hobbesian human state of nature being nasty and brutish, the human being is asocial and amoral. For the purpose of this chapter, however, the most important point is that the human "state of nature" under the Hobbesian philosophy leaves no room for *human agency*. We are, therefore, by our inherent instinct doomed to brutalize one another unless a vicious power inflicts its subjugation upon us.

Within the realm of Enlightenment philosophy, the luminary who most vociferously opposed Hobbes was Jean-Jacques Rousseau. In his *Discourse on the Moral Effects of the Arts and Sciences*,[645] Rousseau decries "the pernicious reflections of Hobbes"[646] and makes an allusion to Hobbes as the philosopher who "informs you that men are only beasts of prey, and may conscientiously devour one another."[647] (Such toxic hostility[648] may be rather common within the domain of philosophy, just like other fields.)

Let's also briefly comment[649] on Rousseau's famous and oft-quoted surmise about "the natural goodness of man." In using an imaginary[650] course of human evolution, Rousseau essentially concluded that man was good-natured originally, in primeval or primitive[651] state, and was spoiled by society.

Paradoxically, the philosopher's solution to regain goodness and overcome the spoilage by society is even more society[652]—and of a legal kind—because "whoever refuses to obey the general will[653] shall be compelled to do so by the whole body. This means nothing less than that he will be forced to be free ... In this lies the key to the working of the political machine."[654]

The Orwellian notion of being "forced to be free" notwithstanding, Rousseau's argument also is that man is naturally non-moral, and it is this civilizing process that allows the human being to become a moral being.[655]

In short, it is not just Hobbes but also Rousseau who considers the original human condition to be non-moral. While Rousseau, more so than Hobbes, accepts the human capacity for choice (ability to act against instinct), it is still the law and the force of the state that promulgate not only the common good but also morality itself. It is, thus, not just the Hobbesian world but also the Rousseauian realm where the presence of adequate human agency seems to be a wishful and dubious concept.

Before referring to scriptures, we'll briefly underscore that, as science advances, our understanding of concepts such as the moral and social aspects of human nature[656] is also evolving to a more balanced and, arguably, more human and rational direction. Ralph Holloway has been a pioneer paleoneurologist (scholar of brain evolution) at Columbia University. In an evolutionary context, Holloway clarifies that "language grew out of a social behavioral cognitive matrix which was basically cooperative rather than aggressive ..."[657]

Harvard's evolutionary biologist Marc Hauser, in *Moral Minds: How Nature Designed Our Universal Sense of Right and Wrong*, theorizes on the basis of his fieldwork that humans have evolved a universal moral instinct that unconsciously guides us towards judgment of right and wrong, and that the brain has a genetically driven system for acquiring moral rules. (We have to keep in mind that these scientists are functioning within and promoting

Darwinian evolutionary theory with scant room for God in the analytical framework.)

With this background, we now refer to the scriptural message about human nature, especially its social and moral aspects. At first glance, it would seem that a species whose essence carries the divine breath and image must be unquestionably good. The reality, though, is quite different. Compared to Enlightenment philosophy, the scriptural lesson about human nature is considerably more sophisticated, nuanced, and enfranchising. The message of our religions seems to be that divine goodness is ever-present in the creation and yet man is a choice-maker—a being with agency. The quotes below illumine the teachings of our religions regarding human nature, morality, and agency. The reader just has to find their own interpretation.

> Consider the human self, and how it is formed in accordance with what it is meant to be, and how it is imbued with moral failings as well as with consciousness of God! To a happy state shall indeed attain he who causes this [self] to grow in purity, and truly lost is he who buries it [in darkness].
>
> —Qur'an 91:7-10

> Finally, brethren, whatever things are true, whatever things are noble, whatever things are just, whatever things are pure, whatever things are lovely, whatever things are of good report, if there is any virtue and if there is anything praiseworthy—meditate on these things.
>
> —Philippians 4:8

> You have been told, O man, what is good,
And what the Lord requires of you:
Only to do justice
And to love goodness,
And to walk modestly with your God.[658]
>
> —Micah 6:8

My grace overspreads everything.

—Qur'an 7:156

He who looks inwardly at the self revels in the self;
He who revels in the self looks inwardly at the self.

—Acaranga Sutra 2.173

I am the self abiding
in the heart of all creatures;
I am their beginning,
their middle, and their end.

—*Bhagavad Gita* 10.20

AND SO, set thy face steadfastly towards the [one ever-true] faith, turning away from all that is false, in accordance with the natural disposition which God has instilled into man: [for] not to allow any change to corrupt what God has thus created—this is the [purpose of the one] ever-true faith; but most people know it not.

—Qur'an 30:30

THE SPIRITUAL NATURE OF MAN (CONFUCIANISM: DOCTRINE OF THE MEAN 16)

Confucius said, "The power of spiritual forces in the universe—how active it is everywhere! Invisible to the eyes and impalpable to the senses, it is inherent in all things, and nothing can escape its operation."

It is the fact that there are these forces which make men in all countries fast and purify themselves, and with solemnity of dress institute services of sacrifice and religious worship. Like the rush of mighty waters, the presence of unseen Powers is felt; sometimes above us, sometimes around us. In the *Book of Songs* it is said,

> The presence of the Spirit:
> It cannot be surmised,
> How may it be ignored!

Such is the evidence of things invisible that it is impossible to doubt the spiritual nature of man.

Insert 15:1

Rabbi Moses Cordovero (sixteenth century) expressed the Creator-creation connection with these words: "The essence of divinity is found in every single thing—nothing but it exists. Since it causes every thing to be, no thing can live by anything else. It enlivens them; its existence exists in each existent."[659] How much the human benefits from the ever-present essence of divinity is still a matter of choice because, as Rabbi Heschel puts it, "without nobility of the spirit, flesh is full of darkness."[660]

And Rumi's advice (*Masnavi* 3:3419-20) in this regard is also clear: the human core is precious and can be sought only purposefully:

> The core of every fruit is better than its rind:
> consider the body to be the rind,
> and its friend, the spirit, to be the core.
> After all, the Human Being has a precious core;
> seek it, inspired by the Divine breath.

Even empirically, the very fact that we have almost a universal discernment and consensus on right and wrong (in a broad sense) shows the innate presence of an internal socio-moral compass within us. Whether we are willing to view it as a divine attribute is a matter of personal discernment and should remain so.

God's Image, Spirit, and Breath Reflected in the Human

There is a common theme in scriptures creating a rather direct connection between the Creator and the creation (at least the human form of it). The quotes below shed some light on it to facilitate the reader's interpretation.

> And God said, "Let us make Adam in our image, after our likeness ..." God created man in His own image, in the image of God He created him, male and female He created them.
>
> —Genesis 1:26-27

> The Lord God formed Adam from the dust of the earth. He blew into his nostrils the breath of life, and Adam became a living being.
>
> —Genesis 2:7

> And then He forms him in accordance with what he is meant to be, and breathes into him of His spirit: and [thus, O people,] He endows you with hearing, and sight, and feelings as well as minds: [yet] how seldom are you grateful!
>
> —Qur'an 32:9

> He gave you the praanaa, the breath of life, and your mind and body.
> He is the Support of the heart.
>
> —Sri Guru Granth Sahib, M.5, 51

> My womb is the great infinite spirit;
> in it I place the embryo,
> and from this, Arjuna, comes
> the origin of all creatures.
>
> —*Bhagavad Gita* 14.3

> For each and every form He is the Model;
> it is His form that is to be seen everywhere.
>
> —*Rig Veda* 6.47.18

As these excerpts indicate, the idea of Divine "breath" is shared by many religions. While the excerpts from Gita and Rig Veda do not mention "breath," it is worth noting that the *Maitri Upanishad* fully details the five types of divine breath—Prana, Apana, Samana, Udana, and Vyana. The scripture describes the upward and downward movement of breath within the human body and throughout each limb, clarifying their relationship to life and death: "So he [Prajapati, the Lord of Creation] divided himself fivefold—he who is spoken of as the Prana breath, the Apana breath, the Samana breath, the Udana breath, the Vyana breath."[661]

It is the understanding enunciated in these scriptural messages that is central to our concepts of worship, servitude, as well as our relationship to other creation—further developing to inform even our concept of prayer and its efficacy. This understanding, though, has myriad ways of expanding our horizon in finding our place within creation and, perhaps more importantly, in finding our relationship with the rest of the creation.

Love: The Foundation of All Relationship

How then do we locate and manifest this spiritual connection? Various traditions have used different expressions with similar connotations (such as union, samadhi, nibbana, mukti, moksha, fa'na, etc.) in describing *unio mystica*, the ultimate goal of a human's spiritual journey. The emotion that powers the journey, however, can be most fittingly captured using the word "love." The emanation of this emotion is from the relationship with the Creator, and then spreads within the creation.

The "love" we are talking about here, though, is quite a bit different from the popular amorous sentiment in today's global society. Intrinsically, it is not limited to a very small circle, and it also is not connected with our own desire. Even T. S. Eliot's "love beyond desire" may fall short if it carries a physical connotation or conditionality to it. Viktor Frankl, an eminent twentieth-century neuroscientist, captures the idea closely: "Love is the only way to grasp another human being in the innermost core of his personality. No one can become fully aware of the very essence of another human being unless he loves him." This expression leads us to a love beyond desire, beyond recompense, beyond need. Love as a search and a quest—love for the sake of love alone. Simply a manifestation of the inner being, love is the expression of the innate essence a soul carries.

In his book *Love in Action*, Thich Nhat Hanh highlights the capacities love endows: "Love enables us to see things that those who are without love cannot see."[662] In *Strength to Love*, Dr. King elaborates upon his own Love in Action doctrine, that real love only shines its light when it is woven in action.

> First, it is a marvelous expression of Jesus' ability to match words with actions. One of the greatest tragedies of life is that men seldom bridge the gulf between practice and profession, between doing and saying. A persistent schizophrenia leaves so many of us tragically divided against ourselves. On the one hand, we proudly profess certain sublime and noble principles, but on the other hand, we sadly practice the very antithesis of those principles. How often are our lives characterized by a high blood pressure of creeds and an anemia of deeds![663]

As some of the material in this and the surrounding chapters shows, the source of this love in action is transcendental. If the discrepancy Dr. King talks about can be classified as hypocrisy, then it comes from an overreliance on rationalism and pragmatism while undervaluing the spiritual essence we all commonly share (and which our scriptures have clearly highlighted). Ja'ami goes further to classify love as the only way out of the prison of one's own base ego:

> Try even a hundred different things in this world;
> It is love alone that will free you from your self.[664]

PASSIONATE LOVE FOR THE BELOVED

In a teaching titled "The Wedding Celebration," see how the *Zohar* attributes a verse from the *Song of Songs* (7:11) into a proclamation made by Rabbi Shim'on bar Yochai:

> 'I am my beloved's, his desire is upon me.' ...
> I have been bound in a single bond
> with the Blessed Holy One....
> I see all of them rejoicing in this,
> my wedding celebration!
> All of them are invited, in that world,
> to my wedding celebration.[665]

In a similarly intimate exclamation, Guru Arjan Dev Ji worded it this way:

> My Beloved Husband Lord is deep within my heart. How can I see Him? ... The happy soul-bride is loved by her Husband.
>
> —*Sri Guru Granth Sahib*,
> M.5, 80 and 97

Insert 15:2

In Insert 15:2, we see the pure ecstasy of union being expressed by Rabbi Shim'on bar Yochai as well as Guru Arjan Dev Ji. Rabi'a al-Adawiyya had expressed it similarly:

> And my Beloved is with me always,
> For His love I can find no substitute, ...
> Thou wast the source of my life
> and from Thee also came my ecstasy.
> I have separated[666] myself from all created beings,
> My hope is for union with Thee,
> for that is the goal of my desire.[667]

What is the nature of this relationship—between the servant and the Served, the creature and the Creator, the lover and the Beloved—that evokes such a sentiment? How can we understand this intimate relationship that these blessed people are talking about? As narrated by Fariduddin Attar of Nishapur, the famous twelfth-century Persian poet, Rabi'a al-Adawiyya went further in elaborating her understanding when someone asked her to explain what love is: "Love has come from Eternity and passes into Eternity and none has been found in seventy thousand worlds who drinks one drop of it until at last he is absorbed in God, and from that comes the saying 'He loves them (His saints) and they love Him.'"[668]

Understanding this also helps one realize that passionate love for the Ultimate Reality also entails love for creation, all of it, especially the fellow humans—who are the product of the same "Breath," and are shaped in accordance with the same "Image" that shines through one's own self. It is this state of our human spirituality that expresses and manifests itself as human agency in service of the rest of the creation.

Self-knowledge a Requisite to Human Agency

In chapter 17, we'll discuss the human heart as the seat of self-knowledge where the question "who am I" can be answered. It is this self-knowledge that empowers a human being to step up to the agency one is being asked to assume. The concept of this journey being ceaseless and "self-annihilating" is expressed by Rumi in Insert 15:3.

ANNIHILATION IN THE FLAME OF LOVE

In *Fihi ma Fihi*, Rumi says:

> Therefore, the man who can do without God and makes no effort is no man at all; whilst if he were able to comprehend God, that indeed would not be God. Therefore, the true man is he who is never free from striving, who revolves restlessly and ceaselessly

> about the light of the Majesty of God. And God is He who consumes man and makes him naught, being incomprehensible by reason.[669]

In Persian and South Asian poetry, moth's love for flame (of a lamp) is a common motif. The lover (moth) annihilates itself in the beloved (flame). In Rumi's poetry, similarly, reason/self gets annihilated in the "fire" of the Beloved (God), thus reaching its objective. The difference, however, is that the moth may not know the price or the outcome of its love, but the human does. Not only that, this knowledge is the very driver of why the human seeks "annihilation" (fa'na).

Insert 15:3

As Rumi alluded to, it may take some time for the seeker to even realize that what they seek is not up there toward the sky; it is instead the realm of yonder, even beyond; and that the quest begins within. The first challenge is to understand and transcend the sectarian, purposefully divisive and politically convenient notions widely promoted. The second is to find out how to realize one's selfhood (by letting go of and rising above one's own base-ego).

Our spiritual traditions have provided the guidance and have pointed out the challenges of the journey.[670] Rabbi Isaac ben Samuel of Acre (thirteenth century) has some advice to offer: "Strive to see supernal light, for I have brought you into a vast ocean. Be careful! ... Strive to see yet escape drowning. Your soul will see that divine light—actually cleave to it—while dwelling in her palace."[671]

And this from the *Svetasvatara Upanishad* (4.8) further clarifies the importance of seeking the light that resides within our heart: "If the Self of which the scriptures speak is not known by the seeker, what use are scriptures to him?"[672]

Tikkun and its Place in Human Agency

Tikkun (repair or mending) provides a good vehicle to illustrate human relationship with the Divine as well as the rest of the creation. This Jewish mystical concept was introduced by Rabbi Isaac Luria as part of the Kabbalistic tradition. The idea was then adopted and popularized in Hasidic thought. In the present time, in addition to the Hasidic practice of this concept, the Jewish Reform movement has further popularized the term to refer to the *mitzvot* (commandments) that enhance social and environmental repair. Most of us have heard the expression *Tikkun Olam* (literally, world repair or heal the world). As this section shows, the notion is that holiness exists in a broken yet potential form in everything, and it is the role of human agency to reintegrate and repair the sparks of holiness.

The idea of Tikkun used in the theme of this book comes from the captivating Lurianic theory of creation. According to the proposition, before the creation of this world/universe, *Ein Sof* (The Infinite) occupied the complete space of existence. To facilitate the emanation of the world/universe, Ein Sof withdrew itself from some of that "space." The term "*Tsimtsum*," literally contraction, signifies that Ein Sof withdrew[673] "from itself to itself." Ein Sof then emanated a ray of light into that "vacuum" through channels into vessels (*kelim*).

Some of the vessels could not withstand the light and shattered.[674] Along with the shards, some "sparks" also fell within this new creation and became trapped in material existence. As humans, our task is to liberate these sparks and raise or restore them to divinity. Even the most mundane action we take in our lives either promotes or impedes Tikkun, thus influencing our discovery of God. As the Tikkun theory clarifies, the emanation responsible for creation resulted in these "sparks." Human endeavor—to free these sparks, restore them to divinity—is how the concept makes actionably tangible a subtle and mystical understanding introduced centuries ago.

Tikkun as human responsibility is ubiquitous because every human action "reacts somewhere and somehow on this complicated process of Tikkun."[675] We have to be mindful here of something critical the concept leads to: the act that promotes Tikkun is being performed vis-à-vis the creation. The path to God through Tikkun, therefore, is through the rest of the creation.

Then, our disconnection (separation) from the creation is the source of our disconnection from God, and the attenuation of the former reverses the latter. As the *First Epistle of John* would tell us, the way to discover God—better yet, to have "[God's] love perfected in us"[676]—is to realize, reinstate, and reclaim our mutual connection with humans and then with the rest of the creation. There really is no "other" except the illusion that creates this disconnection from God's creation and thus from God. This realization brings forth not just a doctrinal obligation; it becomes a spiritual reservoir emanating responsibility and agency wherein "we are not only masters of our own destiny ... but we also fulfil a mission which reaches far beyond that."[677]

Understanding Spiritual Agency as Responsible Action

Viktor Frankl's experience of captivity at various Nazi concentration camps gave him a unique way of looking at life's lessons. In his book *Man's Search for Meaning*, Frankl emphasized the importance of responsibility in today's world and declared it to be an integral component of the very concept of freedom:

> Freedom, however, is not the last word. Freedom is only part of the story and half of the truth. Freedom is but the negative aspect of the whole phenomenon whose positive aspect is responsibleness. In fact, freedom is in danger of degenerating into mere arbitrariness unless it is lived in terms of responsibleness.[678] That is why I recommend that the Statue of Liberty on the East Coast be supplemented by a Statue of Responsibility on the West Coast.[679]

Frankl's observation was not just a theoretical understanding. It was about the prevalent state of mind as he observed in the middle of the last century. From the viewpoint of spiritual agency also the meaning becomes much clearer if we parse the notion of Freedom[680] into its two halves: Liberty and Responsibility.

In addition to legal constraints, our sense of responsibility comes from our internal moral compass that comprises instinct, intuition, intellect, and imagination.[681] All these faculties are formed by a society's culture, which is usually influenced by one or more spiritual systems. As explained in this chapter and others, our connection with the spiritual core is central to our human agency and its moral instrumentality. Intellect alone is insufficient in the deployment of our moral agency since it is not directly connected with the source of such moral guidance. A culture's main task, therefore, is to exhort the member of the society to adhere to the societal moral compass in spirit and substance.

When a human society no longer functions on the basis of culture, a vacuum is created. In the modern way of thinking, the legal system tries to partly fill that vacuum. And therein lies the problem—since there is an inverse correlation between law and liberty. From the vantage of freedom, therefore, law is an instrument of degradation—not facilitation—of liberty and freedom since it limits human agency.[682]

Part six approaches the discussion from an angle showing the practical and action orientation of our spiritual teachings. The content will exemplify that the guiding light from our spiritual teachings can be a beacon towards the exercise of collective agency.

In a society, an absence of instrumental culture results in a higher need for laws and a reduction in freedoms. The extreme in the Hobbesian paradigm would be the ultimate case of this spectrum. Instead, when our moral compass as its focus honors spiritual principles, we regain our agency to be who we are.

PART SIX:

RECLAIMING OUR SPIRITUAL CORE AND AGENCY

The heart in my bosom is made with fire of longing,
So that like a burning ember it stays aglow.[683]
—Hakeem Agha Jan Aish Dehlvi[684]

CHAPTER 16:

FAITH MOVES MOUNTAINS

And Jesus said unto them, Because of your unbelief: for verily I say unto you, If ye have faith as a grain of mustard seed, ye shall say unto this mountain, Remove hence to yonder place; and it shall remove; and nothing shall be impossible unto you.

—Matthew 17:20

Friedrich Nietzsche classed faith as the unwillingness to know the truth. Historically speaking, at least some components of the institution of religion seem to have helped develop the image that faith is blind and irrational; that it promotes pure dogma that defies thinking, and even reality. Even eminent people of faith have shared such a concern as was evident in Dr. King's words: "Must we not admit that the church has often overlooked this moral demand for enlightenment? At times it has talked as though ignorance were a virtue and intelligence a crime. Through its obscurantism, closedmindedness, and obstinacy to new truth, the church has often unconsciously encouraged its worshippers to look askance upon intelligence."[685]

Even in today's world, these concerns[686] are very much present within certain segments of most religious establishments—sometimes even loud enough to dominate the discourse.[687] Thus, in a manner of speaking, the image of "faith" being irrational may be justified on some dimension, though not as a whole and perhaps not in the way it is perceived.

Fundamentally though, faith lies not in being blind about reality. It is rather a state wherein we suspend our judgment and expectation that we can grasp or define the ultimate reality in its fullest. Yet, this state of humility is not about suspending our innate perceptivity and discernment that are inherent to our intellectual and spiritual faculties.

Reconciling Faith and Certainty

Doubt, according to Richard Feynman, is essential for morality. In a different sense, no less important though, ambiguity and uncertainty also constitute an essential ingredient of the phenomenon we call faith. The willingness, indeed, the eagerness, to change our minds as our awareness grows should be considered neither contradictory nor incompatible with faith. A mind open to reassessing and refining our beliefs is essential to our spiritual growth.[688] Even so, this openness to empiric perceptivity (that includes reason and rationalism) does not necessarily override our other perceptivities such as imagination, intuition, memory, and understanding.

It would be unwise to develop a firm belief in something without leaving some room for inquiry. Most of us with a firm religious belief would agree to that principle as regards most any domain. When it comes to religion also, we have to be able to discern where to place an unshakeable faith, and where we remain on a voyage of discovery. Religion, as its function, provides us that light which illuminates our path throughout the journey.

Faith and empirical/logical "certainty" can often be two different things, sometimes even diametrically opposed to each other. A reconciliation with this reality sometimes seems to present a significant challenge to religious establishments. And yet it behooves us to realize that the landscape of the "certainty" of our various non-religious beliefs may also be peppered with nuances, contradictions, and doubts.

Just like any other field of knowledge, virtually everyone will face some degree of difficulty in grasping certain concepts in religion.[689] Moreover, in the case of religion, the limitation is not just our sensory abilities. Our logical mind and intuitive faculties also struggle to readily comprehend spiritual wisdom. The transmission of spiritual knowledge, therefore, necessitates the use of fables, parables, analogies, and heart-based teachings. When it comes to more complex topics, even the human language and other constructs simply cannot provide an adequate description. Paradox and contradiction, of whatever type, don't have to be always looked upon as incompatibility, especially when it comes to our understanding of God.

Feynman once also defined science as a belief in the ignorance of experts (though scientists today do not generally acknowledge, or perhaps even do not seem to comprehend, what he meant). He goes on to class "the scientific spirit of adventure" as "the humility of the intellect."[690] As a corollary, faith is to be looked upon as the humility of one's spirit. In short, a belief system anchored in question, inquisitiveness and exploration is more likely to lead us where we are trying to go in any field that requires comprehension of complexity.

Another way to understand this is by way of the concept of contingency.[691] Every piece of our empirical knowledge (or science) rests upon various other empirical phenomena and assumptions. Any movement in that base of information can drastically alter our understanding of the "piece" under discussion (Newtonian physics is a good example). We simply cannot know when and if one of those underlying assumptions will change—and shake the foundation that other parts of science are based upon.

Faith in God, though indeed still a belief, rests on stronger ground. We can see here that the ground itself, while unknowable, is non-contingent; it does not rely upon some other factor for its own validity. In a manner of speaking, the "direction" of our understanding that produces faith can be the opposite of how empiricism works. Here, we reflect upon the signs available to us; this would include every aspect of the physical world and its existence as well as the subtle wisdom in our scripture. It is thus reflection, not rationalism, that strengthens our faith.

Reflection—The Doorway to Knowledge and Faith

It is through the augmented perceptivity that we, mostly on an individual basis, reach something we call faith. The deeper that process of "reflection," the more secure our faith can be as evidenced by respect for and accommodation of others' belief systems. On the other hand, the shallower our process of reflection, the more insecure we would be in our faith. Even though one may paradoxically think one has a "strong" faith in this state, the rigidity would bring "brittleness" instead of flexibility, as well as intolerance of others. We can also be certain: this tendency to reflect or ponder does not provide us formal proofs of the existence of the Way, or the Dharma, or God. It's about "discovering" that Truth by the full deployment of our various perceptive faculties, and by "lifting any veils"[692] on our minds and hearts. Here's a translation of Iqbal's famous verse implying faith's potential in the following manner:

> The hallmark of one without faith is that he is lost
> within the universe;
> The hallmark of one with faith is that lost within
> him is the universe.[693]

We humans have access to myriad modes of perceptivity. Sensory, empirical, and logical modes provide us the fundamental vehicles to comprehend the physical and sensory phenomena. Our understanding of the divine, however, is not by sensory and logical modes. The spiritual journey of understanding begins with reflection and cannot be arrived at through empiric experimentation or strictly logical convincing by an authority. Reflection, though, is just the beginning of accessing our deeper perceptive faculties since the spiritual journey is not consummated through reflection alone; other modes of perceptivity are needed to go further.

> When the mind is cleansed
> by the grace of wisdom,
> he is seen by contemplation
> —the One without parts.
>
> —Mundaka Upanishad, 3.1.8

Religion quite frequently provides spiritual guidance using reminders and signs visible to us so we may discern. Such reflection and discernment take us beyond empiricism alone. Even what we take for granted as "natural" can open up deeper levels of meaning through the process of reflection. As the *Qur'an* (45:12) says: "God it is Who has subjected to you the sea that ships may sail therein by His command, that you may earn of God's bounty [through trade] and that you may be grateful... therein are signs for people who reflect."

The verse above, for example, is an invitation to reflect upon—with gratitude—how the laws of physics support all existence in a myriad of ways, including human commerce. With this gratitude comes humility for all that we have at our disposal, and a sense of responsibility to the trust placed upon the human race. This would mean that we don't pollute the oceans, we protect the purity of the air we breathe and, in general, refrain from plundering the natural resources made available to us. If we abdicate the concept of service to the rest of the creation in pursuit of purely selfish interests, then the human race defies the responsibility we carry.

The process of such spiritual reflection and discernment does not follow some prescribed method or formula. (For example, to describe this reflection process, the *Qur'an* uses words such as *tadhakkur*, *tadabbur*, *tafakkur*, *faqaha*, and *hikma*. Comprehending what's implied is difficult enough; the difficulty of translating such words is evident.) Such expression of one's spiritual faculties involves a continual interplay of seeking, observing, testing, asking, receiving, listening, contemplating, and learning. If we allow that process to work beyond doctrine, our inner truth then takes over as the guide. Even here, humility and *adab* (applied & practical ethics), for example, would be part of the recipe.

A well-known hadith says: "An hour's reflection is better than a year's worship." When questioned if reflection was even better than reading the *Qur'an*, Prophet Muhammad's response was: "And, can the *Qur'an* be useful without knowledge?"[694]

The *Qur'an* itself, at 41:53, goes much further: "In time We shall make them fully understand Our messages [through what they perceive] in the utmost horizons [of the universe] and within themselves, so that it will become clear unto them that this [revelation] is indeed the truth. [Still,] is it not enough [for them to know] that thy Sustainer is witness unto everything?"

Understanding Reflection: An Example

The "signs" within nature and within us, when combined with the message in the scripture, support our journey towards realizing our full spiritual potential. This paradigm of reflecting upon the "signs," while subjective, may yield rather strong and foundational understandings. Our cultural and spiritual understandings of various phenomena are full of examples that show human possession of wisdom and knowledge well before science had access to such knowledge.

For example, half a century ago, my mother explained to me that our physical and spiritual being is strongly influenced by our thoughts and even the words we use. And that those thoughts as well as words can manifest within us—even physically. The need thus to exercise care and prudence in that regard. My understanding from that teaching always was that words and thoughts act as bio-symbols. (Bio-symbol could be understood as a message interpreted by the human mind and body; and then manifested in a psychological or physical sense.)

Author of *The Mindbody Code*, Mario Martinez is a renowned neuropsychologist. Using empiric methods, his groundbreaking global research has led him to a new scientific discovery: Our thought patterns, and even the words we use, create bio-symbols that our body interprets, directly impacting not just our emotional state but also our physical well-being.

How did my mother, who did not even have a secondary-school diploma, know what science would "discover"[695] half a century later? The answer is simple: She had been educated through the transmission of cultural wisdom emanating from her Islamic faith. She then transmitted it to me. I reflected upon it at some point in time and decided to adopt it as a matter of a belief system (without any "scientific" proof, yet after a rigorous process of reflection). Consequently, I have been careful all my life about the words I use and the thoughts I entertain. In this case, for a very long time, faith carried the wisdom that science just recently discovered.

To promote reflection and discernment, our religions may sometimes evoke ambiguity and uncertainty. It would be more fruitful to have the reaction of reflection to deepen our understanding rather than a thoughtless literal belief in everything. The profession of faith thus becomes an expression of our humility—we humans may be fundamentally unequipped and ill-equipped to "scientifically" know God, the Way, the Shari'ah, or the Dhamma.

Divine Wisdom for Human Benefit

In the book of Ecclesiasticus (the *Apocrypha)*, the divine Wisdom speaks in a female[696] voice to inform us of the following:

> I am the word spoken by the most High;
> it was I who covered the earth like a mist.
> My dwelling place was in high heaven;
> my throne was in a pillar of cloud.
> Alone I made a circuit of the sky
> and traversed the depth of the Abyss.
> The waves of the sea. the whole earth,
> every people and nation were under my sway...
> Before time began He created me.
> and until the end of time I shall endure
> In the sacred tent I ministered in his presence.[697]

It's indeed no surprise, therefore, that our scriptures may even contain information that was simply not on the human radar until relatively recently. The following are from the *Qur'an*:

> NOW, INDEED, We create man out of the essence of clay,[698] and then We cause him to remain as a drop of sperm in [the womb's] firm keeping, and then we create out of the drop of sperm a germ-cell, and then We create out of the germ-cell an embryonic lump, and then We create within the embryonic lump bones, and then We clothe the bones with flesh—and

> then We bring [all] this into being as a new creation (23:12-14); ... and that it is He who creates the two kinds—the male and the female—out of a mere drop of sperm as it is poured forth (53:45-46); ... Was he not once a [mere] drop of sperm that had been split, and therefore became a germ-cell—whereupon He created and formed [it] in accordance with what [it] was meant to be, and fashioned out of it the two sexes, the male and the female? (75:37-39).
>
> ARE, THEN, they who are bent on denying the truth not aware that the heavens and the earth were [once] one single entity, which We then parted asunder, and [that] we made out of water every living thing? Will they not, then, [begin to] believe? (21:30); ... AND IT IS We who have built the universe with [Our creative] power, and, verily, it is We who are steadily expanding it (51:47).

How is it that, fifteen hundred years ago, the scripture provided information about embryonic development, sex determination through sperm, origin of life in water, and the expanding universe—when those subjects were not even being explored, let alone understood? Should we really be surprised that other scriptures, such as the Rig Veda, may contain information that could not have been readily "knowable" in ancient times?

Clearly, however we justify it, a belief in God cannot be classified as scientific—or even rational, the way we understand these terms. (And that's consistent with atheism, which can be classified neither as scientific nor rational.) Informed believers understand that point and feel no need to deny whatsoever that scientific knowledge does not always comport with certain elements of religious belief. Accepting that complementarity and seeming incompatibility between faith and science may be the best way for us to continue to expand our awareness towards greater understanding and knowledge in both the domains. As history shows, science continues to discover new realities that bring about a change in its own belief system.

The Not-So-Advanced Science

It should be no surprise to find examples where religion has been ahead of science in promoting scientific knowledge. The divergent incentives perhaps keep science from being of full service to humanity. The practice of fasting would be a good example. For reasons of spiritual and physical health, fasting has been prescribed by most religions—in some cases as a mandatory practice. For thousands of years, the practice has been a norm and its benefits known. Yet, even today, most physicians would have no understanding of it. Arguably, only one discipline (known as functional medicine) within the conventional Western system of medicine has started clinically applying the practice of fasting for its health benefits. And the results being discovered are truly eye-opening.

Why has "scientific" medicine been such a laggard in exploring a practice that religion has practiced for millennia? Should we really be so surprised to find other areas where science is similarly way behind in its understanding? There may be another question to ask though: who will provide financial incentives to the current industrial structures (medicine and pharmaceutical) to promote the benefits of fasting, or other phenomena that do not offer commercial benefit? It is these aspects of structural incentives that get overlooked when evaluating the reasons behind decisions in structured domains.

Probing from a different angle, it's not just the overall concept of fasting that seems to elude science. The Buddha advised us some 3,000 years ago to avoid eating late in the day. As reported in 2020 by *The Journal of Clinical Endocrinology & Metabolism*, a new study[699] at Johns Hopkins shows that eating late at night worsens glucose tolerance and reduces fatty acid oxidation.

Bertrand Russell was a big proponent of science and went so far as to say: "What science does not tell, humanity will never know." If we use Aristotelian syllogism in reference to Russell's statement and the Buddha's advice, the logical conclusion is inescapable: the Buddha was a scientist, so advanced that it took modern science some three millennia to catch up on only one of his discoveries. Where did the Buddha's scientific knowledge come from? What all else, within the Buddha's teaching, will science accept to be scientific in the near future? How about the rest of the unfathomable wisdom in the teachings of other prophets and sages?

Stating that science and religion are complementary—not rivals—to each other, Dr. King had clearly defined such complementarity: "Science keeps religion from sinking into the valley of crippling irrationalism and paralyzing obscurantism. Religion prevents science from falling into the marsh of obsolete materialism and moral nihilism."[700] Incidentally, a closer observation of today's world shows evidence of both paralyzing obscurantism and moral nihilism—leveraging each other to worsen the intellectual and spiritual impoverishment of the human race. This understanding further promotes the importance of reflection and discernment in our thinking patterns, not blind adherence to the belief systems that various institutions or individuals promote, whether in the name of religion or science.

As Zen Master Dogen Zenji clarifies in his *Genjokoan*: "Those who have great realization about delusion are buddhas. Those who are greatly deluded within realization are sentient beings."[701] And Lao Tzu (*Tao Te Ching* 41:5-8) expressed it this way:

> When the inferior man hears the Way,
> he laughs at it loudly.
> If he did not laugh,
> it would not be fit to be the Way.

The Ethical Calling of Faith

In religion, as in other facets of the human phenomenon, to understand and be understood offers us all the best path for growth and evolution. Our refusal to understand others, however, also creates the risk that if we choose not to exercise our God-given critical faculties, we open ourselves to be psychologically exploited by opportunists.

A dispassionate look tells us that the scriptures almost universally have man's conduct as their primary aim. That statement definitively applies to the *Qur'an*. In religions where the absolute centrality of God in the entire system of existence is evident, it provides another powerful beacon in the journey so that one's conduct may become fully commendable—even in God's eyes, so to speak.

The relationship between God and man is that of the Served and the servant, respectively. And it is this acceptance that informs the human's connection to the rest of the creation. If all the creation has been created to serve, then that places a special responsibility on humans to understand the interdependence that is needed for coexistence. In other words, the human being is not in service if the human race keeps upsetting the natural balance for the rest of the creation. This understanding is the catalyst that cannot be replaced by science, or the state, or rationalism, or even philosophy. And that realization, when we have clarified the difference between authority and power,[702] is what allows man to pursue his interests without becoming autocratic, blithely selfish, and hazardous to his own well-being.

Faith, in its deeper meaning, therefore, is not about a blind set of beliefs or a thoughtless disregard for what is prima facie evident or scientifically irrefutable. Quite to the contrary, faith can bring authority and agency in our lives that is otherwise almost inconceivable. Faith (with or without institutionalized religion) can therefore be looked upon as:

- surrendering to what we do not have the capability to understand
- accepting what is not within our control
- allowing perceptivity, imagination, and inventiveness to go beyond physical or other constraints imposed by the prevalent orthodoxy of other systems of knowing
- being in the world with a purpose; acquiring an internal mode of thinking, feeling, and acting meaningfully (instead of merely following external regulations)
- serving without the expectation of recompense; being hopeful when facing desperate circumstances

- finding the meaning in existence and in the transcendence of our own existence
- learning how to respect the rest of the creation
- developing the courage and willingness to give one's life to save that of a complete stranger
- looking in the eyes of someone from another continent and feeling the connectedness of mutual respect, of commonality, indeed of oneness that the material world cannot feel

Our concept of what we call science simply does not offer the benefits as enunciated here. Most other current fields of knowledge do not offer any such guidance. To find that "something else" that is needed to fill the vacuum, we have to look for a system of moral and ethical principles such as culture, philosophy and religion. No other social institution can meet this need. Culture in today's "legal" world is arguably a devitalized, if not a decommissioned, concept—except for some indigenous societies who have not gone through the conversion to extreme materialism and substitution by legal systems. Thus, all we are really left with is philosophy and religion. The two fields are not mutually exclusive at all—even within the orthodoxy of Enlightenment thought—and can work together. As Dr. Pfau's example in Insert 16:1 illustrates, there are certain domains where religion becomes a unique and singular force in the motivation and agency we humans need to work for our collective interest.

A HUMAN BEING WHO DEFINED HUMANITY[703]

On a Saturday in August 2017, Pakistani soldiers carried the flag-draped coffin of Dr. Ruth Pfau, a German-born Catholic nun, to a state funeral.

Born in Leipzig, Germany, Ruth Pfau studied medicine and subsequently joined the Order of the Daughters of the Heart of Mary. In

1960, she visited the Marie Adelaide Leprosy Center ("MALC") in Karachi and decided to stay and help. She stayed there the rest of her life. Leprosy is now under control in Pakistan; the country is on its way to becoming leprosy-free—thanks to the work done by Dr. Pfau.

"Not only did she treat the leprosy patients, she also gave them back their dignity ... a human being who defined humanity." said Adibul Hasan Rizvi, a well-known physician, at her memorial. According to journalist Zubeida Mustafa, "She visited patients' homes to speak to their families about leprosy and raise awareness about it. This was how she changed people's thinking [about leprosy]."

Honored by various states, Dr Pfau received numerous awards, including the Order of the Cross (Germany), Hilal-e-Imtiaz (Pakistan), the Damien-Dutton Award (USA), Albert Schweitzer Gesellschaft Award (Austria), and the Ramon Magsaysay Award for Public Service (the Philippines).

As described by Mutaher Zia, a physician at MALC, "Her day used to start with her attending the early morning service at the St Patrick's Cathedral when there would be few people there. When she died, the St Patrick's Cathedral was filled to brim with people from all faiths. She was a unifying force in life and death."

Insert 16:1

Dr. Pfau's example would move any human being, religious or not. Given how human ideologies are driving the human race into inexplicable misery, is there one ideology we can name that is capable of producing such an example of selfless service? Is there any human construct that is likely to move a human being to manifest the immense ocean of love as Dr. Pfau did? The agency exercised by one person, Dr. Pfau, far outweighed the non-agency of millions in society.

Religion, perhaps more than some other constructs of identity, can create an unusual human bond of kinship even among strangers. Through this bond, religion can create a multiplier effect that is unusual in the power it generates. And this is in addition to spirituality being a rather potent source of agency within the human heart and mind—as we see in Dr. Pfau's example. Chapters 17 and 18 clarify the central role of human heart in manifesting the human-Divine connection, and how this connection is the key to manifesting human agency.

The collective human goal should be to realize the vitality of the force that can move a human to extraordinarily positive decisions and actions. The human agency can then be leveraged for our collective benefit. And that is the fundamental thesis of this book.

CHAPTER 17:

HUMAN HEART—THE CENTER OF WISDOM AND DIVINE INSPIRATION

O my brother! A pure heart is as a mirror; cleanse it with the burnish of love and severence from all save God, that the true sun may shine within it and the eternal morning dawn.[704]

—Haft-Vadi, Chahar-Vadi
Seven Valleys, Four Valleys, 21

Nanak seeks the Sanctuary of God, the Master of all hearts. He is contained deep within each and every heart. He is always with you, as your Helper and Support.

—Sri Guru Granth Sahib. M.5, 48.2

The Self, rising in the firmament of the heart—sun of wisdom, darkness-dispersing, all-present, all-supporting— shines forth and illumines all.

—Adi Shankara. *Atma Bodha*, 114

In the popular modern expression, the heart is the source of feelings and emotions. Historically, going back to the Greek and Roman cultures, we see that heart was seen as the seat of life, intellect, soul, and emotion. Aristotle honored the heart by calling it the seat of the noblest emotions.[705]

Even within the context of rationalism, Enlightenment philosophy employed the concept of non-physical, non-observable "soul" or "spirit." Hegel's proclamation (quoted in chapter 15) about human spirit is one such example. Also, the notion of "beautiful soul" was promoted by German luminaries such as Goethe and Schiller. In "*On Grace and Dignity*" (1793), Friedrich Schiller expounds: "It is thus in a beautiful soul, that sensuousness and reason, duty and inclination harmonize, and grace is its epiphany."[706]

The realization of human soul as stated here by Schiller,[707] at least superficially,[708] seems to accept the inescapability of some type of a "spiritual" force. This occasional invocation of some form of human soul by Enlightenment philosophers seems to paradoxically protest the Enlightenment paradigm wherein "the Western scientific vision of a mechanical universe has created a philosophical or conceptual alienation from our own inherent spiritual nature."[709] Enlightenment thought, though, tells us nothing about where this "soul" comes from, or its relationship with the human body.

Heart: Abode of the "Inner Light"

Our spiritual cultures face no such limitation. In spirituality, heart's place has historically been quite central. The Quaker teaching about reliance on the "Inner Light" or the "Light of Christ," delves into a concept that is beyond our understanding of moral sensibility, intellectual insight, or even conscience. It would rather be fair to say that this Quaker concept is referring to the divine spirit and wisdom within us. Words from Bahá'u'lláh, Guru Arjan Dev Ji, and Adi Shankara in the epigraph above clarify that our heart is that abode where the soul resides and is the divine connection for human beings. And, as we can see in these teachings, there even seems to be a similarity in the description of something that may not be easily describable.

SAMPLE REFERENCES TO "HEART" IN THE UPANISHADS

The shining Self dwells hidden in the heart.
Everything in the cosmos, great and small,
Lives in the Self. He is the source of life,

> Truth beyond the transience of this world.
> He is the goal of life. Attain this goal!
>
> —Mundaka Upanishad 2.2.1-2
>
> The ignorant think the Self can be known
> By the intellect, but the illumined
> Know he is beyond the duality
> Of the knower and the known.
>
> —Kena Upanishad
>
> Insert 17:1

In Hinduism, as explained by Pandit Vamadeva Shastri, heart (*hridaya*) is:

> [The] seat of the Self or Atman in Vedantic thought. Realization of the Self in the heart is the main Vedantic formulation of Moksha or liberation... The heart is the source of our entire being. All our different faculties are like different rays branching out from the central light of the heart which is like the Sun... Yet the heart is not just the source of our individual existence (Atman). It is also our place of unity and connection with the cosmic existence (Brahman). It spreads not just through our entire individual beingness but throughout the entire universe... This heart or hridaya is obviously not the mere physical organ. Nor is it simply the heart center, the anahata chakra of the subtle body, though it is closely related to it. This heart is the core of our being, which is the core of Being itself. The heart is where we experience our own self-being and through it contact the nature of all things. This hridaya could be better called the 'spiritual heart' in distinction to the physical and subtle heart centers.[710]

In the *Qur'an*, the heart (*al-qalb*) is mentioned well over a hundred times, and only two of those instances seem to be a possible reference to the physical organ. Other closely-related words (*fu'ad, lubb/albab, sad'r, aq'l, naf's, sarira*) are also prevalent. The expression "eye of the heart" (*ayn al-qalb*) further shows the centrality of this faculty in comprehending the divine Reality. (To be clear, this "spiritual heart" is much more than the physical organ as well as the psychological faculty of feelings such as the "heart that melts.")

There's a canonical hadith qudsi: "My earth and My heaven do not encompass Me, but the heart of My servant who has faith does encompass Me." A short Sufi expression goes like this: "The heart of *mumin* (the person of faith) is the Throne of the All-Merciful" (*al-qalb al-mumin Arsh al-Rahman*). This doctrine highlights the significance and proximity of this perceptive human faculty to the knowledge of God. Heart was created to know ("see," *irfan*) God as the eye was created to see objective forms. Indeed, intellect does not have the capacity to "know" God since it lacks the spiritual "power" of the heart. As the *Qur'an* (50:37) says: "Surely in that is a reminder for whoever possesses a heart ..."

It is worth noting that the *Qur'an* does not say that the reminder is for whoever possesses an intellect. That is because, as Ibn Arabi explains, "the intellect restricts and seeks to define the truth within a particular qualification, while in fact the Reality does not admit of such limitation. It is not a reminder to the intellectuals and mongers of doctrinal formulations who contradict one another and denounce each other."[711]

SAMPLE REFERENCES TO "HEART" IN THE QUR'AN

Verily, in the remembrance of God do hearts find tranquility.

—*Qur'an* 13:28

Say [O Prophet]: Whoever is an enemy of Gabriel should know that he revealed this [Qur'an] to your heart by God's Will, confirming what came before it—a guide and good news for the believers.

—*Qur'an* 2:97

NOW, BEHOLD, this [divine writ] has indeed been bestowed from on high by the Sustainer of all the worlds: trustworthy divine inspiration has alighted with it from on high upon thy heart, [O Muhammad,] so that thou mayest be among those who preach in the clear Arabic tongue.

—*Qur'an* 26:192-195

And thus did [God] reveal unto His servant whatever He deemed right to reveal. The [servant's] heart did not give the lie to what he saw.

—*Qur'an* 53:10-11

We will show them Our signs in the universe and within themselves ...

—*Qur'an* 41:53

Insert 17:2

Heart: the Source of Self Knowledge

Ali ibn Uthman al-Hujwiri[712] (eleventh century) is considered the most revered Sufi saint of South Asia. (He is commonly known as *Daata Gunj Bakhsh*, munificent bestower of the treasure.) In his extant seminal treatise *Kashf al-Mahjub* (Revelation of the Hidden), he says, "The spirit in the body is like fire in fuel; fire is the creation (*makhluq*), and coal is manufactured (*masnu*)."[713] The inference delivered by al-Hujwiri's words is significant. It is the human spirit that has the primal status vis-à-vis the human body, which is a shell for the primal entity. One could also understand it as the spirit and the body being two entities representing the same essence in two different realms.

The Islamic Philosophy of Illumination (*hikmat al-Ishraq*)[714] was expounded by Shihab ad-Din al-Suhrawardi (twelfth century). This concept emphasizes, "... there is no real distinction in the essence of all beings, only in their degree of illumination with Divine Light."[715] This concept came to be known as the "grades of Being." Al-Hujwiri's teaching can be further explained by al-Suhrawardi's message that the distinction among the essence of all beings is that of degree only. This chapter talks about the vehicle in human possession: the heart which, through the choices it makes, can augment the degree of "possessing" the light.

The human heart sits at the threshold between the two realms, the physical and the spiritual. It is, therefore, the meeting point of our outer and inner knowledge. With its capacity to comprehend deep levels of quality and subtlety, this is the place where all human faculties, worldly and divine, are aggregated. This perceptive ability of the heart gives it the capacity to reach higher levels of knowledge not available to intellect, reason, or emotion. That is why it is said to be the only human "organ" and faculty that receives divine inspiration.

In our spiritual teachings, a heart is capable of knowing its own self. It is through this self-knowledge that the heart knows the creation and the Creator. "He who knows himself knows his Lord" (*man 'arafa nafsahu faqad 'arafa rabbahu*) is an Islamic tradition that highlights the importance of self-awareness as the path to proximity to God and awareness of God's infinitude. In her poetry, my grandmother expressed it as follows:

> In the rose it was You Manifest,
> I hadn't perceived.
> Every vista in the garden was You Manifest,
> I hadn't perceived.
> You are the First, You are the Last;
> being is the proof.
> My heart was the "Home of the Being,"
> I hadn't perceived.[716]

In *Shiur Qomah* (Ohr Yakar), Rabbi Moses Cordovero highlights the difference between the two states of being: first, where one's perceptivity is confined to the physicality of existence; and second, where one learns to unfold the mystery of existence by asking a simple question: Who am I? (I have added some notes for clarification.)

THE ENLIGHTENMENT OF ASKING "WHO AM I?"

An impoverished person thinks that God is an old man with white hair, sitting on a wondrous throne of fire that glitters with countless sparks, as the Bible states: 'The Ancient-of-Days sits, the hair on his head like clean fleece, his throne—flames of fire.'[Note a] Imagining this and similar fantasies, the fool corporealizes God. [Note b] He falls into one of the traps that destroy faith. His awe of God is limited by his imagination.

But if you are enlightened, you know God's oneness, you know that the divine is devoid of bodily categories—these can never be applied to God. Then you wonder, astonished: Who am I? [Note c] I am a mustard seed in the middle of the sphere of the moon, which itself is a mustard seed within the next sphere. So it is with that sphere and all it contains in relation to the next sphere. So it is with all the spheres—one inside the other—and all of them are mustard seeds within the further expanses. And all of these are mustard seeds within further expanses.

Your awe is invigorated, the love in your soul expands.[717]

Note a: Referring to Daniel 7:9

> **Note b**: Referring to a comment by Maimonides in *the Guide of the Perplexed.*
>
> **Note c**: *Mi anochi* (*Exodus* 3:11). King David also asks this question in *Samuel* II, 7:18. As indicated in chapter 9, Ramana Maharshi is well-known for this same question. Iqbal's religious philosophy of *khudi* (selfhood) revolves around a similar fulcrum.
>
> Insert 17:3

When we have not consciously encountered Rabbi Cordovero's question, we remain lost in the vast distractions of the world. Showing us the universe within is our reflective attitude towards that question, sometimes even leading to a discovery similar to that of Meister Eckhart: "God is closer to me than I am to myself"[718] as also stated in my grandmother's poetry above. The question, however, can only be addressed by the heart, not the intellect. A heart thus functions simultaneously as a mirror and a microcosm with an infinite capacity for knowledge. The following excerpt from a Sufi book talks about this infinite capacity carried by every heart:

> [Our spiritual aim is] to experience both the manifestation of God and the transcendence of God as a unity. Most of us are caught in the stage where we experience the manifestation of the universe and all its forms as something separate. However, manifestation is not really separate. It is individualized, but not separate. All manifestation is pervaded by the same reality. There is an inseparability of the limited and the absolute... The beautiful quality of the heart is it can simultaneously look at the separation and union of the soul. It can see both working at the same time. The heart has the capacity to accept simultaneously both your experience of separation from God and your feeling of union with the source.

> That is why the heart is so important in Sufism—because it has an almost infinite capacity. A sacred tradition has Allah affirming: 'The heavens and the earth cannot contain me, but the heart of my loving servant can.' Everything is taking place within the globe of the heart. It is in the infinite space of the heart that the possibility exists for the integration of the limited and the absolute.[719]

The story of Sadr al-Din al-Shirazi (commonly known as Mulla Sadra,[720] an eminent seventeenth-century Muslim philosopher) is worth mentioning here. Sadra propounded that ancient philosophies "conjoined to revealed truths as imparted to the prophets and the sages [formed] the highest expression of truth."[721]

A time came in Sadra's life when he withdrew from the world for a long time until, as described in his masterwork, his "heart caught fire, and the light of the divine world shone forth upon me ... and I was able to unravel mysteries which I had not previously suspected."[722] As a consequence, his *i'lm* (learning) took on new dimensions that he shared in the form of his magnum opus *kitab al-hikmah al muta'aliyah* (Book of Transcending Wisdom) also known as *kitab al-asfar al-arba'ah* (Book of Four Journeys), which refers to the journey of the Soul from and to the Creation and the Reality.

This detail simply clarifies the following: just like some other first-rate intellectuals such as al-Ghazali, mind alone proved insufficient as a perceptive vehicle to Sadra. Until he finally received the light in his heart, which he perceived to be from the grace of God, his intellect could not open the windows into the dimensions that resided within—only his "heart" could.

Heart and Health: New Frontiers of Scientific Research

The prevalent medical science has so far treated the heart as merely a pump in the body. The limited available scientific research, however, is now showing a very different picture. But the research we are about to see is not as commonly known as it should be—even within the clinical domain. Much of the research on the subject of "heart beyond a pump" has been conducted by the HeartMath

Institute, established circa 1990. (Except the heading in Insert 17:4, the information in the following paragraphs, presenting the research conducted by the HeartMath Institute, is a direct quote.)

> New research shows the human heart is much more than an efficient pump ... [it] also is an access point to a source of wisdom and intelligence that we can call upon to live our lives with more balance, greater creativity and enhanced intuitive capacities. All of these are important for increasing personal effectiveness, improving health and relationships and achieving greater fulfillment.[723]
>
> HeartMath research has demonstrated that different patterns of heart activity (which accompany different emotional states) have distinct effects on cognitive and emotional function. During stress and negative emotions, when the heart rhythm pattern is erratic and disordered, the corresponding pattern of neural signals traveling from the heart to the brain inhibits higher cognitive functions. This limits our ability to think clearly, remember, learn, reason, and make effective decisions. (This helps explain why we may often act impulsively and unwisely when we're under stress.) The heart's input to the brain during stressful or negative emotions also has a profound effect on the brain's emotional processes—actually serving to reinforce the emotional experience of stress.[724]
>
> In contrast, the more ordered and stable pattern of the heart's input to the brain during positive emotional states has the opposite effect—it facilitates cognitive function and reinforces positive feelings and emotional stability. This means that learning to generate increased heart rhythm coherence, by sustaining positive emotions, not only benefits the entire body, but also profoundly affects how we perceive, think, feel, and perform.[725]

Insert 17:4 indicates that the heart is a source of perceptivity and intelligence, and also has its own "brain" to process information that influences other organs in the body including the cranial brain. The heart is also the source of "energy" in the body.

SCIENCE CATCHING UP WITH SPIRITUALITY

We also observed that the heart acted as though it had a mind of its own and could significantly influence the way we perceive and respond in our daily interactions. In essence, it appeared that the heart could affect our awareness, perceptions and intelligence.[726]

Our and others' research indicates the heart is ... in fact, a highly complex information-processing center with its own functional brain ... that communicates with and influences the cranial brain via the nervous system, hormonal system and other pathways. These influences affect brain function and most of the body's major organs and play an important role in mental and emotional experience and the quality of our lives.[727]

We have learned, however, that communication between the heart and brain actually is a dynamic, ongoing, two-way dialogue, with each organ continuously influencing the other's function.[728]

[The] magnetic fields produced by the heart are involved in energetic communication... The heart is the most powerful source of electromagnetic energy in the human body, producing the largest rhythmic electromagnetic field of any of the body's organs ... more than 100 times greater in

> strength than the field generated by the brain and can be detected up to 3 feet away from the body, in all directions ... we have performed several studies that show the magnetic signals generated by the heart have the capacity to affect individuals around us.[729]
>
> —Excerpted from: The HeartMath Institute
>
> Insert 17:4

There is clearly much more information available on this subject. What needs emphasis, however, is the following: a large percentage of clinicians, even cardiologists and neurologists, would not have an adequate enough understanding—even awareness—of this research. What does it say about the present-day scientific research that is mostly funded by the pharmaceutical industry? (Chapter 3 and Appendix A cover the topic of how and why a structured institution revolves around self-benefit, rather than societal benefit.)

Heart: the Source of Wisdom

In John 15:5, Jesus says: "I am the vine; you are the branches. Anyone who dwells in me, as I dwell in him, bears much fruit; apart from me you can do nothing." The implication here seems to be that of an integral and intricate divine-human connection. It is thus the awareness of what resides inside of us that plays a key role in every facet of the life we lead. Our heart, being the central seat of discernment, is the faculty that can perceive and know the essence and the spirit that dwells within.

Sitting at the threshold, however, the heart can turn in any direction. In other words, whatever a heart is attached or attracted to provides the essential qualitative definition of that heart. An obsession with worldly attractions rusts the heart and takes away its capacity to manifest its innate qualities. Blameworthy qualities of heart that allow it to accumulate "rust" were listed by Abu Hamid al-Ghazali (eleventh century) under two classifications: Anger-related vices would include irascibility, arrogance, vengeance, violence, etc. Appetence-related vices would include greed, deception, possessiveness, stinginess, etc.[730]

The heart of one who craves worldly power and riches, for example, would have a qualitative disposition similar to such craving and would manifest appetence-related vices. This can paradoxically empower that heart and could be seen as a self-fulfilling prophecy. And that's the reason religious teachings exhort us to deliberately seek what would benefit our hearts.

The role of heart, versus the intellect, being the locus of wisdom may sound counterintuitive in the present time. Yet, this role needs to be recognized and understood. Our current life patterns and conditioning are inhospitable to accepting the heart's place to be higher than that of intellect. The limitation of the intellect, therefore, is important to be understood. In the *Futuhat al-Makkiyya* (I, 255-258), Ibn Arabi explains it:

> [If] these kinds of knowing were the result of thinking and reflection, human being (*insaan*, the inner reality of fully realized human being) could be circumscribed in a short period. But instead, these acts of knowing arrive from the Truly Real (*al-Haqq*), continually flowing into the heart of the (true) servant: they are His devoted spirits descending upon the servant from the world of His Unseen through His Lovingmercy.[731]

The place of heart as the locus of human wisdom is captured further by the condensed version of a hadith tradition (*an-Nawawi* #27): "Seek the guidance (*fatwa*)[732] of your heart, whatever opinion legal experts may give."[733]

In addition to the blameworthy qualities listed by al-Ghazali, the four tyrannies we discussed earlier (fear, want, victory, identity) act as a barrier to this awareness. A heart dominated by these tyrannies faces the limitations and perils created by them. As the spiritual connection is lost, so is the internal joy—which then gets replaced not just by day-to-day happiness from external stimuli, but also by the momentary pleasure obtained from fleeting distractions and hollow entertainment. It is not that there is anything wrong with pleasure. What's problematic is not realizing the propensity of what we seek and the state within which we seek it. Conditioning that limits our perceptivity limits our self-actualization and disables our heart from being our guide—disempowering us from achieving our potential.

Heart: the Locus of Human Agency

In the epigraph of this chapter, the message from Bahá'u'lláh advises of the need to burnish the mirror of the heart. The explanation below of this concept comes from the Sufi tradition, though there would be significant mutual similarity when we review the teachings in depth. Here is Rumi (*Masnavi*, 1:33-34):

> Love wants its tale revealed to everyone,
> But your heart's mirror won't reflect this Sun,
> Don't you know why we can't perceive it here?
> Your mirror's face is rusty—scrape it clear!

Our avoidance of the blameworthy qualities does serve a strong ethical and societal purpose. The spiritual aspect, though, may not be so apparent until we pay attention to it. Yet it is this connection that deserves much more awareness. To allow the divine to reflect within us, we are told to polish the mirror. To do that, one has to avoid the blameworthy qualities of the heart and acquire the praiseworthy qualities instead. Scriptures teach that every heart sways between good and evil, depending upon various drivers. These religious precepts (explained in chapter 18) are meant to help us gain self-mastery and are relatively similar in the various religious frameworks.

When the heart is clean, one controls the base instincts. When the heart is rusted,[734] the base instincts control one's psyche and intellect. It is important to realize the wisdom of these teachings since they connect to the state of the heart. The chapter's epigraph highlights the heart's place as the divine abode—the locus of empowerment and realization of full human potential—possessing the key to our individual and collective transformation.

CHAPTER 18:

DISCOVERING CONNECTION–HUMAN & DIVINE

Preceded by perception are mental states,
For them is perceptions supreme,
From perception have they sprung.
If, with perception polluted, one speaks or acts,
Thence dukkha follows
As a wheel that draught ox's foot.

—Dhammapada 1:1

Preceded by perception are mental states,
For them is perception supreme,
From perception have they sprung.
If, with tranquil perception, one speaks or acts,
Thence sukha follows
As a shadow that never departs.

—Dhammapada 1:2735

When we evaluate the problems humanity faces, the Hobbesian ideology of "every man at war with the other" emerges to be at the core of the human crisis. It, therefore, behooves us to recognize the coordinates, micro and macro, of this paradigm and then ameliorate their impact on human society. In its place, we may choose to deploy some other precepts commonly recommended by our spiritual systems. This chapter briefly explains how we can connect with our reality using these precepts.

In the previous chapter, we discussed the "blameworthy qualities" that can disconnect the human heart from its spiritual essence. Unfortunately, our modern societal institutions (Hobbesian in nature) tend to promote such disconnection by the emphasis on materialism, coupled with the attitude of the individual's supremacy to the society at any cost.[736] Determining the source of the present human condition, therefore, requires a closer look into how the various societal systems function to influence us individually and collectively. The disconnection that we really should ponder is internal as well as external, individual and societal, national and international, spiritual and civic, moral and material. Dealing with the external becomes feasible only when one also engages with the internal challenge.

To grasp the drivers of the problems in today's world, a clear understanding of the common practice of reductionism and trivialization in public communication systems is crucial. What would be central to such understanding is that, even without an intention to that end, ordinary communication systems can result in misinformation, disinformation, and conditioning.

Oversimplification, jocundity, and rendition of complex phenomena into black and white are all part of the paradigm in today's socio-political systems. Such reductionism and trivialization in day-to-day living conditions causes a disconnection of the individual from the collective. For example, it would be rather easy in the United States to find Republicans and Democrats who have been conditioned to loathe each other based upon one rationale or the other. An almost nihilistic atmosphere thus displays itself in the manifestation of the current ideological and adversarial reality.

Human Disconnection Sources: Reductionism, Trivialization and Tyrannies

Humanity, however we interpret the content of the word, exists in our realization and bestowal of relationship with the other. The disinclination of our current societal paradigm to fully embrace that reality makes it even more incumbent upon us to give up some of our psychic investiture in the prevalent sense of individualism.

Here, let's expand on the various drivers of modern disconnection between the individual and the society. The systemic place of "tyrannies" (fear, want, victory, identity) weakens a culture and creates a disconnection between individual and society. Societal structures, leveraging reductionism and trivialization, play an important role in creating and sustaining this disconnection. Religious establishments may not be an exception to that rule. Understanding this interplay becomes essential in completing the picture. Given the complicated nature[737] of the theme, this section will extensively rely upon scholars so as to bring forth the most reliable elucidation of the topic.

1. Trivialization & Reductionism

Charles Black was a towering American jurist in the second half of the twentieth century. In a 1953 scholarly piece published in the *Columbia Law Review*, Black did not just "tremble for the sanity of a society," he also pointed to a "sinister symbol" coming from the inconsistency between professed belief and practiced reality.

> If your flesh crawls as did mine on first reading this phrase[738] ["delivering a guaranteed audience"] as applied to American citizens ... then you will see why I think it only fair to throw up at this time any pretense of neutrality on the captive-audience question. I am revolted by the whole business. I see only one side to it...
>
> But I tremble for the sanity of a society that talks, on the level of abstract principle, of the precious integrity of the individual mind, and all the while, on the level of concrete fact, forces the individual mind to spend a good part of every day under bombardment with whatever some crowd of promoters want to throw at it ...
>
> Subjecting a man, willy-nilly and day after day, to intellectual forced-feeding on trivial fare, is not itself a trivial matter; to insist, by the effective gesture of

> coercion, that a man's right to dispose of his own faculties stops short of the interest of another in forcing him to endure paid-up banality, is not itself banal, but rather a sinister symbol of relative weighting of the independence of the mind of man and the lust to make a buck.[739]

In a world that was not yet inundated with television and social media, Black was warning us against the sinister nature and consequence of "intellectual forced-feeding on trivial fare." Even though most of us would neither accept nor perhaps even realize the intellectual and spiritual "forced feeding" that most of us routinely go through and how it shapes the way we think and feel—essentially influencing who we are.

A generation later, the same sentiment was aired by Professor Neil Postman, who, in the 1980s warned that spiritual devastation in the age of advanced technology is more likely to come from an enemy with a smiling face; and that this devastation could amount to a cultural death.

> When a population becomes distracted by trivia, when cultural life is redefined as a perpetual round of entertainments, when serious public conversation becomes a form of baby-talk, when, in short, a people become an audience and their public business a vaudeville act, then a nation finds itself at risk; a culture-death is a clear possibility.[740]

In the socio-political context, the corollary to Postman's observation is the following precept from legendary American journalist Walter Lippman:[741] "There can be no liberty for a community which lacks the means by which to detect lies."

In evaluating the words of Postman and Lippmann, the concern is not just about means of detecting falsehood, it is rather about the relevance of such distinction—when the very concept of true-false is frequently made so partisan (in all senses) that everything on one side becomes "true" whereas everything on the other side becomes "false." Thus, every picture gets looked at (in a mostly pre-determined sense) in terms of pure black or pure white. The palatability of shades of gray, perhaps even such a possibility, is not entertainable and is frequently frowned upon or squashed. Consequently, the very concept of truth and falsehood is essentially rendered irrelevant in the socio-political discourse. In the United States, a sizable percentage of Democrats and Republicans would provide a good embodiment of this phenomenon.

The same would be true in the partisan domains of nationality and religion the world over. While one can argue the extent of the individual-society disconnection from one place to the other, what Postman wrote would apply to the citizenry of all nation-states in the world.[742]

Tocqueville prognosticated this element of individual-society disconnection as a precursory symptom of despotism[743] within a democratic society: "The first thing that strikes the observation is an innumerable multitude of men ... incessantly endeavoring to procure the petty and the paltry pleasures with which they glut their lives. Each of them, living apart, is as a stranger to the fate of all the rest, ... he exists but in himself and for himself alone."[744]

Even though spread over almost two centuries, we cannot help but notice the thematic similarities within these proclamations by Tocqueville, Black, and Postman. Whether at a personal or societal level, these observations highlight the undeniable impact of reductionist thought and trivialization upon the individual and the society. This has become a global phenomenon that urges us to look at a global level for its causes.

2. Application of the "Tyrannies" towards Human Disconnection

Chapter 4 discussed the tyrannies of human psyche: fear, want, victory, identity. We would find an irrefutable presence of these tyrannies, and their conditioning, in our current state of individual and societal disconnection.

Because the concept we want to discuss is that of connection and disconnection, we should clarify what is being referred to here. In this context, "connection" means our link, bond, affinity, or affiliation with other facets of "creation"— nature, animals, humans, etc. It can also mean a connection with something beyond or larger than one's own self—a sense of purpose or faith in God. Society thus is the human collective, with a thread of commonality, that is interdependent or connected with one another. It may be a clan, a village, a whole country, or all of humanity. Loss of this bond leads to a sense of disconnection.

The two examples below show us the disconnection caused at the opposite ends of the wealth index in very different parts of the world. We can see a reflection of the tyrannies of want, and perhaps victory, in these examples. Referring to how a crisis prompted her to re-examine her concept of possessions, and perhaps even the notion of relationship, Lee Randall, a US journalist who became unemployed in 2016, wrote that year:

> Arriving at middle age on the brink of my very own economic meltdown, I'm having to question my relationship to things ... I held my own for years, until the newspaper employing me eliminated numerous jobs, including mine. Now, with the redundancy money gone, I have resorted to selling things... The trouble is that I am my things and my things are me. I don't want to relinquish them. This reluctance is not acquisitiveness: it is that I don't want to abandon myself. Single, childless, I'm all I've got: me.[745]

In reading Randall's statement, two things stand out. First, there seems to be a developing awareness or realization that one's material pursuits (or attachment to things) may not be adequate in achieving self-fulfillment.[746] (Such realization may not be as common in today's world as one would think.) In that sense, she may be at the cusp of further self-discovery.

Second, in a societal sense, how is it that—in a functional and vibrant society—she should be "all I've got: me?" Could it then be that such a system of living—that creates an "epidemic"[747] of isolation and loneliness—is detrimental and does not indicate a functional and vibrant society?

A 2020 article published in a British paper takes us to Mumbai, on the other side of the planet. It also takes us to the personal concerns of those at the other extreme of the economic divide:

> When Saurabh Goswami's phone rings, the VIP Indian marriage matchmaker [whose company is named Ultra Rich Match] has no idea quite what to expect. 'They could insist on marrying into a family with a helipad, a fleet of luxury cars, private shoppers and even a certain number of servants for their every need.' ... Dr Vishnu Modi, a VIP astrologer in Mumbai further elaborates: 'As India modernizes, couples can face more and more problems as life is more complex, whether it is in their jobs or relationships.'[748]

In both the examples above—of the unemployed US journalist and the ultra-rich Indian matrimony-seeker—the emergent common theme, even in such extremely divergent circumstances, is that of an individual whose happiness in life revolves mostly around pursuits best captured by the concept of materialism. What also comes across these writings is that the subjects in the two pieces may not have much of a perceptual connection—let alone a spiritual one—with the rest of the human society around them. As Tocqueville would say, each subject of these narratives "living apart, is as a stranger to the fate of all the rest." The extreme individualism ultimately yields a societal disconnection with weakening results for the collective.

These examples are not meant to say that one should not enjoy what life has to offer. Clearly, not everything material adds up to naked materialism. And material things do have an unavoidable importance in human life—things do lubricate the process of life, connect us with others, store our memories, drive our decisions, influence our feelings, and shape how we think. One example of such mutually nourishing material/physical relationship completely guided by spirituality[749] is that of human connection with land (and other elements of the living environment) within the various traditions of indigenous peoples all over the world.

Identifying the Stakes Unleashed by the Disconnection

Our collective capacity to correctly identify problems is critical to their solution. And that faculty has been significantly weakened by the disconnecting factors already mentioned in this chapter. The consequences of our multi-dimensional disconnection may even be existential. With the combined momentum of powerful structures and rapidly accelerating technology, we are dealing with unprecedented problems in virtually every domain: human, ecological, civic, political, and economic. Just the environmental domain provides us problems that may be too daunting to solve: climate change; accelerated extinction of plant and animal species; plasticized oceans; toxic air, water, and food; deforestation; toxic waste disposal; soil erosion, etc. Each one of these conundrums brings a galaxy of its own sub-problems. The unsustainability of our systems is written on the wall. Whether we can read it is not a function of our ability but rather that of our proclivity (to face the reality). The same human vulnerabilities that made us create these problems are now thwarting our ability to even recognize their in-our-face presence.

Without denying the division and sectarianism that is openly created by this or that religious establishment, our religious traditions do provide us the theoretical and practical basis for a transformation. And that resource can be leveraged, individually and collectively. The sections below focus on the importance of referring to our spiritual teachings and some relevant ideas from those teachings that would be helpful in our social conscience.

Religious Guidance to Mitigate the Disconnection: Spiritual and Societal

As a call to find the true inner self, Rumi begins his poem *Seeking the Source* with the following words:

> a voice out of this world
> calls on our souls
> not to wait any more
> get ready to move
> to the original home.[750]

Our spiritual traditions provide fairly clear frameworks of traits, habits, and practices that are harmful and that disconnect us from our spiritual essence (causing "rust" in our hearts). The Decalogue (Ten Commandments) are universally known. Other religions provide similar guidelines for social practices and moral observances. Societal concepts of service and sharing are also highly emphasized.

In Jainism and Hinduism, the *vratas* (vows) and the *yamas* (restraints) recommend mutually similar principles: non-injury, truthfulness, non-stealing, chastity, non-attachment (*ahimsa*, *satya*, *asteya*, *brahmacharya*, and *aparigraha*). This goes on to constitute a comprehensive framework. Jainism adds conduct and discipline vows (*guna* and *shiksha vratas*), and then there are differences in requirements separating the lay person from the monk. In yoga philosophy, the five *yamas* listed above are supplemented by five *niyamas* (virtuous observances)—purity, contentment, self-discipline, self-study, and surrender.[751] The Five Precepts in Buddhism as well as Taoism also provide similar teachings.

In his treatise titled *On Detachment*, Meister Eckhart writes:

> After a thorough study of these writings I find, as well as my reason can testify or perceive, that only pure detachment surpasses all things, for all virtues have some regard to creatures, but detachment is free of all creatures. Therefore our Lord said to Martha, '*unum est necessarium*' (*Luke* 10:42), which is as much as to say, 'Martha, he who would be serene and pure needs but one thing: detachment.'[752]

Aparigraha (non-attachment) is a conceptual repository that provides incessant guidance and helps set a state of mind inherently conducive to every teaching of every spiritual system. Non-attachment is about release, relief, or relinquishment—bringing about a state of freedom. For the lay-person, renunciation—complete rejection—is usually not the path being promoted as the manifestation of non-attachment. By definition, the concept of Middle Way in Buddhism as well as in Islam, for example, would not be promoting extremes: the middle way is the middle way. One could thus live a comfortable life, responsibly enjoying nature's bounty and still be practicing non-attachment.

Sikhism identifies five vices to be avoided: lust, anger, greed, attachment, pride/ego (*kam*, *krodh*, *lobh*, *moh*, and *ahankar*).[753] The avoidance of these vices is then to be supplemented with the observance of five virtues (truthfulness, contentment, compassion, humility, love), remembrance of God (*Simran*, *Naam-Japna*), and complying with God's directions (*Hukam*) as well as the civic responsibilities of service and sharing (*seva*, *vand chakkna*). An example of seva (service) is found in the *langar*—community meal—which is served at every *gurdwara* without any distinction accorded to one's status, gender, religion, etc. Everyone is welcome and everyone will be served as an equal.

There is something intriguing and instructive about the five vices in Sikhism. "*Punj chor*" is the Punjabi expression used for these vices. The term literally means "five thieves." That's a novel and revolutionary way of looking at religious proscription. These vices are not just things one should avoid to meet some external requirement. Rather, these are "thieves" that, if allowed to operate within one's psyche, would steal something from that person—something extremely valuable that is inherent in, and innate to, that person.

We must therefore answer the cardinal question: what is that something these thieves are trying to steal? When deliberately pondered, we can see that these thieves are out to rob us of our potential to reach our spiritual destination. Another way would be to say that these thieves take away from us the tendency to ask the question: Who am I?[754] The irony is that after the theft, one would mostly be robbed even of the awareness of a loss (though the awareness may be regained, and the theft may be undone). Simply put, these thieves reduce the human to its lower self that has lost its depth in intellect, perceptivity and spirituality—one would be left to live as another animal who functions just on its base instincts.

We'll summarize two key points here. First, it is important to realize that these simple dos and don'ts contain within them an aspect of deep spiritual transformation. To understand them simply as ethical rituals or moral niceties would miss the point: that these injunctions are doorways to the spiritual journey and attainment. Second, in many ways, these goals are not as difficult to attain. Grasping the essence of even one such teaching inevitably leads to facility with other teachings, thus helping us overcome the disconnection.

In a way, the message of this section was encapsulated in Krishna's advice to Arjuna:

> Knowing the self beyond understanding,
> sustain the self with the self.
> Great Warrior, kill the enemy
> menacing you in the form of desire.
>
> —*Gita* 3:43

Turning Around and Remedying the Disconnection

If we humans are willing to collectively effectuate the needed directional change, then what is our guiding approach or framework that we can agree upon? If we believe that Dr. King's formula (restructuring and revolution of values) still offers a good approach, then what "source of values" do we consult to bring about such a "revolution?" Would the Enlightenment philosophers be able to guide us? Or perhaps our current legal system or Hollywood; or perhaps the corporation, politician, and media; or even the university? If current structures are not sufficient enough to deal with the challenge, what options then do we have?

Current and the previous centuries have seen numerous movements that brought together various civic circles and spiritual traditions to achieve a common objective to serve humanity (the movement to abolish Apartheid in South Africa is an example). Such movements represented "religious" as well as "secular" elements in the society. The need of the present time also is a confluence of such waves so we may collectively enunciate, and coalesce around, shared principles that are true to the pluralistic beauty of our existence in all dimensions.

Non-Separation—The Key to Connection

Dr. Warren Ward, who teaches psychiatry and psychotherapy at the University of Queensland, Australia, narrates the following:

> Ten years ago, I was diagnosed with melanoma. As a doctor, I knew how aggressive and rapidly fatal this cancer could be. Fortunately for me, the surgery seemed to achieve a cure (touch wood). But I was also fortunate in another sense. I became aware, in a way I never had before, that I was going to die—if not from melanoma, then from something else, eventually. I have been much happier since then. For me, this realisation, this acceptance, this awareness that I am going to die is at least as important to my wellbeing as all the advances of medicine, because it reminds me to live my life to the full every day. I don't want to experience the regret that Ware[755] heard about more than any other, of not living 'a life true to myself.'[756]

For someone to say that his close encounter with death has made his life happier is rather curious. And yet the truth of what he means is readily pouring over the brim of his expression. There are myriad ways to finding the "connection" we are discussing here. For the psychotherapist himself, it was the realization of the finitude of his own physical existence that led him to more deeply discover the meaning in life. For someone else, it may be a very different or unexpected occurrence or phenomenon that turns the bulb on. What's important is that we do not resist and deny the message when it appears.

Sufis use the language of "separation" and "non-separation" to describe that connection. Even scientifically, whatever we know of emerged out of a dot a few billion years ago. As Walt Whitman had observed, "every atom belonging to me as good belongs to you." The separateness is thus as much a product of human insecurity as it is that of our physical perceptivity. Let's apply the idea in this time of the pandemic and working from home. This example, in a very personal sense, shows the place of non-separation and connection in our intimate, spousal lives.

Just this past week I received an email from an ordained clergy member whose work is in family counseling. As an expression of difficulty in finding time for non-work activities, the email contained the following: "The world of family therapy and divorce is on fire ..."[757]

We should at least be able to locate the paradox in this phenomenon. Two people who supposedly "love" each other end up deepening their mutual incompatibility when they actually have to spend more time together. The connection of this problem with the adversarial societal ethos may be undeniable and inevitable. How is it that a little more company and intimacy is leading couples to a discovery of their mutual inharmoniousness and mutual intolerability?[758]

What is it, then, that we call love? Kahlil Gibran provides some guidance in his famous book:

> You were born together, and together
> you shall be forevermore.
> You shall be together when the white wings of death
> scatter your days....
> Love one another, but make not a bond of love:
> Let it rather be a moving sea
> between the shores of your souls.
>
> —Kahlil Gibran, *The Prophet*, 15

Gibran's words may sound like separation; yet the expression tries to combine non-separation with non-attachment—an even better formula. Another way to express it would be to say that our individuation is not our separation. Science tells us that the company of family and friends generates a good feeling within us because we become part of the mutual regulation of our nervous systems—literally. In other words, the person giving us company is directly engaged in the processes going on in our brains.[759] A *supportive* relationship with one's parent, spouse, sibling, child, friend, neighbor, or coworker may thus be the best medicine for mind and heart.

The domain of non-separation encompasses individual and collective human pursuit of truth, beauty, and tranquility—captured by Dr. King as the "inescapable network of mutuality." Elaborated below are some basic vehicles that may be instrumental in achieving these goals.

1. Connection via Ihsan (Beauty in Action)

Our religious traditions provide conceptual and functional guidance to help us avoid the habits that derail us from our spiritual path, as well as those that help us practice divine attributes so as to accelerate the journey. The Qur'anic notion of "*Ihsan*" sets the bar yet lets the individual exercise judgment and agency in its performance.

The triconsonantal root word for this concept is H-S-N, which translates to beauty, excellence, or good. Ihsan (doing beautiful deeds, beauty in one's action; pursuit of excellence, etc.) forms an umbrella concept with ubiquitous application. Other conjugations of the word include *ahsanu* (do good, act excellent) and *muhsin* (one who engages in Ihsan, pl. *muhsineen*). This concept is repeated again and again in the *Qur'an* well over 100 times, likely in the vicinity of 200 times. On the average, thus, every single chapter in the *Qur'an* would contain more than one exhortation to bring beauty in one's deeds. Insert 18:1 provides a small sampling.

GOD LOVES THE MUHSINEEN

And perform beautiful deeds. Truly, God loves the Muhsineen [those who perform beautiful deeds].

—Qur'an 2:195

And, truly, God is with the Muhsineen.

—Qur'an 29:69

And those who endured patiently ... and spent out of what We have provided them ... and they repel evil with excellence: for them is the Ultimate Abode.

—*Qur'an* 13:22

And not equal are the good deed and the bad. Drive back [evil] with the excellent [deed]. Then, behold he who between you and him is enmity [will be] as if he were a loyal friend.

—Qur'an 41:34

He Who created death and life so that He may test as to which of you is best in deeds [by being in a state of Ihsan].

—Qur'an 67:2

[Those] who spend in gladness and tribulation and the ones who choke their rage and the ones who pardon humanity. And God loves the Muhsineen.

—Qur'an 3:134

Insert 18:1

Examining some more verses reveals the word Ihsan being clad in a long list of connotations: aesthetics, beauty, love, God consciousness (*taqwa*), excellence, humility, deference, patience, forgiveness, graciousness, gallantry, modesty, dedication, generosity, compassion, justice, etc. Putting it together, though, we can see that this is not about specific actions alone. It is about living in a state of being, mind, and heart that is beautiful all the time. Every action in this state would indeed classify as that which heals the world (Tikkun), making the two concepts complementary.

Umm al-Fadl al-Wahatiyya, a Persian Sufi saint, lived in the tenth century. Her clarification, which dovetails with the famous Hadith of Gabriel,[760] connects the seeking of knowledge to Ihsan and then with witnessing God:

> [The] one who seeks knowledge is the one who acts on it. Acting in one's knowledge is not in the amount of fasting, almsgiving, and praying that one does. Rather, acting in one's knowledge is in sincerely dedicating one's actions to God with correct intention and awareness that God Most High is observing him, even if he is not observant toward his Lord and witnessing Him at all times.[761]

When seeking knowledge can be meaningful only in the action it generates—and when that action is permeated with the Love of God as a witness—the definition of Ihsan is complete.

A hadith goes so far as to say: "God is beautiful and He loves beauty."[762] In this light, we can tell that there is divinity within an action or sentiment that carries beauty, and also that such an action or sentiment attracts the Divine Love. And as we can see from the verses in Insert 18:1, there are no prerequisites to be a Muhsin; anyone who chooses to be one can be.

2. Connection via Compassion

Connection begins where our own self stops being the prime center of our concern. We can then connect with others; and through them we reconnect with our own self (sometimes in a way that we did not know earlier). Only then are we able to actually understand our own deeper concerns. Chapter 13 discussed compassion being a central message of the Indic as well as the Abrahamic religions.

In the famous Parable of the Good Samaritan[763] (Luke 10:25-37), Jesus answers the question "And who is my neighbor?" By declaring a stranger to be a neighbor, Jesus's response provides a revolutionary definition of the word "neighbor"—transcending any notion of proximity, kinship, tribal identity, etc. And that may be the only definition we really should use. By extension, Jesus may also have invited us to redefine our definitions of family, kin, and clan based upon the values we practice.

Hebrews 13:2-3 further consolidates the message: "Do not neglect to show hospitality to strangers, for thereby some have entertained angels unawares. Remember those in prison as if you were there with them, and those who are being maltreated, for you are vulnerable too."

Earlier, this book emphasized the influential role that Thomas Hobbes had in shaping thought patterns during the Age of Reason. The zeitgeist that prevails in our world still might disproportionately be influenced by the negative messages of the Enlightenment era, especially the attitude of Thomas Hobbes. His message, war of every man against everyone else, cemented adversarial relationships even at the interpersonal level within a society.

In chapter XX (i.e. twenty, titled "Of Dominion Paternall and Despoticall") of his magnum opus *Leviathan*, Hobbes strongly promotes the necessity of absolute despotism and totalitarianism given his maxim of a man's neighbor being his enemy.

Hobbes also claims that his viewpoint is the product of the scriptures he has consulted ("So it appeareth plainly, to my understanding, both from Reason, and Scripture ..."[764]). The question, however, is the following: Is Hobbes's interpretation of Jesus's message even remotely correct? It would be rather difficult to find a scripture in any religion that would deliver an overall expression anywhere close to Hobbes's wholesale decrees of despotism, totalitarian control, and violent mutual animus within the human race. Not that every single Enlightenment philosopher[765] walked lockstep with Hobbes. Yet, as chapter 4 shows, the weighty influence of someone considered a giant thinker should not be underestimated in the direction history took.

Instead of accepting innate human nature as belligerent and vile—a belief that ultimately demands totalitarian control—it may be time we altogether gave up this "religion" of animosity and returned to the real teachings of Jesus—and those of all other prophets, founders, and sages in our religions. As the evidence in this book shows again and again, our spiritual teachings exhort us to see the inner beauty (the divine image) of the human soul—leading us away from the adversarial mindset and towards a state of mutual respect and respect of nature.

3. Connection via Service

Sincere social service is an integral component of the teaching within any religious or spiritual system. What was prescribed at the time was in accordance with the needs of that time. The purpose, though, was twofold: to effectively address the societal need at any given time, as well as to effectively (and deeply) build the spiritual depth of the practitioner (adherent). As for the latter, a direct action, though in-line with the humble intent of anonymity (viz. Matthew 6:3 or BB 9b in the *Babylonian Talmud*),[766] is considered the best means to achieving the objective.

In Mark 10:43-45, Jesus makes contingent the very definition of greatness and leadership upon one's attitude to be a servant: "whoever wants to become great among you must be your servant, and whoever wants to be first must be slave of all. For even the Son of Man did not come to be served, but to serve." The notion of service here springs from clarity in terms of humility and compassion.

And even beyond that, as Dr. King explained, "compassion is more than flinging a coin to a beggar. It comes to see that an edifice which produces beggars needs restructuring."[767] The question we may have to ask is: does our present concept of social service channeled almost entirely through NGOs, foundations controlled by the wealthy, and even large corporations[768] serve the intended objectives? Does such conversion of this important responsibility into institutionalized benevolence—coupled with desensitization to the roots of social problems—undermine its intended objectives? What does it do to our concept of society?

Sometimes, it seems that our current understanding of "charity" has evolved to carry certain weaknesses, including a patronizing connotation—which is odd given the original sense of "love" and "esteem" associated with the word "charity." Then we have the emergence of the concept of philanthropy, in which it seems that only the ultra-rich can be philanthropic even though research[769] shows that the poor are more generous and caring. If our spiritual teachings tell us that "your smile ... is charity,"[770] why can't a pauper be celebrated as a philanthropist?

As a society, we do need to include a higher component of duty, obligation, responsibility, service, justice, and fairness to our understanding and practice of charity, as is commonly taught by our religions. Especially, our current concept of charity seems to have turned the spirit and purpose of the teaching on its head. "Who's doing whom a favor?" would be a pertinent question to ask and answer so we can deeply understand the real spiritual meaning of service.

4. Connection via Forgiveness

Hence, forgive with graceful forbearance.

—Qur'an 15:85

Let's begin with Dr. King who, in referring to the decided practical human difficulty (or, as he puts it, a "strange dichotomy") between proclamation and action, says:

> This agonizing gulf between the *ought* and the *is* represents the tragic theme of man's earthly pilgrimage. But in the life of Jesus we find that the gulf is bridged. Never in history was there a more sublime example of the consistency of word and deed. During his ministry in the sunny villages of Galilee, Jesus talked passionately about forgiveness... 'I say not unto thee, Until seven times: but, Until seventy times seven.'[771] In other words, forgiveness is not a matter of quantity, but of quality. A man cannot forgive up to four hundred and ninety times without forgiveness becoming a part of the habit structure of his being. Forgiveness is not an occasional act; it is a permanent attitude. This was what Jesus taught his disciples.[772]

Despite the exhortations of this concept in all religions, forgiveness is still not well understood, especially in the spirit it is promoted by our spiritual systems. The multi-dimensional and multi-directional place of this moral and spiritual virtue goes well beyond the commonly understood purpose of patching up a broken relationship. The notion carries foundational implications for relationships regarding the creation as well as the Divine because one "who is devoid of the power to forgive is devoid of the power to love."[773]

The act and attitude of forgiveness are, ultimately, for one's own self and one's own spiritual growth. It is not necessarily a decision to reconcile with the one who may have caused the injury. It neither condones nor pardons any wrongdoing. The point is to release or relinquish any grudge or ill will we still hold, thereby purifying our own selves spiritually. In effect, it is also an act or attitude of kindness towards our own selves. (As in other spiritual virtues, forgiveness also is not merely a deed; it is a disposition.)

Forgiveness simply helps us to overcome our own burden of hurt, rage and fear because these emotions, however justified, have a deeply debilitating effect on our psyche, judgment, and the very sense of right and wrong. The self-liberation from the prison created by the hurt feelings is the best "revenge" one can get. To stay submerged in the pain is to create the psychological prison, to disempower one's own self and to give more "power" to the one who originally caused the pain. To unload the emotional rucksack, let go of the pain, and hold no grudge is a mode of self-healing that brings solace, contentment, and tranquility into our soul. It also helps to keep in mind that what gets hurt often is the lower self (ego); and that's where all the anger resides. Forgiveness is also a good exercise to gain mastery over that part of our ego.

We can truly forgive only when we do it through practicing compassion for our own selves; this we do by allowing our own feelings and sentiments to not be suppressed but rather acknowledged and then reconciled with the nobility and mercy within us to bring about the release and emancipation needed for the mental and psychological shift. This is not an easy task. By practicing the virtues taught by our religions, however, our spiritual heart can expand and give us the courage to let go.

The other side of the coin is to ask for forgiveness—we apologize or we say we are sorry. Once again, this is not always an acceptance of wrongdoing or a feeling of guilt. When a hurt is caused despite there being no wrongdoing, an apology is then an expression of our magnanimity in that we are helping the other reach the place of forgiveness and overcoming an unnecessary hurt. Whether we forgive or ask for forgiveness, the act exhibits a maturity within our self that then multiplies with every such act!

5. Connection via Gratitude

Gratitude is another highly advised habit and state of mind. This state of mind reduces the need for forgiveness and apology—because the one in gratitude is less likely to cause an offence or be offended. As we know, those who are usually grateful neither complain nor frequently dwell in negativity, thus ensuring more harmonious relationships. Reducing the occasion when forgiveness becomes necessary is tremendously beneficial to an individual and a society—and gratitude provides an easy path to that goal. As HeartMath Institute's research shows, the state of appreciation or gratitude also induces a coherent Heart Rate Variability rhythm associated with many health benefits.[774]

Human nature, with all its weaknesses, also has a primordial element of goodness,[775] which can be leveraged and deployed with a basic quest to find the meaning in our existence. We can rediscover our sense of connection with deliberate, considerate, purposeful, and responsible exercise of our choice-making capacity. That may well be the most effective way to strengthen our connection: with the Divine, our fellow human beings, and nature—in turn fully realizing the agency that resides within.

CHAPTER 19:

TIKKUN—THE CONCEPTUAL FOUNTAINHEAD OF AGENCY

For many of us the march from Selma to Montgomery was about protest and prayer. Legs are not lips and walking is not kneeling. And yet our legs uttered songs. Even without words, our march was worship.
I felt my legs were praying.

—Rabbi Abraham Joshua Heschel

The words in the epigraph came from Rabbi Heschel on March 21, 1965—soon after returning from participating in the March from Selma to Montgomery, Alabama. These words became etched in human history as the very definition of our spiritual commonality.

What emerges right off is the implication that worship is not just about a specific action; it is a state of heart and mind, a state of being. Heschel himself points out: "What is the objective of observance if not to be sensitive to the spirit, to the spirit in oneself and in all things?"[776]

Earning God's Love

A Muslim should be able to identify more with Heschel's words in terms of faith—given the close connection with a well-known *hadith qudsi* in Islamic tradition. The teaching says: "My servant continues to come nearer to Me through the further acts of devotion until I love him. Then when I love him I am his hearing with which he hears, his sight with which he sees, his hand with which he holds, and his foot with which he walks..."[777]

Heschel's statement implies that his action was an expression of his devotion to and love for God. As the hadith points out, he in turn becomes God's beloved.[778] The blessing of being God's beloved then means that, in the context of the march, Heschel's human faculties (of hearing, seeing, walking, etc.) are manifestations and expressions of God's love. In a metaphorical manner of speaking, it was God who was walking with Heschel's legs.[779] And this would apply to all who were marching that day.[780]

What we see here is a spiritual interplay between the individual's sense of responsibility (manifested through the effort to bring about societal change) and the human sense of devotion to and worship of the Ultimate Reality and Creator. And that is how one's religious obligation of worship—through the transformative power of divine Mercy and Love—becomes one's societal obligation of service extended on behalf of and with the other.

Abu Abd ar-Rahman as-Sulami, a tenth-century Muslim scholar and theologian, narrates a saying of Fatima[781] of Nishapur (a ninth-century Sufi saint): "When God ignores a person, he will wander aimlessly in every city square and will prattle constantly with every tongue. When God does not ignore a person, He silences him except for the truth (*as-sadq*) and compels him to hold Him in reverence and sincerity."[782]

The truth in word and action (as we'll see throughout this chapter) coming from Heschel places him in Fatima's definition of those who gain God's Proximity and Favor. And this becomes another affirmation of the above-narrated hadith's application vis-à-vis Heschel.

We can also model Heschel's example from the angle of Prophet Abraham's piety and godliness. The *Qur'an* (6:79) presents Abraham's proclamation as follows: "Behold, unto Him who brought into being the heavens and the earth have I turned my face, having turned away from all that is false ..."

It is clear that those marching that day had turned away from falsehood (of otherness, of fear, of powerlessness) and were marching within God's Love. There is a critical point needing emphasis. Rabbi Heschel's effort that day (and that of so many other non-Black participants in the march) was primarily a statement of solidarity with the "other." It was an expression that the pain of and the injustice to the "other" was pain and injustice to one's own self, making its amelioration one's own responsibility. In effect, the notion of "other" had been nullified or merged into "us"—and it is this definition of religion and faith that, in the language of the hadith qudsi, brings one so close to God that divine actions are manifested through those of the servant.

The scope of the action is further illustrated by the *Diamond Sutra* in a dialogue between the Buddha and Subhuti, one of his disciples. The question is how to give rise to the highest, awakened mind. The Buddha confers the following: "We have to do our best to help every living being cross the ocean of dukkha. But after all beings have arrived at the shore of liberation, no being at all has been carried to the other shore. If you are still caught up in the idea of a self, a person, a living being, or a life span, you are not an authentic bodhisattva."[783] Using his concept of interbeing, Thich Nhat Hanh explains "self" in the teaching as follows:

> Life is one. We do not need to slice it into pieces and call this or that piece a 'self.' What we call self is made only of non-self elements. When we look at a flower, for example, we may think that it is different from 'non-flower' things. But when we look more deeply, we see that everything in the cosmos is in that flower. Without all of the non-flower elements—sunshine, clouds, earth, minerals, heat, rivers, and consciousness—a flower cannot be. That is why the Buddha teaches us that the self does not exist. We have to discard all distinctions between self and non-self.[784]

Realizing Spiritual Motherhood

Spiritual otherness is a grave infirmity that ails the current foundation of our patterns of thought and action. The excerpt in Insert 19:1 is from a papal mass[785] on January 1, 2017, at the Vatican Basilica commemorating the World Day of Peace.

SOLEMNITY OF MOTHER MARY

To celebrate Mary as our mother at the beginning of the new year means recalling a certainty that will accompany our days: we are a people with a Mother; we are not orphans. Where there is a mother, there is tenderness.

Mothers are the strongest antidote to our individualistic and egotistic tendencies, to our lack of openness and our indifference. A society without mothers would not only be a cold society, but a society that has lost its heart, lost the "feel of home." A society without mothers would be a merciless society, one that has room only for calculation and speculation. Because mothers, even at the worst times, are capable of testifying to tenderness, unconditional self-sacrifice and the strength of hope. Where there is a mother, there is unity, there is belonging, belonging as children.

To begin the year by recalling God's goodness in the maternal face of Mary, in the faces of our own mothers, protects us from the corrosive disease of being "spiritual orphans". It is the sense of being orphaned that the soul experiences when it feels motherless and lacking the tenderness of God, when the sense of belonging to a family, a people, a land, to our God, grows dim.

The loss of the ties that bind us, so typical of our fragmented and divided culture, increases this sense of orphanhood and, as a result, of great emptiness and loneliness. This sense of being orphaned lodges in a narcissistic heart capable of looking only to itself and its own interests. It grows when we forget that life is a gift we have received—and owe to others—a gift we are called to share in this common home.

Mary gave us a mother's warmth, the warmth that shelters us amid troubles. We too want to receive her into our homes, our families, our communities and nations. We want to meet her maternal gaze. The gaze that frees us from being orphans; the gaze that reminds us that we are brothers and sisters, that I belong to you, that you belong to me, that we are of the same flesh. The gaze that teaches us that we have to learn how to care for life in the same way and with the same tenderness that she did: by sowing hope, by sowing a sense of belonging and of fraternity.[786]

Insert 19:1

In a 1972 essay titled the "Reasons for My Involvement in the Peace Movement", Rabbi Heschel went on to clarify the underpinning of the development of his thought: "indifference to evil is worse than evil itself.... There is immense silent agony in the world, and the task of man is to ... prevent the desecration of the soul and the violation of our dream of honesty."[787]

The papal homily talks about we humans becoming "spiritual orphans" in the absence of an environment that is suffused with metaphorical "motherhood." Rabbi Heschel's expression "desecration of the soul" conveys the same message as the metaphor of "spiritual orphanhood." The point is presented by both the Rabbi and the Pope as a situation of mutual exclusivity. Therefore, it behooves us to fully grasp this common message because they both signify that our choice is to live either in a system governed by "motherhood" or in a system that dwells in "otherhood."

Revisiting the Kabbalistic notion of tikkun,[788] we see that the word has many meanings. To repair, improve, and heal are the most common translations. The concept of tikkun can be applied in so many ways. And all those ways of looking at it are commendable and beneficial.

While tikkun's application to "prevent the desecration of the soul and the violation of our dream of honesty" seems abstract, it is crucial to our ability to bring about real repair. That is because it is not possible to achieve the objective of preventing the desecration of the soul and the dream of honesty without introspection towards our own soul and our own dream of honesty—personally, and only then collectively. And it is the individual, one at a time, where the repair begins.[789] As we look inside and repair our own soul and dream, spreading our understanding of tikkun becomes sounder and more effective.

Relative freedom from base-instinct and self-centeredness allows a soul's effort to be more meaningful—bringing others together—thus creating a multiplier effect. This notion is in synch with the message from the *Analects of Confucius* (4:25), where the Master tells us, "Moral force (*Te*) never dwells in solitude, it will always bring neighbors."

Confucius's words carry a double-edged sword and need careful understanding. Heschel's ranking of "indifference to evil" as "worse than evil itself" was further clarified when he stated that indifference (and not evil) is the opposite of good. In that context, according to the Confucian teaching, our indifference promotes, or multiplies, further indifference in the society. The evildoer is legally guilty. But we are morally responsible for the wrongdoing. And that point must not be underestimated—certainly not within the domain of spirituality and morality. In a way, our "non-tikkun" behavior or attitude, and self-imposed lack of agency, promotes corruption—which has been especially decried in the *Qur'an* again and again. The following example of how different people would approach extremism illustrates this essential message:

There is one type or another of extremism within various nationalistic ideologies and religions. While not an exhaustive list, most people claiming such identities can be classified in the following categories of those who: clearly see the problem and its source; perceive the problem but don't know what's really going on behind the curtain; blame someone else to have created the problem; believe that someone else should deal with it because it's too complex; want to have "unity" within the identity-based community (to deal with the external "threat"); deny that there is any such problem; sympathize with the extremists; or are themselves extremists.

Having abdicated a central responsibility, many of these groups would then fall in the "desecration of the soul" category and it would be fair to say that, using Heschel's words, their "indifference to evil is worse than evil itself," especially in the sense of the collective impact. That simple message from Heschel, Francis, and Confucius carries significant import.

Honoring All of Divine Creation

Contemplation and pursuit of divine truth is not limited to "religion" alone. True, India, China, Persia, and the Middle East are the points of emergence for most of the world's religions, yet there is more to it. In Greek history, we can go as far back as Pythagoras to see the quest for spirituality and truth. The *Enneads* by Plotinus is an inspiration from Plato's message. Then we have the amazingly rich history of African cultures, as well as indigenous spiritual traditions and cultures of America and Australia. In *The Dawn of Everything*, David Graeber and David Wengrow point out that the indigenous American intellectuals "actually played a role in this conceptual revolution [of Enlightenment]. It is very strange that this should be considered a particularly radical idea, but among mainstream intellectual historians today it is almost a heresy."[790]

With the impact of imperialism and then colonialism, we may never know what all we lost. Given this background, it is truly remarkable that these indigenous cultures are still fighting for the integrity of the planet's ecosystems and fundamental human values—thus providing an immense service and much needed leadership to all humanity.

An important mode of realizing spiritual motherhood is by honoring non-human creation with whom we share the planet. And here, we have a lot to learn from indigenous societies. A study by the University of British Columbia (covering Australia, Brazil, and Canada) found that the highest biodiversity is on lands managed by indigenous communities—even higher than on wildlife preserves.

As the study's lead author Richard Schuster says, it is the approach of the "indigenous communities that are keeping species number high." Schuster went on to say that collaboration with indigenous land stewards will "be essential in ensuring that species survive and thrive."[791] As indicated by the Whanganui example (which I put together based on information from various listed sources), what the indigenous spiritual traditions still offer us covers both theory and practice. The rest of the human race just needs to open its mind and heart so we can all contribute towards the solutions to the common problems we face.

WHANGANUI AND GANGES: THE TALE OF TWO RIVERS

Ko au te awa, ko te awa ko au (I am the River, the River is me). These words describe the inseverable connection of the Maori tribes (of Whanganui, New Zealand) to their ancestral river. For centuries, the tribes cared for and depended upon the river.

The tribes' traditional authority and spiritual guardianship was extinguished by government decree when European settlers took over the land in the mid-1800s. The river has since then been damaged and degraded even though it was promoted as "the Rhine of New Zealand" for tourism purposes.

For 140 years, the local Maori tribe of Whanganui has been fighting this legal battle. Hundreds of tribal representatives wept with joy as the longest-running litigation in New Zealand's history came to an end, and the status of the river was passed into law: in March 2017, the government of New Zealand recognized in law that the river is a living being. Parliament passed legislation declaring that *Te Awa Tupua*—the river and all its elements—constitute an indivisible, living whole with "all the rights, powers, duties, and liabilities" of a legal person. Te Urewera, a former national park had already, and then in December Mount Taranaki too, gained the same status as a living person.

Still, the law does not replace what was taken away by colonialism. The Maori people believe that the focus on legal rights is misplaced. What matters is a new orientation of humans to the natural world, one based not on rights but responsibilities. Gerrard Albert, the lead negotiator for the Whanganui iwi [tribe], expressed it this way: "We can trace our genealogy to the origins of the universe. And, therefore, rather than us being masters of the natural world, we are part of it. We want to live like that as our starting point. And that is not an anti-development, or anti-economic use of the river but to begin with the view that it is a living being, and then consider its future from that central belief."

While there is still a long way to go, the magnanimity and enlightenment of the people and the government of New Zealand has to be recognized. In this legislation, as the National Geographic reports, "the Crown issues an apology for its historical wrongdoing, acknowledging that it breached the treaty, undermined the ability of Whanganui tribes to exercise their customary rights ... and compromised their physical, cultural, and spiritual well-being."

The inspiration caused by this legal action was instantaneous. Within days, the High Court of Uttarakhand province in India had declared River Ganges (and its tributary Yamuna) as persons with rights. Within weeks of that decision, however, the state government appealed—and the Supreme Court of India overturned the decision. Ganges is arguably the world's most polluted river. Commonly referred to as Ma Ganga or Ganga Mata (Mother Ganges), it is understood to be a goddess in the Hindu religion who came down from heaven to cleanse the Earth; bathing in her waters washes away a person's sins. Once again, however, the politico-economic institutions ensured that the goddess who is here to cleanse the earth will not be cleansed of the unfathomable deluge of toxic chemicals and human excrement routinely and indiscriminately dumped into it.

—*BBC*, the *Guardian*, the *Hindu*,
the *National Geographic*,
the *Smithsonian* magazine

Insert 19:2

Let's further examine the "indifference" Heschel decries in his statement quoted above. This word can be interpreted as self-imposed absence of agency. Undoing the "indifference" thus manifests agency in our words and actions—restoring the responsibility and innate freedom we were born with. Agency is not about official power or authority to create an impact; it is rather the presence of internal will and purpose regardless of the external factors. "Whanganui and Ganges: The Tale of Two Rivers" shows a decades-long struggle that the officially "powerless" Mauri tribes in New Zealand engaged in. Their resoluteness in following their ancestral culture finally yielded an inspiring fruit—the Whanganui River regained, even in the eyes of non-Mauri people, its status that it had enjoyed since time immemorial and had just lost less than two centuries ago.

We can contrast that with the situation of River Ganges that—despite being called "Mother"—carries millions of tons of toxic and carcinogenic pollution. And when the few who are fighting against all odds win a court decision, the structures of the politico-economic system quickly move to undo their effort. Where is the agency of over a billion people who deem Mother Ganges sacred? In a society where the concept of "mother" is much more hallowed than the concept of "father," what forces are denying this agency to the Indian public?

In *The Palm Tree of Deborah*, Rabbi Moses Cordovero's explanation sheds light on the above problem and its solution: "the essence of the divine image is action." Referring to Genesis 1:26-27, Cordovero clarifies: "If you resemble the divine in body but not in action, you distort the form."[792] Thus, the nature of human role is to be like the ten sefirot that present themselves in our world as divine activity. (Sefirot defined in chapter 13, subtitle "Unique and Incomparable Divine Nature.") It is "by enacting the spiritual on the stage of life, we perceive our kinship with the divine."[793] In one form or the other, every scripture, prophet, sage, and spiritual teacher has placed tremendous emphasis on the importance of action that is aligned with the message of the Ultimate Reality. The pivotal place of such action in our lives simply cannot be ignored by a person of faith.

We end this section by summarizing a few themes already mentioned above. First, the spiritual grounding that has been so clearly highlighted above by the words of Rabbi Heschel and Pope Francis is pivotal in our ability to manifest the societal changes many are striving for. When we understand this message in light of the Diamond Sutra (quoted above) and its explication by Thich Nhat Hanh, we notice the strong kinship being implied—not just with fellow humans, but with all of the creation. We just saw how the Whanganui tribe considers itself to be in kinship with all creation, not just humans. Heschel's description of the prophets' concern with "no limit" points to the erasure of the demarcations that create the "other," especially based upon identities, that become a limitation unless consciously addressed. If there is still the "other," we have a long ways to go. Our having a "spiritual mother" reflects our common spiritual bond. *Qur'an* (2:115) emphasizes the Divine reflection within the creation with these words: "... and wherever you turn, there is God's countenance."

Second, the foremost effort is essentially internal. It is in manifesting what already resides inside (faith, ethics, aesthetics, morals, principles, etc.) and then applying it to the world around us. If our effort does not begin internally, and its result is not visible to those within our close circle, then we remain handicapped in effectiveness. An important milestone, therefore, is our ability to ask ourselves the same question that Moses wanted an answer to: who am I?

Third, being under the umbrella of a spiritual "motherhood" provides us the essential immunity and resilience we need in our struggle in mastering the *punj chor* (vices), the *yamas* (restraints), the *vratas* (vows). Insert 19:1 provides one way of symbolizing this spiritual shield—"motherhood"--that keeps us from the "spiritual orphanhood" that has become the trademark of our extremely materialistic world.

Fourth, given the practical erasure of our traditional cultures by the developments in our politico-economic systems, the concept of tikkun (repair) provides us a platform for the renewal of our cultures. At the least, renewal and restoration becomes a much-needed rallying cry to make us realize the need of the hour.

Consecration of the Soul via Action

Almost two decades ago, a group of Japanese nuclear abolitionists visited the United States to lobby at the United Nations against nuclear weapons. They stayed at our home when they came to Connecticut. The group included Miyoko Matsubara,[794] one of the "Hiroshima Maidens," a group of school-age girls who were irradiated and disfigured by the bombing. What I found most striking about

Miyoko was the absence[795] of bitterness, sense of victimhood, or self-pity. Instead, she carried a soul that was full of life, compassion, and agency.

The experience of having lived through what she described as "hell on earth" had given her unusual tenderness, wisdom, and courage. Her compassion and concern were directed completely towards others. The concern was not limited to nuclear threat alone; it was about the violence of war in general: "My mission is to continue telling my experience as a survivor ... talking about the folly of war and the preciousness of life, to as many people as possible."

Even in moments when her facial expression betrayed a sense of helplessness at the collective human inability to understand what she understood so well, Miyoko's attitude was of agency and tikkun—every small change she could make mattered.[796]

While Heschel's words discuss the avoidance of the "desecration" of the soul, the work he did was to manifest the "consecration" of the soul. Miyoko Matsubara's mission was no different. They had both realized that there is no "other," and they lived their lives true to that precept, true to the manifestation of human agency inherent to them. In that context—promising that humans will be made into "*light*" (agents of good)—*Isaiah* 49:6 declares that "It is too little that you should be My servant" only.

Finally, while the spiritual concepts in different religious traditions stand on their own, the beauty with which they can come together is also remarkable. If the agency of pursuing "spiritual motherhood" and "sanctification of the soul"—as promoted by Francis and Heschel respectively—is a tree named *Radical Revolution of Values*, then we can take *Tikkun* as the trunk of the tree. Attached to the trunk—as main branches of the tree—are *Aparigraha* (non-attachment), *Ihsan* (beauty in action), *Panna/Prajna* (discernment), *Santosha* (contentment), *Seva* (service), *Te* (moral force), etc. The foliage and flower of this tree are completely imbued with *Agape* (unconditional love)—which, in addition to being Jesus's principal message, is also a central concept in all our spiritual traditions.

It would be apt to note the component of struggle for social reform within the effort of all prophets and sages, for example

Moses, Jesus, Muhammad, and Nanak. Their messages similarly pointed to the injustice of the prevalent systems that controlled the socio-political and economic power. The agency for change and restoration of normative and just balance, therefore, has been part of our religious traditions, and will always be a struggle in process.

CONCLUSION:
MANIFESTING THE MESSAGE

In a well-known consolation letter to a stranger who had lost a young son, Einstein stated:

> A human being is part of a whole, called by us the 'Universe' a part limited in time and space. He experiences himself, his thoughts and feelings, as something separated from the rest—a kind of optical delusion of his consciousness. The striving to free oneself from this delusion is the one issue of true religion. Not to nourish the delusion but to try to overcome it is the way to reach the attainable measure of peace of mind.[797]

Different religions provide all the necessary guidance their adherents need when they keep open the spirit of reflection so that they may free themselves from this experiential prison as described by Einstein. Remarkably, the great scientist refers to man's sense of separation from the rest of the creation as an "optical delusion of consciousness." One of the goals of this book has been to broaden the horizon of information for further development of this understanding.

The spark of tikkun, pointed out by the Kabbalistic tradition, already resides within us, waiting all along for its discovery. A similar understanding within the teachings of our own faith may be sufficient in our ability to harness the agency the human race needs in our collective journey towards justice, peace, and harmony in this world.

There is an indigenous American parable in which the grandfather is telling the grandson about two wolves—one good and one bad—engaged in a never-ending fight inside every one of us. The grandson asks: which one of them will ultimately win. "The one we feed" is the grandpa's response. Whatever wolf the external politico-economic forces want us to feed, the ultimate *agency* is within us, and no one can take it away. We can be certain about it because we know that the "spark" resides within us.

Sage Vyasa brings the *Bhagavad Gita* to a conclusion with the following words by Sanjaya, the visionary narrator:

> There do fortune, victory, abundance,
> and morality exist, so I think.

The epic poem thus ends with "so I think," three words of enigmatic contingency. As if the mantle and gavel of agency has been surreptitiously handed to the unsuspecting reader.

By being the spark, we fulfill the responsibility of tikkun. May God allow this effort to be received in that light. As Rumi would say, may the Lord of the two worlds bless you. And in Ghalib's words:

> Flow it would, the inexorable lifeblood,
> in the veins of a rock;
>
> What you deem melancholy, lo and behold,
> if only it were a spark.[798]

APPENDIX A:

CULTURE/STRUCTURE COMPARISON

Dimension of Comparison	CULTURE	STRUCTURE
Target of Benefit	Supra-Self, Amorphous	Self-benefit, Self-bound
Benefit Outlook	Society-centric	Self-centric
Beneficiary	Society	Self
Value Promotion	Beneficial/Harmful, Fair/Unfair	Right/Wrong, Win/Lose
Transmission Modality	Moral, Ethical, Customs, Mores	Procedural, Process-oriented
Transmission Format	Oral Tradition, Literature	Written Code, Manuals
Agency & Empowerment	Promotes Agency	Limits & Suppresses Agency
Room for Non-Conformity	Relatively High	Relatively Low
Tolerance of Non-Conformity	High, Some Non-Conformity a Source of Evolution	Low, Non-Conformity Causes Disruption
Usual Application Domains	Societies, Self-governing Democratic Entities	"Institution", States, Legal Entities
Sphere of Influence	Societal / Universal	Institutional
Emphasis (on)	Substance & Meaning	Forms & Appearances
Interpretation	Varied, Diffused, Agent the Interpreter	Uniform, Consistent, Central Authority that Interprets
Enforcement	"Soft," Social Pressure, Contextual Hermeneutic	"Hard," Code, Regulation, Law, Prescription/Proscription
Impetus for Enforcement	Perceived Societal Well-being, Promotion of Tradition, Justice	Protection of the "Institution"
Implementation (via)	Exhortation, Social Pressure	Complusion, Discipline, Policies
Signs of Implementation	"Mindful" Rule Application (Agent the Lever of Application)	"Mindless" Application, Follow the Rule
Mode of Spreading	Abstract	Specifically Defined
Change Process	Diffused, Expansive, Autopoietic	Procedural, Reactive, Determined by Hierarchy

APPENDIX B:

GLOSSARY OF CONCEPTS, PERSONS, AND PLACES

Acaranga Sutra: Sacred text in the Jain religion. Contains teachings of Mahavira.

Adab: Applied and practical ethics; respect, courtesy, and politeness; good behavior, manners and etiquettes.

Adhem, Abou Ben: See Ibn Adham.

Adi Shankara: See Shankara.

Agape: The highest form of love and charity. It is also the love God has for man and vice versa. The phrase "God is love" appears two times (4:8 and 4:16) in the *First Epistle of John*.

Agency: The inherent human capacity of decision-making and action—somewhat independently of other (external) factors, yet in consort with those factors. See chapter 15.

al-Ghazali: Eleventh-century Persian polymath. A highly influential Islamic philosopher, logician, and theologian.

Aparigraha: Non-attachment. This trait is one of the vows (*vratas*) in Jainism and one of the restraints (*yamas*) in Hinduism.

Apophasis: "Theology by Negation." Describing something by stating which characteristic it does not have. Especially applicable in theology since human language, thought, and intellect are considered inadequate in grasping various concepts such as the Divine nature or essence.

Atma Bodha: A short text in Sanskrit attributed to Adi Shankara (see Shankara below). It describes awareness of self-knowledge.

Avicenna: See Ibn Sina.

Bahá'u'lláh: Nineteenth-century prophet-founder of the Baha'i Faith. One of the two considered by the Baha'is to be Divine Messengers. The other is The Bab, who is the Herald of the Baha'i Faith. (Several phrases in this definition directly copied from Wikipedia and Bahai.org.)

Bhagavad Gita: A scripture comprising of several hundred verses; part of the epic *Mahabharata*. It is a holy scripture in Hinduism. Sometimes, *Bhagavad Gita* is shortened to *Gita*. (Literally means Divine Song or

Song by God.) Traditionally, Sage Vyasa is considered to be the author of the *Mahabharata* (and *Gita*).

Bodhisattva: One who travels on the path towards Buddhahood.

Cordovero, Moses: Sixteenth-century rabbi and Talmudic scholar who lived in Safed (in Galilee, now Israel). He is a central mystical figure in Judaism whose seminal works have been influential in the development of Kabbalah.

Deen/Din: Literally, submission or following. See chapter 10, section Structural Linguistic Limitations....

Dhammapada: One of the best-known Buddhist scriptures; a collection of the Buddha's sayings in verse form.

Dharma or Dhamma: A fundamental concept in Indic religions with many meanings and connotations. "Moral and religious duty" would perhaps provide the simplest understanding today. Dharma in Sanskrit and Dhamma in Pali signify the same concept.

Diwan: A complete collection of poems by one poet. Sometimes this may exclude the really long poems (such as Rumi's *Masnavi*). The word simply implies a form of poetry collection; it does not reflect the type of poetry in that collection.

Dukkha or Duhkha: A foundational concept in Indic religions especially Buddhism. In Buddhist thought, it indicates the nature of all existence. "Suffering" is the usual translation into English, though there is more to the word's connotations. Sukha would be one of its antonyms.

Eckhart: See Meister Eckhart.

Ein Sof: In Kabbalah, refers to God prior to any self-manifestation. The expression's translation would be "without end" or "unending." It is understood to mean "infinite." It is believed that Rabbi Azriel of Gerona may have been the first person to make such use of the expression.

Enlightenment: The intellectual and philosophical movement in Europe in the 17th and 18th centuries. Various ideas (liberty, tolerance, separation of church and state, etc.) considered so fundamental today to the Western civilization came out of this period. Also known as the Age of Reason or the Age of Enlightenment.

Enneads: Six-volume collection of the writings of Plotinus, a Hellenistic philosopher who was born in Roman Egypt around 200 AD. Porphyry, a student of Plotinus, compiled the work.

Erasmus: Sixteenth-century Dutch philosopher and Catholic theologian, considered to be a noted scholar of his time. His place in

Renaissance humanism can be seen by the "Prince of the Humanists" sobriquet he still enjoys.

Etymology: Study of the history of words and linguistic forms; analysis of a word to find its origin or original meaning.

Exegesis: Critical interpretation and explanation of a text, usually a religious one.

Faiz, Faiz Ahmed: Famous twentieth-century Pakistani poet and intellectual. His people-centered and inspiring poetry is well known the world over.

Fatwa: Consult, Opinion, Advice, Ruling. In Islam, it means a legal-theological consult; the notion finds its origin in the *Qur'an* (4:127, 176 etc.). The opinion-seeker goes to an expert for a consult. (The seeker may even be a civil judge or a ruler.) The advice of the expert is non-binding and does not apply to any person or institution other than the fatwa petitioner. Just like other concepts in the hands of religious establishments, the notion of fatwa has also evolved into all kinds of opportunistic interpretations. For further clarification, see Berger, Maurits S. "Fatwa." In *The Oxford Encyclopedia of Islam and Politics. Oxford Islamic Studies Online*, http://www.oxfordislamicstudies.com/article/opr/t342/e0003 (accessed Apr 24, 2022).

Genjokoan: Well-known and influential essay by Dogen Zenji, founder of Soto School in Zen Buddhism. As Shohaku Okumura explains, "Genjokoan begins with an explanation of Zen and then goes on to elucidate delusion and realization, wholehearted practice, and the relationship of self to realization and environment." (*Realizing Genjokoan: The Key to Dogen's Shobogenzo*, p 23-24.)

Ghalib: Mirza Asadullah Baig Khan Ghalib is considered the all-time greatest Urdu poet. He lived in India in the nineteenth century.

Gita: See *Bhagavad Gita*.

Gurdwara: Place of assembly and worship for Sikhs. People from all backgrounds and faith are welcomed to any Gurdwara Sahib.

Guru Arjan Dev Ji: Fifth of the Sikh Gurus, who compiled the first official edition of Adi Granth, which later expanded to become the *Guru Granth Sahib*. Lived in the sixteenth century. ("Ji" is an honorific in Indic languages and signifies love and respect.)

Guru Granth Sahib: The holy religious scripture in Sikhism.

Guru Nanak Dev Ji: Founder of Sikhism and the first Guru of the religion. Lived in the fifteenth and sixteenth centuries.

Hadith: Collection of Prophet Muhammad's reported sayings and actions. The earliest one was compiled some two centuries after the Prophet's death. The word literally means tradition. Hadith Qudsi (sacred tradition) is something Prophet Muhammad said to convey God's message (this is different from the *Qur'an* which is God's direct revelation).

Haft Vadi, Chahar Vadi: Two mystical treatises in the Persian language written by Bahá'u'lláh, founder of the Bahai Faith. Literal meaning: Seven Valleys, Four Valleys.

Hobbesian: In accordance with political philosopher Thomas Hobbes's doctrines and ideas, especially the belief that humans naturally compete and fight exclusively for their own interests.

Holistic: Theory that systems (biological, physical, social) can be optimally viewed as wholes, not a mere collection of parts. This is in contrast to the concept of reductionism. Holism is a neologism coined by Jan Christian Smut of South Africa.

Ibn Adham, Ibrahim: An eighth-century Sufi saint, he was born in Balkh, currently in Afghanistan—the same place where Rumi was born. Rumi wrote about Ibrahim in the *Masnavi*. Ibrahim was born a prince and became the monarch of his kingdom. He, however, left everything and chose an ascetic life. It is believed that a Christian monk named Simeon was Ibn Adham's earliest spiritual teacher.

Ibn Arabi: A twelfth and thirteenth century Arab Andalusian Muslim scholar, philosopher, poet, and mystic. He would arguably be one of the most prolific authors who ever lived. His place as a recognized saint (*waliallah* in Islam) earned him the honorific *al-Shaykh al-Akbar* (the Greatest Shaykh). Even in medieval Europe, he enjoyed the sobriquet *Doctor Maximus* (the Greatest Teacher). As for the present time, Yale's Professor Robyn Creswell says that Ibn Arabi "represents a grand synthesis of Sufi thought. Ignorance of his works in the West is one of the great scandals of intellectual history."

Ibn Sina: Avicenna. Eleventh-century Persian polymath whose works span the field of medicine, philosophy, physics, mathematics, theology, logic, psychology, geology, geography, and astronomy. His *Canon of Medicine* (*al-qanun fi al-tibb*) was used as a standard medical text in Europe until the eighteenth century.

Identity: The term "identity" in this book is used mostly in the sense of social, group, and collective affiliation based upon such classifications as national, religious, gender, racial, ethnic, etc. See chapter 4 for a fuller discussion.

Ihsan: Beauty in action or pursuit of excellence. A Qur'anic concept mentioned scores of times in the holy book. (See chapter 18, subtitle "Non-Separation …").

Iqbal, Muhammad: Twentieth-century South Asian Muslim philosopher and politician. An acclaimed poet, he wrote his verse in Urdu and Farsi.

ISI: Inter-services Intelligence. Pakistan's military intelligence agency.

ISIL or ISIS: Islamic State of Iraq and the Levant. Also known as Islamic State and Daesh. A militant and extremist group that derives its inspiration from its version of Islamic teachings. Saudi Arabia is known to have been its biggest supporter (before developing its own curriculum, ISIL even used Saudi textbooks in its "education" system). In 2014, ISIL came to prominence when it conquered certain areas in Iraq and Syria—establishing a state and engaging in various types of atrocities.

Janissary: A loyal or subservient supporter or troop who exhibits unquestioning loyalty and enthusiasm for a leader or a cause.

Kaaba: The cube-shaped building in Mecca that is considered the most sacred site in Islam. This is the point (qibla) Muslims face towards when performing the daily ritual prayers.

Kabbalah: Esoteric discipline and school of thought in Judaism. It provides the foundation of mystical religious thought, interpretation, and practice within Judaism.

Lao Tzu or Laozi: Ancient Chinese philosopher considered to be the author of *Tao Te Ching* and the founder of philosophical Taoism. He is believed to have lived somewhere in the 6th–4th century BCE time period. The name is an honorific title that translates to "old and venerable master."

Luria, Isaac: Sixteenth-century leading rabbi and mystic, who has a central place in today's Kabbalah. His literary works are few, yet his spiritual enlightenment drew followers towards him. Some traditions say that Luria arrived in Safed the exact day of Rabbi Cordovero's funeral. There also are accounts that he was Cordevero's student for a short time. The concept of Tikkun is part of Lurianic Kabbalah.

Maharshi, Ramana: 19th and 20th century Indian Hindu sage. He prescribed self-enquiry and self-awareness as the main paths towards removing ignorance and gaining happiness.

Mahavira: Spiritual guide in Jainism. As Britannica says, "Technically, the 24th of the Tirthankaras (meaning ford-maker or savior of the Jain community), Lord Mahavira is believed to have lived around the 6th century BCE." The honorific Mahavira translates to "great hero." He is believed to have been an older contemporary of the Buddha.

Masnavi: Rumi's magnum opus. See Chapter 11 for a fuller discussion.

Meister Eckhart: 13th–14th century Christian theologian, mystic, and philosopher. He was born in what is now Germany in the Holy Roman Empire.

MI6: Formally Secret Intelligence Service (SIS), is the foreign intelligence service of the United Kingdom. MI6 may be considered the equivalent of the CIA. (**MI5** is responsible for domestic counterintelligence.)

Mysticism: Spirituality that is aware and accepting of human relation and connection with God, resulting in an integral and inseparable consciousness of the unceasing Divine Presence. Religion (way of life, state of being) as it emerges from such consciousness is simultaneously passionate, profound, and humble.

Nihilism: The most common and popular implication is the rejection of all social and political institutions, or that life itself is without intrinsic purpose and values. More formally, the philosophy has more complex facets.

Obscurantism: Resistance to, or effort to disallow, the spread of knowledge; a policy of withholding knowledge from the general public.

Operation Cyclone: Code name for CIA's program to arm and finance the Afghan mujahideen in Afghanistan (against the Soviet invasion) from 1979 to around 1992. See chapter 1.

Panna or Prajna: Discernment; used as an important concept in Indic philosophy and religions.

Rabi'a al-Adawiyya: Also called Rabi'a of Basra. Eighth-century Sufi Muslim. She is considered one of the cardinal saints (waliallah) in Islam.

Ramakrishna: Nineteenth-century Indian Hindu mystic from Bengal. After his spiritual practice and deliberation, he came to the conclusion that various religions represent various paths to the same goal.

Reductionism: Idea or philosophy that a phenomenon can be understood in terms of other simpler or more basic phenomena. Also, a position that interprets or understands a complex system as the sum of its parts. See holism also as a contradictory concept.

Rig Veda: Ancient Indian collection of hymns. One of the four sacred canonical texts in Hinduism, it is the oldest known Vedic Sanskrit text and among the oldest extant texts in Indo-European language. (Rig Veda would translate to praiseful knowledge.)

Rousseau, Jean Jacques: Eighteenth-century Genevan philosopher whose political philosophy influenced the progress of Enlightenment in Europe (and may have had some influence on the French Revolution). Highly influential in modern political thought, Rousseau is today considered one of the most important Enlightenment thinkers.

Rumi: Jalal ad-Din Muhammad Balkhi; author of the *Masnavi*. See chapter 11.

Samadhi: In Indic religions, a state of meditative consciousness attained by practicing dhyana (withdrawing the mind away from sensory perceptions into a state of equanimity and awareness).

Santosha: Contentment and satisfaction; an important ethical and practical concept in Indian philosophy.

Sefirot: In Kabbalah, the Ten Sefirot—singular Sefirah—are Ein Sof's revealed attributes / emanations that interact with each other and the world. See chapter 13 for more information.

Seva: A common word in Indian languages denoting service. In Indic religions, it signifies selfless dedication to others and service performed without the expectation of anything in return.

Shankara: Eighth-century Indian Vedic scholar who is the preeminent proponent of the Advaita Vedanta tradition. Same person as Adi Shankara.

Shari'ah: For nuances in the concept, see chapter 10, subtitle "Structural Linguistic Limitations ...".

Society: The human collective, with a thread of commonality, that is interdependent or connected with one another. It may be a clan, a village, a whole country, or all of humanity. This extended community network creates kinship bonds on various possible dimensions: moral, traditional, spiritual, sartorial, linguistic, artistic, culinary, commercial, etc. Society thus is that collective where mutual dependence and forming take place. "Value" then is the most salient aspect of this process of mutual dependence and formation.

Sri Guru Granth Sahib: See Guru Granth Sahib.

Sufism: See Tasawwuf.

Structure: See chapter 3, subtitle "Structure and Corruption: Defining ... the Concepts."

Sukha: A concept in Indic religions that translates to bliss, happiness, ease. Dukkha would be one of its antonyms.

Systematic: Methodical. Following a set methodology, schedule, arrangement, or pattern.

Systemic: What relates to or affects an entire system. In an interconnected system, change at point A may cause a change at Point M.

Tagore, Rabindranath: 19th–20th century Indian polymath from Bengal. He was a philosopher, composer, playwright, and painter. As a poet, he is known for the beautiful verse in Gitanjali, for which he received the Nobel Prize in Literature. In 1915, King George V awarded knighthood to Tagore, which he repudiated in 1919 in the wake of the Jallianwala Bagh Massacre by the British forces. In his renouncement letter, he wrote: "The time has come when badges of honour make our shame glaring in their incongruous context of humiliation ..."

Tao Te Ching: Classic Chinese text traditionally credited to Lao Tzu. It is believed to have been written in the fourth century BCE. Along with *Zhuangzi*, *Tao Te Ching* is a fundamental text for Taoism (both religious and philosophical). Next to the *Bible* and the *Bhagavad Gita*, *Tao Te Ching* is the world's most translated book.

Tasawwuf: Also known as Sufism. Within Islam, a school of thought that emphasizes spirituality, esotericism, and relative asceticism. It has also been defined as Islamic mysticism (which is a bad definition since the word "mysticism" does not have an objective definition and is generally used pejoratively). Rumi and his *Masnavi* are examples of Tasawwuf.

Te: Moral force, character, virtue, personality, integrity, etc. See chapter 10, subtitle "Shifting Meaning of Words."

Teshuva: In Judaism, repentance with the primary purpose of ethical self-transformation.

Tikkun: See chapter 15, subtitle "Tikkun and its Place" for an elaboration of the concept.

Upanishads: Hindu philosophy texts of the late Vedic era. Commonly referred to as Vedanta, the Upanishads deal with diverse topics such as meditation, consciousness, philosophy, and ontology. Around a hundred Upanishads are known, of which a dozen or so are considered the principal Upanishads.

Uttaradhayana Sutra: An important sacred book in Jainism that deals with aspects of doctrine and discipline.

Wahhabism: A Sunni Muslim revivalist movement associated with the doctrines of Muhammad ibn Abd al-Wahhab, an eighteenth-century preacher. The Kingdom of Saudi Arabia and Qatar are the only two countries with Wahhabi majority, though Saudi Arabia has spent tens of billions of dollars to promote its religiopolitical ideology all over the world.

Waheguru: Word used for God in Sikhism. The word "wah" in this name comes from Persian and is an interjection of awe, admiration, and delightful bewilderment. "Wondrous Teacher" would be the literal translation of the word.

Yochai: Rabbi Shimon bar Yochai was a second century sage and teacher in ancient Judea.

Zeitgeist: A German concept meaning spirit of the time or age. It signifies an invisible force influencing a certain era in human history. Rev. Martin Luther King used this word frequently.

Zenji, Dogen: Thirteenth-century Japanese Buddhist philosopher and poet who founded the Soto school of Zen.

Zohar: Foundational text in Kabbalah. It addresses various theological subjects and includes commentary on the mystical aspects of the *Torah*. Within Orthodox Judaism, the traditional view has been that Rabbi Shimon bar Yochai is the author of Zohar. Gershom Scholem's research in the twentieth century, however, established that Rabbi Moses de Leon (thirteenth century) authored it. Now it is widely believed, especially within academic circles, that de Leon was the author of this key text.

Zoroaster: Also Zarathushtra, Zardosht. Ancient Iranian spiritual leader (prophet); founder of what is now called Zoroastrianism. While there is no consensus, he is believed to have lived around the sixth century BCE.

Zhuangzi (Chuang Tzu): Along with *Tao Te Ching*, it is one of the two ancient Chinese foundational texts of Taoism. It is attributed to and named after its traditional author Zhuangzi (Master Zhuang). Though mainly philosophical, it also enjoys a prominent place amongst the greatest literary works in Chinese history. It is believed to have been authored around 400 BCE.

SELECTED BIBLIOGRAPHY

BOOKS, ACADEMIC JOURNALS, ACADEMIC STUDIES, AND GOVERNMENTAL REPORTS

Abdel Haleem, Muhammad. *Understanding the Qur'an: Themes and Style*. London: Tauris, 2001.

Abou El Fadl, Khaled. *The Search for Beauty in Islam: A Conference of the Books*. Lanham, MD: Rowman & Littlefield, 2006.

Abou El Fadl, Khaled, Joshua Cohen, and Ian Lague. *The Place of Tolerance in Islam*. Boston: Beacon Press, 2002.

Ahmad, Eqbal, Carollee Bengelsdorf, Margaret Cerullo, and Yogesh Chandrani. *The Selected Writings of Eqbal Ahmad*. New York: Columbia University Press, 2006.

Ahmed, Shahab. *What Is Islam? The Importance of Being Islamic*. Princeton, NJ: Princeton University Press, 2016.

Aish, Hakeem Agha Jan Dehlvi. *Kulliyaat-e Aish*. Compiled by Habiba Bano. New Delhi: Taraqqi-e Urdu Bureau, 1992.

al-Ghazālī, Abu Hamid Muhammad. *Kitāb sharḥ 'ajā'ib Al-Qalb = The Marvels of the Heart: Book 21 of the Iḥyā' 'ulūm Al-dīn, the Revival of the Religious Sciences*. Trans. Walter James Skellie. Louisville, KY: Fons Vitae, 2010.

al-Hujwīrī, 'Alī. *Kashf Al-Mahjūb*. Interpreted by Maulvi Feroz-ud-Din. Lahore: Ferozsons, 2003.

al-Hujwīrī, 'Alī Ibn-'Uṯhmān al-Jullābī. *The Revelation of the Veiled: An Early Persian Treatise on Sufism*. Translated by Reynold A Nicholson. Warminster, UK: Aris & Phillips, 2000.

Alter, Robert. Foreword to *Major Trends in Jewish Mysticism*, xi-xxvii. By Gershom Scholem. New York: Schocken, 1995.

Anderson, Paul. *Platonism in the Midwest*. Philadelphia: Temple University Publications, 1963.

Arab League. "The Arab Convention For The Suppression Of Terrorism." United Nations Office on Drug and Crime. Accessed May 12, 2021. https://www.unodc.org/images/tldb-f/conv_arab_terrorism.en.pdf.

Armstrong, Karen. *A History of God: the 4000-Year Quest of Judaism, Christianity, and Islam*. New York: Knopf, 1993.

Armstrong, Karen. *The Battle for God*. New York: Ballantine Books, 2001.

Asad, Muhammad. *The Message of The Qur'an*. Gibraltar: Dar al-Andalus. 1980.

Bailey, Olivia. *Hidden Marks: A study of women students' experiences of harassment, stalking, violence and sexual assault*. London: National Union of Students, 2010.

Baldwin, James. *Nobody Knows My Name*. New York: Vintage Books, 1993.

Bennoune, Karima. *Cultural Rights*. United Nations General Assembly, A/71/317, August 9, 2016. https://undocs.org/en/A/71/317.

Birgivî, Mehmet Efendi, and Tosun Bayrak. *The Path of Muhammad: A Book on Islamic Morals and Ethics*. Bloomington, IN: World Wisdom, 2005.

Black, Charles L. "He Cannot Choose but Hear: The Plight of the Captive Auditor." *Columbia Law Review* 53, no. 7 (November 1953): 960-72. Accessed August 27, 2020. doi:10.2307/1119180.

Browne, Edward G. *A Literary History of Persia: From the Earliest Times until Firdawsi*. London: Unwin, 1908.

Brzezinski, Zbigniew. *The Grand Chessboard: American Primacy and Its Geostrategic Imperatives*. New York: Basic Books, 1997.

Burke, Edmund. "Reflections on the French Revolution." *From the Harvard Classics*, Vol. XXIV, Part 3. Accessed September 17, 2020. https://www.bartleby.com/24/3/6.html.

Cone, James H. "Martin Luther King, Jr., and the Third World." *The Journal of American History* 74, no. 2 (September 1987): 455-67.

Cordovez, Diego, and Selig S. Harrison. *Out of Afghanistan: The Inside Story of the Soviet Withdrawal*. Oxford: Oxford University Press, 1995.

Curtis, Mark. *Secret Affairs: Britain's Collusion with Radical Islam*. London: Serpent's Tail, 2018.

de Waal, Frans, Robert Wright, Christine M. Korsgaard, Philip Kitcher, and Peter Singer. *Primates and Philosophers: How Morality Evolved*. Edited by Stephen Macedo and Josiah Ober. Princeton: Princeton University Press, 2016.

Dickens, Charles, and Patricia Ingham. *American Notes for General Circulation*. London: Penguin Books, 2000.

Dixon, Howard Lee. "Low Intensity Conflict: Overview, Definitions, and Policy Concerns." CLIC, Langley AFB Virginia. June 1989. https://apps.dtic.mil/dtic/tr/fulltext/u2/a209046.pdf

Durant, Will, and Ariel Durant. *Lessons of History*. New York: Simon & Schuster, 1968.

Eckhart von Hochheim [Meister]. *Complete Mystical Works of Meister Eckhart*. Translated and Edited by Maurice O'Connell Walshe. New York: Crossroad, 2009.

Edwards, Marc A, and Siddhartha Roy. "Academic Research in the 21st Century: Maintaining Scientific Integrity in a Climate of Perverse Incentives and Hypercompetition." *Environmental Engineering Science* 34, no. 1 (January 2017): 51-61. doi: 10.1089/ees.2016.022351.

Eichrodt, Walther. *Man in the Old Testament, Studies in Biblical Theology*. Translated by K. and R. Gregor Smith. London: SCM Press, 1951.

Fakhry, Majid. *A History of Islamic Philosophy*. New York: Columbia University Press, 1983.

Feynman, Richard P., and Michelle Feynman. *Perfectly Reasonable Deviations from the Beaten Track: The Letters of Richard P. Feynman*. New York: Basic Books, 2005.

Faiz, Faiz Ahmad. *Nuskha Ha'ey Wafa*. Lahore: Maktaba-e Karava'n.

Freke, Timothy. *The Illustrated Book of Sacred Scriptures*. Wheaton, IL: Theosophical Publishing House, 1998.

Ghalib, Mirza Asadullah Baig Khan. *Divān-e Ghalib*. Lahore: Ferozsons, 1989.

Gibbs, David. *Afghanistan: The Soviet Invasion in Retrospect*. International Politics 37, no. 2 (2000): 233-245.

Gibran, Kahlil. *The Prophet*. New York: Alfred A. Knopf, 1992.

Gilens, Martin, and Benjamin Page. "Testing Theories of American Politics: Elites, Interest Groups, and Average Citizens." *Perspectives on Politics* 12, no. 3 (September 2014): 564-81. doi: 10.1017/S1537592714001595.

Graeber, David, and David Wengrow. *The Dawn of Everything: A New History of Humanity*. New York: Farrar, Straus and Giroux, 2021.

Gu, Chenjuan Nga Brereton, Amy Schweitzer, Matthew Cotter, Daisy Duan, Elisabet Børsheim, Robert R Wolfe, Luu V Pham, Vsevolod Y Polotsky, and Jonathan C Jun. "Metabolic Effects of Late Dinner in Healthy Volunteers—A Randomized Crossover Clinical Trial." *The Journal of Clinical Endocrinology & Metabolism* 105, no. 8 (August 2020): 2789-802. doi: 10.1210/clinem/dgaa354

Hanh, Thich Nhat. *Love in Action: Writings on Nonviolent Social Change*. Berkeley: Parallax Press, 1993.

Hanh, Thich Nhat. *Being Peace*. Edited by Arnold Kotler. Berkeley: Parallax Press, 1996.

Hazen, Don. *After 9/11: Solutions for a Saner World*. San Francisco: AlterNet.org, 2001.

Helminski, Camille Adams. *Women of Sufism: A Hidden Treasure—Writings and Stories of Mystic Poets, Scholars & Saints*. Boston: Shambhala, 2003.

Heschel, Abraham Joshua, and Susannah Heschel. *Moral Grandeur and Spiritual Audacity: Essays*. New York: Farrar, Straus and Giroux, 1997.

Hixon, Lex. *Coming Home: The Experience of Enlightenment in Sacred Traditions*. New Delhi: New Age Books, 2004.

Ho, Mae-Wan. *The Rainbow and the Worm: The Physics of Organisms*. Singapore: World Scientific, 2006.

Hobbes, Thomas. *Leviathan*. Originally published 1651. Project Gutenberg (EBook #3207), January 25, 2013. http://www.gutenberg.org/files/3207

Hume, Robert Ernest. *The Thirteen Principal Upanishads: Translated from the Sanskrit with an Outline of the Philosophy of the Upanishads and an Annotated Bibliography*. London: Oxford University Press, 1921.

Ibn al-ʻArabī, Muhyi-d Din, and R W J Austin. *The Bezels of Wisdom* [Fusus al-Hikam]. Mahwah, NJ: Paulist Press, 1980.

Illich, Ivan. *Toward a History of Needs*. New York: Pantheon Books, 1978.

Iqbal, Muhammad. *Kulliyaat-e Iqbal*. Islamabad: Alhamra Publishing, 2000

Jefferson, Thomas. "From Thomas Jefferson to Benjamin Rush, 23 September 1800," *Founders Online,* National Archives, https://founders.archives.gov/documents/Jefferson/01-32-02-0102. [Original source: *The Papers of Thomas Jefferson*, vol. 32, *1 June 1800–16 February 1801*, ed. Barbara B. Oberg. Princeton: Princeton University Press, 2005, pp. 166–169.]

Jefferson, Thomas. "From Thomas Jefferson to St. John de Crèvecoeur, 15 January 1787," *Founders Online,* National Archives, https://founders.archives.gov/documents/Jefferson/01-11-02-0041. [Original source: *The Papers of Thomas Jefferson*, vol. 11, *1 January–6 August 1787*, ed. Julian P. Boyd. Princeton: Princeton University Press, 1955, pp. 43–45.]

Kadish, Sanford H. "The Crisis of Overcriminalization." *The Annals of the American Academy of Political and Social Science* 374 (1967): 157-70. http://www.jstor.org/stable/1037202.

King, Martin Luther. *Where Do We Go from Here: Chaos or Community?* Boston: Beacon Press, 1968.

King, Martin Luther. *Strength to Love*. Philadelphia: Fortress, 1981.

King, Martin Luther, and James Melvin Washington. *A Testament of Hope: The Essential Writings of Martin Luther King, Jr.* New York: Harper & Row, 1986.

Knox, Bernard. *The Norton Book of Classical Literature*. New York: Norton, 1993.

Korten, David C. *When Corporations Rule the World, Second Edition*. San Francisco: Berrett-Koehler Publishers, Inc., 2001.

Kriwaczek, Paul. *In Search of Zarathustra: The First Prophet and the Ideas That Changed the World*. New York: Knopf, 2003.

Lao Tzu. *Tao Te Ching: The Classic Book of Integrity and the Way*. Translated by Victor H. Mair. New York: Quality Paperback Book Club, 1998.

Leakey, Richard E. *The Origin of Humankind*. New York: Basic Books, 1994.

Magee, Bryan. *The Story of Thought*. New York: DK Publishing, 1998.

Mair, Victor H. Preface to *Tao Te Ching: The Classic Book of Integrity and the Way*, xvii-xxii; by Lao Tzu. New York: Quality Paperback Book Club, 1998.

Martinez, Mario E. *The Mindbody Code: How to Change the Beliefs That Limit Your Health, Longevity, and Success*. Boulder, CO: Sounds True, 2014.

Matt, Daniel C. *The Essential Kabbalah: The Heart of Jewish Mysticism*. New York: Quality Paperback Book Club, 1998.

Mays, Benjamin. *Born to Rebel: An Autobiography*. New York: Scribner, 1971.

McAdams, Richard H. "The Political Economy of Criminal Law and Procedure: The Pessimists' View." *Criminal Law Conversations*, P.H. Robson, K. Ferzan and S. Garvey, eds., Oxford University Press, 2009, U of Chicago, Public Law Working Paper No. 243 (October 22, 2008). doi: 10.2139/ssrn.1288158.

McGrew, Sarah, Teresa Ortega, Joel Breakstone and Sam Wineburg. "Evaluating Information: The Cornerstone of Civic Online

Reasoning." *Stanford History Education Group*. November 22, 2016.

Meyer, Wali Ali, Bilal Hyde, Faisal Muqaddam, and Shabda Kahn. *Physicians of the Heart: A Sufi View of the Ninety-Nine Names of Allah*. San Francisco: Sufi Ruhaniat International, 2011.

Miller, Barbara Stoler. *The Bhagavad-Gita: Krishna's Counsel in Time of War*. New York: Quality Paperback Book Club, 1998.

Moniquet, Claude. "The Involvement of Salafism/Wahhabism in the Support and Supply of Arms to Rebel Groups around the World." *The European Parliament—Directorate-General for External Policies*, June 2013.

Morris, James Winston. *The Reflective Heart: Discovering Spiritual Intelligence in Ibn Arabi's Meccan Illuminations*. Louisville, KY: Fons Vitae, 2005.

Nasr, Seyyed Hossein. "Rumi and the Sufi Tradition." *Studies in Comparative Religion*, Vol. 8, no. 2 (Spring 1974). Accessed August 16, 2020. http://www.studiesincomparativereligion.com/uploads/ArticlePDFs/230.pdf

Nietzsche, Friedrich Wilhelm. *On the Genealogy of Morality*. Edited by Keith Ansell-Pearson; translated by Carol Diethe. Cambridge: Cambridge University Press, 2006.

Nováček, Karel, Simone Mühl, Seán Fobbe, Roger Matthews, Rafał Koliński, and Olivier Nieuwenhuijse. *The Intentional Destruction of Cultural Heritage in Iraq as a Violation of Human Rights: Submission for the United Nations Special Rapporteur in the Field of Cultural Rights*. Munich: RASHID International e.V. August 28, 2017. doi: 10.5281/zenodo.3835895

Orwell, George. *1984: a Novel*. New York: Signet Classics, 1961.

Paine, Thomas, Sidney Hook, and Jack Fruchtman. *Common Sense, Rights of Man, and Other Essential Writings of Thomas Paine*. New York: Signet Classics, 2003.

Paul, James, and Céline Nahory. *War and Occupation in Iraq*. New York: Global Policy Forum. June 2007. https://archive.globalpolicy.org/images/pdfs/full.pdf.

Phillips, Adam, and Barbara Taylor. *On Kindness*. London: Penguin, 2010.

Pinheiro, Paulo Sérgio, Karen Koning AbuZayd, Vitit Muntarbhorn, and Carla Del Ponte. *Report of the Independent International Commission of Inquiry on the Syrian Arab Republic*. United Nations General Assembly, A/HRC/31/68, February 11, 2016.

Pope Francis. *Evangelii Gaudium of the Holy Father*. Vatican Press: http://www.vatican.va/content/dam/francesco/pdf/apost_

exhortations/documents/papa-francesco_esortazione-ap_20131124_evangelii-gaudium_en.pdf.

Pope Francis. *Holy Mass on the Solemnity of Mary, the Holy Mother of God. Vatican Library*, January 1, 2017. http://www.vatican.va/content/francesco/en/homilies/2017/documents/papa-francesco_20170101_omelia-giornata-mondiale-pace.pdf.

Postman, Neil. *Amusing Ourselves to Death: Public Discourse in the Age of Show Business*. New York, NY: Penguin Books, 1986.

Radhakrishnan, Sarvepalli. *The Philosophy of The Upanisads*. London: Allen & Unwin, 1924. [*The Philosophy of the UpaniShads* was a reprint of chapter IV from Radhakrishnan's *Indian Philosophy*, Volume I.]

Raḥmān Fazlur. *Islam*. Chicago: University of Chicago Press, 1979.

Raḥmān Fazlur. *Major Themes of the Qur'ān*. Minneapolis, MN: Bibliotheca Islamica, 1994.

Rousseau, Jean-Jacques. *The Social Contract & Discourses*. Translated by George Douglas Howard Cole. New York: E. P. Dutton, 1920. Project Gutenberg (EBook #46333), July 19, 2014. https://www.gutenberg.org/files/46333.

Rūmī, Jalāl al-Dīn. *The Masnavi*. 6 vols. Translated by Jawid Mojaddedi. Oxford: Oxford University Press, 2008.

Rūmī, Jalāl al-Dīn, and Kabir Edmund Helminski. *The Rumi Collection: An Anthology of Translations of Mevlana Jalaluddin Rumi*. Boston: Shambhala, 2000.

Russell, Bertrand. *Unpopular Essays*. London: Routledge, 2009.

Sa'dī, and W. M. Thackston. *The Gulistan (Rose Garden) of Sa'di: Bilingual English and Persian Edition with Vocabulary*. Bethesda: Ibex Publishers, 2008.

Sardar, Ziauddin. Foreword to *Force and Fanaticism: Wahhabism in Saudi Arabia and Beyond*, ix-xii. By Simon Ross Valentine. London: Hurst & Company, 2015.

Schiller, Friedrich. *On Grace and Dignity*. Translated by George Gregory. Schiller Institute. Accessed November 10, 2020. http://r.schillerinstitute.org/educ/aesthetics/Schiller_On_Grace_and_Dignity.pdf.

Schimmel, Annemarie. *I Am Wind, You Are Fire: the Life and Work of Rumi*. Boston: Shambhala, 1996.

Schmid, Alex. "Terrorism - The Definitional Problem." *Case Western Reserve Journal of International Law* 36, no. 2 (2004): 375.

Scholem, Gershom. *Major Trends in Jewish Mysticism*. New York: Schocken, 1995.

Sells, Michael. *Mystical Language of Unsaying*. Chicago: University of Chicago Press, 1994.

Shaheed, Farida. *Report of the Independent Expert in the Field of Cultural Rights*. United Nations General Assembly, A/HRC/17/38, March 21, 2011. https://undocs.org/A/HRC/17/38.

Skellie, Walter James. Translator's Introduction to *Kitāb sharḥ 'ajā'ib Al-Qalb = The Marvels of the Heart: Book 21 of the Iḥyā' 'ulūm Al-dīn, the Revival of the Religious Sciences*, ix-xxxv. By Abu Hamid Muhammad al-Ghazālī. Louisville, KY: Fons Vitae, 2010.

Smith, Margaret. *Muslim Women Mystics: the Life and Work of Rábi'a and Other Women Mystics in Islam*. Oxford: One World Publications, 2002.

Steele, Bridget, Elizabeth Nye, Mackenzie Martin, Alessandra Sciarra, G J Melendez-Torres, Michelle Degli Esposti, and David Humphreys. "Global prevalence and nature of sexual violence among higher education institution students: a systematic review and meta-analysis." *The Lancet* 398, Special Issue, S16 (November 2021). doi: 10.1016/S0140-6736(21)02559-9.

Stone, Christopher D. "Should Trees Have Standing?–Toward Legal Rights for Natural Objects." *Southern California Law Review* 45 (1972): 450-501.

Stuntz, William J. "The Pathological Politics of Criminal Law." *Michigan Law Review* 100, no. 3 (2001): 505-600. https://repository.law.umich.edu/mlr/vol100/iss3/2.

Sulamī, Muḥammad ibn al-Ḥusayn. *Early Sufi Women: Dhikr an-Niswa Al-muta'abbidāt aṣ-Ṣūfiyyāt*. Translated by Rkia E. Cornell. Louisville, KY: Fons Vitae, 1999.

Tagore, Rabindranath. Foreword to *The Philosophy of The Upanisads*, ix-x. By Sarvepalli Radhakrishnan. London: Allen & Unwin, 1924.

Tasbihi, Eliza. "Sabzawārī's Sharḥ-i Asrār: A Philosophical Commentary on Rūmī's Mathnawī" in *Mawlana Rumi Review*, Volume 7, no. 1 (January 2016): 175-96. doi:10.1163/25898566-00701009

Tocqueville, Alexis de. *Democracy in America*. Edited by Richard D. Heffner. New York: Penguin, 1984.

Twain, Mark. *Autobiography of Mark Twain, Vol. 2*. Edited by Benjamin Griffin and Harriet Elinor Smith. Berkeley: University of California Press, 2013.

U.S. Food & Drug Administration. "Coronavirus (COVID-19) Update: FDA Revokes Emergency Use Authorization for Chloroquine and Hydroxychloroquine." FDA News Release, June 15, 2020. [Press Release 1] https://www.fda.gov/news-events/press-announcements/coronavirus-covid-19-update-fda-revokes-emergency-use-authorization-chloroquine-and.

U.S. Food & Drug Administration. "Coronavirus (COVID-19) Update: FDA Warns of Newly Discovered Potential Drug Interaction That May Reduce Effectiveness of a COVID-19 Treatment Authorized for Emergency Use." FDA News Release, June 15, 2020. [Press Release 2] https://www.fda.gov/news-events/press-announcements/coronavirus-covid-19-update-fda-warns-newly-discovered-potential-drug-interaction-may-reduce.

U.S. Health and Human Services. "Checklist of information to complete the VAERS form." VAERS. Accessed December 31, 2021. [VAERS Checklist] https://vaers.hhs.gov/docs/VAERS 202.0_Checklist.pdf

U.S. Health and Human Services. "Report an Adverse Event." VAERS. Accessed December 31, 2021. [VAERS Report] https://vaers.hhs.gov/reportevent.html.

U.S. Secretary of State. "Terrorist Finance: Action Request for Senior Level Engagement on Terrorism Finance." *U.S. Department of the State*, December 30, 2009. [Canonical ID: 09STATE131801_a] Accessed 2021-07-13. https://wikileaks.org/plusd/cables/09STATE131801_a.html.

Valentine, Simon Ross. *Force and Fanaticism: Wahhabism in Saudi Arabia and Beyond*. London: Hurst & Company, 2015.

Washington, James Melvin. Introduction to *A Testament of Hope: The Essential Writings of Martin Luther King, Jr.*, xi-xxvi. By Martin Luther King and James Melvin Washington. New York: Harper & Row, 1986.

Watt, William Montgomery. *Companion to the Qurʾān*. Oxford: Oneworld, 1994.

Watts, Alan W. *The Way of Zen*. New York: Vintage Books, 1957.

Whitman, James Q. *Hitler's American Model: The United States and the Making of Nazi Race Law*. Princeton: Princeton University Press, 2018.

Yakir, Michal. *Wondrous Order: Systematic Table of Homeopathic Plant Remedies. Book One: Flowering Plants*. Kandern, Germany: Narayana Verlag, 2017.

Yasutani, Hakuun. *Flowers Fall: A Commentary on Dōgen's Genjōkōan*. Translated by Paul Jaffe. Boston: Shambhala, 1996.

NEWSPAPERS, MAGAZINES, ENCYCLOPEDIAS, INTERNET SOURCES

Aguirre, Anthony. "Multiverse." *Encyclopedia Britannica*. Accessed December 10, 2020. https://www.britannica.com/science/multiverse.

Ahmad, Eqbal. Interview by David Barsamian. *Himal Magazine*, March 01, 1999. https://www.himalmag.com/eqbal-ahmad-distorted-histories/.

Alliance for Human Research Protection. "Lancet Published a Fraudulent Study: Editor Calls it 'Department of Error.'" AHRP. June 2, 2020. https://ahrp.org/the-lancet-published-a-fraudulent-study-editor-calls-it-department-of-error/.

Appiah, Kwame Anthony. Review of *Irrationality: A History of the Dark Side of Reason* by Justin E.H. Smith. *New York Review of Books*, May 9, 2019.

Arizona Department of Emergency and Military Affairs (DEMA). "Various Definitions of Terrorism: Controversy in Defining Terrorism." Accessed February 06, 2021. https://dema.az.gov/sites/default/files/Publications/AR-Terrorism%20Definitions-BORUNDA.pdf.

Associated Press. "Bin Laden, Albania Link Reported." November 29, 1998. https://apnews.com/article/6d844d0d31d7cf39ccd52891567235be.

Bacon, Perry Jr. "In America's 'Uncivil War,' Republicans Are the Aggressors." FiveThirtyEight. February 8, 2021. https://fivethirtyeight.com/features/in-americas-uncivil-war-republicans-are-the-aggressors/

Bagaria, Joan. "Set Theory." *The Stanford Encyclopedia of Philosophy* (Spring 2020 Edition), Edward N. Zalta (ed.). https://plato.stanford.edu/archives/spr2020/entries/set-theory/.

Bahaipedia. "God." Accessed October 06, 2020. https://bahaipedia.org/God.

Baker, Kevin. "Easy Chair: Losing My Religion." *Harper's Magazine*, March 2020.

Banville, John. Review of *The Unnamable Present* by Roberto Calasso, trans. Richard Dixon. *New York Review of Books*, September 26, 2019.

Batty, David, Helena Bengtsson, and Josh Holder. "Sexual harassment allegations: find figures for UK universities." *The Guardian* (London, England), March 5, 2017.

Beall, Jc, Michael Glanzberg, and David Ripley. "Liar Paradox." *The Stanford Encyclopedia of Philosophy* (Fall 2020 Edition), Edward N. Zalta (ed.). https://plato.stanford.edu/archives/fall2020/entries/liar-paradox/.

Begley, Sharon. "Are We Becoming Smart Fools?" *Mindful Magazine*, December 2017: 20-22.

Beha, Christopher. Review of *Seven Types of Atheism* by John Gray. *New York Review of Books*, February 21, 2019.

Bernstein, Joseph. "Bad News: Selling the Story of Disinformation." *Harper's Magazine*, September 2021.

Biden, Joseph. Interview by Kingsbury, Kathleen, Binyamin Appelbaum, John Broder, Michelle Cottle, Nick Fox, Mara Gay, Aisha Harris, Jeneen Interlandi, Lauren Kelley, Alex Kingsbury, Brent Staples, Charlie Warzel, and Jesse Wegman. *The New York Times*, January 17, 2020. https://www.nytimes.com/interactive/2020/01/17/opinion/joe-biden-nytimes-interview.html.

Biello, David. "The Nuclear Odyssey of Naoto Kan, Japan's Prime Minister during Fukushima." *Scientific American*, October 16, 2013.

Bissett, James. "We Created a Monster." *DeltaX.net*, July 31, 2001. https://www.deltax.net/bissett/a-monster.htm.

Bissett, James. "War on terrorism skipped the KLA." *Center for Research on Globalization*, November 13, 2001. https://archives.globalresearch.ca/articles/BIS111A.html.

Blair, David. "Qatar and Saudi Arabia 'have ignited time bomb by funding global spread of radical Islam.'" *The Telegraph* (London), October 4, 2014

Boer, Roland. "Savage peoples: the racism of Adam Smith in Wealth of Nations." *The Conversation*, May 11, 2015. https://theconversation.com/savage-peoples-the-racism-of-adam-smith-in-wealth-of-nations-35675.

Bradley, Omar. "No Armistice." *New York Times* (New York), November 11, 1986. https://www.nytimes.com/1986/11/11/opinion/no-armistice.html.

Brenan, Megan. "Americans' Trust in Media Dips to Second Lowest on Record." *Gallup.com*, October 7, 2021. Accessed January 9, 2022.

https://news.gallup.com/poll/355526/americans-trust-media-dips-second-lowest-record.aspx.

Brigham and Women's Hospital. "Two Remdesivir Clinical Trials Underway at Brigham and Women's Hospital." Brigham and Women's Hospital News Web Portal, March 26, 2020. https://www.brighamhealthonamission.org/2020/03/26/two-remdesivir-clinical-trials-underway-at-brigham-and-womens-hospital/.

Burns, John F. "House of Graft: Tracing the Bhutto Millions–A special report; Bhutto Clan Leaves Trail of Corruption." *New York Times* (New York), January 9, 1998.

Buruma, Ian. "The Great Wall of Steel: Xi Jinping remakes Chinese nationalism." *Harper's Magazine*, February 2022.

Carter, Stephen L. "Law Puts Us All in Same Danger as Eric Garner." *Bloomberg* (Op-ed), December 4, 2014. https://www.bloomberg.com/opinion/articles/2014-12-04/law-puts-us-all-in-same-danger-as-eric-garner.

Chehata, Hanan. "Saudi 'cultural vandalism' of Muslim heritage continues." *Middle East Eye*. February 12, 2015.

Chittick, William, "Ibn 'Arabî", *The Stanford Encyclopedia of Philosophy* (Spring 2020 Edition), Edward N. Zalta (ed.). https://plato.stanford.edu/archives/spr2020/entries/ibn-arabi/.

Chivers, C, and Eric Schmitt. "Arms Airlift to Syria Rebels Expands, With Aid From C.I.A." *New York Times*, March 24, 2013.

Clemons, Steve. "'Thank God for the Saudis': ISIS, Iraq, and the Lessons of Blowback." *The Atlantic*, June 23, 2014.

Cobain, Ian, Alice Ross, Rob Evans, and Mona Mahmood. "How Britain Funds the 'Propaganda War' Against ISIS in Syria." *The Guardian* (London, England), May 3, 2016.

Cockburn, Andrew. "Spent Fuel: The Risky Resurgence of Nuclear Power." *Harper's Magazine*, January 2022.

Cockburn, Patrick. "Iraq crisis: How Saudi Arabia helped Isis take over the north of the country." *The Independent* (London), July 14, 2014.

Cohen, Nate. "Why Political Sectarianism Is a Growing Threat to American Democracy." *New York Times* (New York), September 8, 2021

"Commission on Information Disorder." *Aspen Institute*. Accessed December 24, 2021. https://www.aspeninstitute.org/programs/commission-on-information-disorder/

Cornell Law School, Legal Information Institute. "22 U.S. Code § 2656f - Annual country reports on terrorism." Accessed February 06, 2021. https://www.law.cornell.edu/uscode/text/22/2656f.

Creswell, Robyn. Review of *Sufism: A New History of Islamic Mysticism* by Alexander Knysh; and *Hallaj: Poems of a Sufi Martyr* by Alexander Knysh. *New York Review of Books*, March 7, 2019.

Crooke, Alastair. "If Syria and Iraq Become Fractured, So Too Will Tripoli and North Lebanon." *Huffington Post*, Updated June 01, 2016. (Originally Published June 01, 2015.) https://www.huffpost.com/entry/syria-iraq-fractured_b_7471540.

Davey, Melissa, Stephanie Kirchgaessner, and Sarah Boseley. "Surgisphere: governments and WHO changed Covid-19 policy based on suspect data from tiny US company." *The Guardian* (London, England), June 3, 2020.

de Waal, Alex. "Lab Leaks." *London Review of Books*, December 2, 2021.

Dejevsky, Mary. "Richard Perle: On the defensive: America's Prince of Darkness." *The Independent* (London), March 29, 2003.

Deresiewicz, William. "The Neoliberal Arts: How college sold its soul to the market." *Harper's Magazine*, September 2015.

Dirda, Michael. Review of *On Kindness* by Adam Phillips and Barbara Taylor. *Washington Post*, August 20, 2009.

Dziadosz, Alexander. Review of *Voices of the Lost* by Hoda Barakat and *God 99* by Hassan Blasim. *London Review of Books*, March 24, 2022.

Enderton, H. and Robert R. Stoll. "Set theory." *Encyclopedia Britannica*. Accessed July 21, 2020. https://www.britannica.com/science/set-theory.

Engelhart, Katie. "Home and Alone: Loneliness is a crisis among older Americans. Can robots keep them company?" *The New Yorker*, May 31, 2021.

Evans, Richard J. Review of *Ruin and Renewal: Civilising Europe after World War Two* by Paul Betts. *London Review of Books*, April 22, 2021.

Faye, Jan. "Copenhagen Interpretation of Quantum Mechanics." *The Stanford Encyclopedia of Philosophy* (Winter 2019 Edition), Edward N. Zalta (ed.), URL = <https://plato.stanford.edu/archives/win2019/entries/qm-copenhagen/>.

Feynman, Richard. "The Relation of Science and Religion: Some fresh observations on an old problem." *California Institute of Technology*

(Transcript of a forum on May 2, 1956). Accessed August 17, 2021. https://calteches.library.caltech.edu/49/2/Religion.htm.

Finlayson, Lorna. "Diary." *London Review of Books*, February 18, 2021.

Finlayson, Lorna. Review of *Complaint!* by Sara Ahmed. *London Review of Books*, May 12, 2022.

Fitzpatrick, Katie. Review of *The Age of Surveillance Capitalism: The Fight for a Human Future at the New Frontier of Power* by Shoshana Zuboff. *The Nation*, May 13, 2019.

Foer, Franklin. "Moral Hazard." *The New Republic*, November 18, 2002.

Freedland, Jonathan. "Disinformed to Death." *New York Review of Books*, August 20, 2020.

Friedman, Matthew. "Just Facts: As Many Americans Have Criminal Records as College Diplomas." *Brennan Center for Justice*, November 17, 2015. https://www.brennancenter.org/our-work/analysis-opinion/just-facts-many-americans-have-criminal-records-college-diplomas.

Fuller, Graham. "Here's What's Behind Erdoğan's New Airstrikes — And Why They Could Backfire." Huffington Post, Updated July 28, 2016. (Originally Published July 28, 2015) https://www.huffpost.com/entry/erdogan-turkey-airstrikes_b_7890014.

Gardner, David. "The toxic rivalry of Saudi Arabia and Isis." Financial Times (London), July 16, 2015.

Gavlak, Dale, and Jamal Halaby. "Arms shipments to Syrian rebels on the rise." *The Times of Israel* (Jerusalem), March 27, 2013.

Gessen, Masha. "The Reichstag Fire Next Time." *Harper's Magazine*, July 2017.

Goodenough, Patrick. "Saudis Deny Supporting ISIS After Former MI6 Head Speaks of 'Substantial and Sustained Funding.'" *CNSNews.com*, July 09, 2014. https://www.cnsnews.com/news/article/patrick-goodenough/saudis-deny-supporting-isis-after-former-mi6-head-speaks-substantial.

Grant, Keisha. "I Owe Them." *NBC Connecticut*, September 25, 2017. https://www.nbcconnecticut.com/news/local/i-owe-them-convicted-mosque-shooter-embraces-islam/23036/.

Greenberg, Jon. "Watch out, 70% of us have done something that could put us in jail." *Politifact*, December 8, 2014. https://www.politifact.com/factchecks/2014/dec/08/stephen-carter/watch-out-70-us-have-done-something-could-put-us-j.

Greenberg, Jon. "Kristof: U.S. imprisons blacks at rates higher than South Africa during apartheid." *Politifact*. December 11, 2014. https://

www.politifact.com/factchecks/2014/dec/11/nicholas-kristof/kristof-us-imprisons-blacks-rates-higher-south-afr/.

Greenwald, Glenn. "Homeland Security's 'Disinformation Board' is Even More Pernicious Than it Seems." *Greenwald.Substack.com*, May 4, 2022. Accessed May 8, 2022. https://greenwald.substack.com/p/homeland-securitys-disinformation?s=r.

Griffiths, Jay. "Schooled in nature." *Aeon*, June 18, 2016. https://aeon.co/essays/schooling-comes-naturally-to-mexico-s-indigenous-people.

Hall, Shannon. "Exxon Knew about Climate Change almost 40 years ago." *Scientific American*, October 26, 2015.

Harrell, Eben. "Neuromarketing: What You Need to Know." *Harvard Business Review*, January 23, 2019.

Hasan, Shazia, "Ruth Pfau remembered as 'a human being who defined humanity.'" *Dawn* (Karachi), September 1, 2017. https://www.dawn.com/news/1355235.

HeartMath Institute. "Exploring the Role of the Heart in Human Performance: An Overview of Research Conducted by the HeartMath Institute" (Chapter: Introduction). [Study-1] Accessed December 10, 2020. https://www.heartmath.org/research/science-of-the-heart/.

HeartMath Institute. "Exploring the Role of the Heart in Human Performance: An Overview of Research Conducted by the HeartMath Institute" (Chapter: Heart-Brain Communication). [Study-2] Accessed December 10, 2020. https://www.heartmath.org/research/science-of-the-heart/heart-brain-communication/.

HeartMath Institute. "Exploring the Role of the Heart in Human Performance: An Overview of Research Conducted by the HeartMath Institute" (Chapter: Coherence). [Study-3] Accessed December 10, 2020. https://www.heartmath.org/research/science-of-the-heart/coherence/.

HeartMath Institute. "Scientific Foundation of the HeartMath System." [Study 4] Accessed December 10, 2020. https://www.heartmath.org/science/.

Henninger, Daniel. " Pull the Plug on the Disinformation Governance Board: Biden and Mayorkas should fire Mary Poppins." *The Wall Street Journal*, May 4, 2022.

Herzog, Lena. "Silencio: The Politics of Silencing." *Lenaherzog.com*, May 16th, 2018. https://www.lenaherzog.com/moma-silencio-talk.

Higgins, Andrew and Moshav Tekuma. "How Israel Helped to Spawn Hamas." *The Wall Street Journal*, January 24, 2009.

Hochschild, Adam. Review of *Hitler's American Model: The United States and the Making of Nazi Race Law* by James Q. Whitman. *New York Review of Books*, October 25, 2018.

Holt, Jim. Review of *The Precipice: Existential Risk and the Future of Humanity* by Toby Ord. *New York Review of Books*, February 25, 2021.

Hubbard, Ben. "Saudis Turn Birthplace of Ideology Into Tourist Spot." *New York Times* (New York, NY), June 1, 2015.

Hulatt, Owen. "Against popular culture." *Aeon*, February 20, 2018. https://aeon.co/essays/against-guilty-pleasures-adorno-on-the-crimes-of-pop-culture.

Human Rights Watch. "Saudi Arabia: New Terrorism Regulations Assault Rights." HRW News Release, March 20, 2014. https://www.hrw.org/news/2014/03/20/saudi-arabia-new-terrorism-regulations-assault-rights.

Human Rights Watch. "US: A Nation Behind Bars." HRW News Release, May 6, 2014. https://www.hrw.org/news/2014/05/06/us-nation-behind-bars.

Hunziker, Robert. "Fukushima Takes a Turn for the Worse." *CounterPunch.org*, January 10, 2022. https://www.counterpunch.org/2022/01/10/fukushima-takes-a-turn-for-the-worse/.

Huxley, Aldous. "Notes on Propaganda." *Harper's Magazine*, December 1936.

In These Times. "Incarceration by the Numbers." April 2020.

Ingersoll, Geoffrey, and Michael Kelley. "REPORT: The US Is Openly Sending Heavy Weapons From Libya To Syrian Rebels." *Business Insider*, December 9, 2012. https://www.businessinsider.com/obama-admin-admits-to-covertly-sending-heavy-weapons-to-syrian-rebels-2012-12.

Institute for Conflict Management. "Pakistan Anti-Terrorism (Amendment) Ordinance, 1999." South Asia Terrorism Portal. Accessed February 06, 2021. https://www.satp.org/satporgtp/countries/pakistan/document/actsandordinences/anti_terrorism.htm.

Jagannathan, Malavika. "The Machine Runs Amok." *University of Washington Magazine*, Winter 2021 (volume 32, number 4).

Jenkins, J. Philip. "Terrorism." *Encyclopedia Britannica.* Accessed January 23, 2021. https://www.britannica.com/topic/terrorism.

Johnson, Samuel. "Corruption of news-writers (Essay No. 30)." *The Idler*, published in the Universal Chronicle, 1758-1760. Accessed

September 17, 2020. https://www.johnsonessays.com/the-idler/corruption-news-writers/.

Kelley, Michael. "How US Ambassador Chris Stevens May Have Been Linked To Jihadist Rebels In Syria." *Business Insider*, October 19, 2012. Accessed 2021-07-11. https://www.businessinsider.com/us-syria-heavy-weapons-jihadists-2012-10.

Kenton, Will. "Economic Man." *Investopedia*. June 8, 2020. https://www.investopedia.com/terms/e/economic-man.asp

Kermali, Shenaz. "The Hajj exhibition is in stark contrast to Saudi Arabia's cultural vandalism." *The Guardian* (London, England), January 27, 2012.

Kessler, Glenn, Meg Kelly, Salvador Rizzo, Michelle Ye Hee Lee, and Leslie Shapiro. "In four years, President Trump made 30,573 false or misleading claims: The Fact Checker's database of the false or misleading claims made by President Trump while in office." *Washington Post*, January 20, 2021. https://www.washingtonpost.com/graphics/politics/trump-claims-database/.

Kessler, Glenn, Meg Kelly, Salvador Rizzo, Leslie Shapiro, and Leo Dominguez. "A term of untruths: The longer Trump was president, the more frequently he made false or misleading claims." *Washington Post*, January 23, 2021. https://www.washingtonpost.com/politics/interactive/2021/timeline-trump-claims-as-president/.

Kessler, Glenn, Adrian Blanco, and Tyler Remmel. "The false and misleading claims President Biden made during his first 100 days in office." *Washington Post*, April 30, 2021. https://www.washingtonpost.com/politics/interactive/2021/biden-fact-checker-100-days/.

Khalaf, Roula, and Abigail Smith. "Qatar bankrolls Syrian revolt with cash and arms." Financial Times (London), May 16, 2013.

Khurana, Simran. "The History of 'My Country, Right or Wrong!'" *ThoughtCo*, March 23, 2018. https://www.thoughtco.com/my-country-right-or-wrong-2831839.

King, Martin Luther. "On Being a Good Neighbor." *The Martin Luther King, Jr. Research and Education Institute, Stanford University*. Accessed May 16, 2022. https://kinginstitute.stanford.edu/king-papers/documents/draft-chapter-iii-being-good-neighbor.

King, Martin Luther. "Beyond Vietnam—A Time to Break Silence." Speech delivered at Riverside Church, New York City, April 4, 1967. https://www.americanrhetoric.com/speeches/mlkatimetobreaksilence.htm

King, Martin Luther. “A Testament of Hope.” *Playboy*, January 1969. https://www.playboy.com/read/martin-luther-king-testament-of-hope

King, Martin Luther. “Sincerity Is Not Enough.” *The Martin Luther King, Jr. Research and Education Institute, Stanford University*. Accessed November 29, 2020. https://kinginstitute.stanford.edu/king-papers/documents/sincerity-not-enough.

Kirkpatrick, David. “ISIS’ Harsh Brand of Islam Is Rooted in Austere Saudi Creed.” *New York Times*, September 24, 2014.

Kunzru, Hari. Review of *Surviving Autocracy* by Masha Gessen. *New York Review of Books*, July 2, 2020.

Lamb, Christina. “Covert US plan to arm rebels.” *The Times* (London), December 09, 2012.

Lantz, Erika. “Four Bullets.” *WBUR*, June 23, 2017. https://www.wbur.org/kindworld/2017/06/23/kind-world-40-four-bullets.

Lee, Michelle Ye Hee. “Does the United States really have 5 percent of the world’s population and one quarter of the world’s prisoners?” *Washington Post* (Washington, DC), April 30, 2015. https://www.washingtonpost.com/news/fact-checker/wp/2015/04/30/does-the-united-states-really-have-five-percent-of-worlds-population-and-one-quarter-of-the-worlds-prisoners/.

Legifrance. “Code penal.” Partie législative (Articles 111-1 à 727-3). Livre IV: Des crimes et délits contre la nation, l’Etat et la paix publique (Articles 410-1 à 450-5). Chapitre Ier: Des actes de terrorisme (Articles 421-1 à 421-8). Accessed February 06, 2021. https://www.legifrance.gouv.fr/codes/id/LEGISCTA000006149845/.

Legislation.gov.uk. “Terrorism Act 2000.” Enacted July 20, 2000. Accessed February 06, 2021. https://www.legislation.gov.uk/ukpga/2000/11/section/1.

Lindstrom, Martin. “You Love Your iPhone. Literally.” *New York Times* (New York), October 1, 2011.

Lloyd, Sharon A. and Susanne Sreedhar. “Hobbes’s Moral and Political Philosophy.” *The Stanford Encyclopedia of Philosophy* (Fall 2020 Edition), Edward N. Zalta (ed.), URL = <https://plato.stanford.edu/archives/fall2020/entries/hobbes-moral/>.

Lucas, Scott. “Russia and Syria: bound together in a mission that is far from accomplished.” *The Conversation*, July 30, 2021. https://theconversation.com/russia-and-syria-bound-together-in-a-mission-that-is-far-from-accomplished-165345.

Macaulay, Thomas Babington. "Minute on Education." Accessed June 28, 2020. http://www.columbia.edu/itc/mealac/pritchett/00generallinks/macaulay/txt_minute_education_1835.html.

Malik, Kenan. "The Great British Empire Debate." *New York Review of Books*, January 26, 2018.

Marlowe, Lara. "The sinking of idealism." *The Irish Times* (Dublin), July 9, 2005. https://www.irishtimes.com/news/the-sinking-of-idealism-1.466454.

McCarthy, Rory, and Maev Kennedy. "Babylon wrecked by war." *The Guardian* (London), January 15, 2005.

MacLeod, Donald. "US lobby could threaten Iraqi heritage." *The Guardian* (London), April 10, 2003.

MacLeod, Donald, and David Walker. "Art falls prey to war." *The Guardian* (London), April 15, 2003.

Mandavilli, Apoorva. "C.D.C. Is Not Publishing Large Portions of the Data That It Collects on Virus." *New York Times*, February 21, 2022.

Mazzetti, Mark, and Matt Apuzzo. "U.S. Relies Heavily on Saudi Money to Support Syrian Rebels." New York Times, January 23, 2016.

Miller, Arthur. "Why I Wrote 'The Crucible:' An artist's answer to politics." *The New Yorker*, October 21, 1996.

Miller, Greg, and Karen DeYoung. "Secret CIA effort in Syria faces large funding cut." Washington Post, June 12, 2015.

Minta, Molly. "Extinction Crisis: Decolonizing Climate." *The Nation*, August 26, 2019.

Mishra, Pankaj. "A Gandhian Stand Against the Culture of Cruelty." *New York Review of Books*, May 22, 2018.

Mulrine, Anna. "Afghan Warlords, Formerly Backed By the CIA, Now Turn Their Guns on U.S. Troops." *US News & World Report*, July 11, 2008.

Murakami, Sakura. "Japan's new PM defends pro-nuclear stance in parliamentary debut." *Reuters*, October 11, 2021.

Nakhleh, Emile. "The Islamic State's Ideology Is Grounded in Saudi Education." *Inter Press Service*, October 31, 2914.

National Center for Complementary and Integrative Health. "Helene Langevin, M.D. Director, NCCIH." National Institutes of Health. Accessed December 12, 2020. https://www.nccih.nih.gov/about/staff/helene-langevin.

O'Connell, Mark. "Why Silicon Valley billionaires are prepping for the apocalypse in New Zealand." *The Guardian* (London) February 15, 2018.

O'Day, Daniel. "An Open Letter from Daniel O'Day, Chairman & CEO, Gilead Sciences." *Gilead*, June 29, 2020. https://stories.gilead.com/articles/an-open-letter-from-daniel-oday-june-29.

Offord, Catherine. "Disputed Hydroxychloroquine Study Brings Scrutiny to Surgisphere." *The Scientist*, May 30, 2020. https://www.the-scientist.com/news-opinion/disputed-hydroxychloroquine-study-brings-scrutiny-to-surgisphere-67595.

Osnos, Evan. "Survival of the Richest." *The New Yorker*, January 30, 2017. Online version published on January 22, 2017 with the headline "Doomsday Prep for the Super-Rich." https://www.newyorker.com/magazine/2017/01/30/doomsday-prep-for-the-super-rich. (Reid Hoffman, co-founder of LinkedIn, attributes the "apocalypse insurance" expression to a friend.)

O'Toole, Fintan. Review of *Yours, for Probably Always: Martha Gellhorn's Letters of Love and War, 1930-1949* edited by Janet Somerville. *New York Review of Books*, October 8, 2020.

Pear, Robert. "Arming Afghan Guerrillas: A Huge Effort Led by U.S." *New York Times* (New York, NY), April 18, 1988.

Piller, Charles, and Kelly Servick. "Two elite medical journals retract coronavirus papers over data integrity questions." *Science* (magazine), June 4, 2020. https://www.sciencemag.org/news/2020/06/two-elite-medical-journals-retract-coronavirus-papers-over-data-integrity-questions.

Pittman, Travis, Amanda Seitz, and Nomaan Merchant. "20 AGs call for end to Disinformation Governance Board, cite threat to free speech." *Abc10.com*, May 5, 2022. https://www.abc10.com/article/news/nation-world/disinformation-governance-board/507-36059d1e-9410-4ce1-8954-03e58b87a07e.

Pope Francis. "The Power of Money." As quoted by *L'Osservatore Romano*, Weekly ed. in English, no. 39, September 25, 2013. http://www.vatican.va/content/francesco/en/cotidie/2013/documents/papa-francesco-cotidie_20130920_power-money.html.

Rabin, Roni Caryn, and Ellen Gabler. "Two Major Covid-19 Studies Are Retracted for Faulty Data." *New York Times* (New York), June 5, 2020.

Rabin, Roni Caryn. "Two Retractions Hurt Credibility Of Peer Review." *New York Times* (New York), June 15, 2020.

Randall, Lee. "For the love of stuff." *Aeon*, August 3, 2016. https://aeon.co/essays/why-i-love-my-possessions-as-a-mirror-and-a-gallery-of-me.

Ray, Tarence. "United in Rage: Half-truths and myths propelled Kentucky's war on opioids." *The Baffler*, July-August, 2021 (No. 58).

Roose, Kevin. "Reclaiming Reality From Chaos." *New York Times* (New York), February 4, 2021.

Sanger, David E. "Obama Order Sped Up Wave of Cyberattacks Against Iran." *New York Times* (New York), June 01, 2012.

Saul, Heather. "President Obama claims rise of Isis is 'unintended consequence' of George W. Bush's invasion in Iraq." *Independent* (London), March 18, 2015.

Sawyer, Wendy and Peter Wagner. "Mass Incarceration: The Whole Pie 2020." *Prison Policy Initiative*, March 24, 2020. https://www.prisonpolicy.org/reports/pie2020.html.

Schwarz, Jon. "Legendary Journalist in Private: 'It Is All Fraudulent, All of It, Everywhere.'" *The Intercept*, May 28, 2015. https://theintercept.com/2015/05/28/legendary-journalist-private-fraudulent-everywhere/

Scott Aaronson. "The great mystery of mathematics is its lack of mystery." *Aeon*, April 1, 2016. https://aeon.co/ideas/the-great-mystery-of-mathematics-is-its-lack-of-mystery.

Sengupta, Kim. Review of *Secret Affairs: Britain's Collusion with Radical Islam* by Mark Curtis. *Independent* (London), October 23, 2011.

Shamah, David. "Stuxnet, gone rogue, hit Russian nuke plant, space station." *Times of Israel* (Jerusalem), November 11, 2013. https://www.timesofisrael.com/stuxnet-gone-rogue-hit-russian-nuke-plant-space-station/.

Shane, Scott. "Both Arsonists and Firefighters." *New York Times* (New York), August 26, 2016.

Shastri, Pandit Vamadeva. "A Vedic Consecration to the Spiritual Heart." *American Institute of Vedic Studies*, November 27, 2020. https://www.vedanet.com/a-vedic-consecration-to-the-spiritual-heart.

Shulman, David. Review of *Rooted Cosmopolitans: Jews and Human Rights in the Twentieth Century* by James Loeffler; and *The Wall and the Gate: Israel, Palestine, and the Legal Battle for Human Rights* by Michael Sfard, trans. Maya Johnston. *New York Review of Books*, June 28, 2018.

Skidelsky, William. "Niall Ferguson: 'Westerners don't understand how vulnerable freedom is.'" *The Guardian* (London), February 19, 2011.

Spencer, Richard. "US and Europe in 'major airlift of arms to Syrian rebels through Zagreb.'" The Telegraph (London), March 08, 2013.

Spillius, Alex. "Wikileaks: Saudis 'chief funders of al-Qaeda.'" The Telegraph (London), December 5, 2010.

Stanford University. "Strength to Love." The Martin Luther King, Jr. Research and Education Institute. Accessed November 29, 2020. https://kinginstitute.stanford.edu/encyclopedia/strength-love.

Stephens, Joe, and David B. Ottaway. "From U.S., the ABC's of Jihad." *The Washington Post* (Washington), March 23, 2002.

Stevenson, Peter. Review of *On Kindness* by Adam Phillips and Barbara Taylor. *New York Times*, July 29, 2009.

Stevenson, Tom. Review of *AngloArabia: Why Gulf Wealth Matters to Britain* by David Wearing. *London Review of Books*, May 9, 2019.

Sultan, Bandar bin. Interview by Larry King. *Larry King Live (CNN)*, October 1, 2001. http://transcripts.cnn.com/TRANSCRIPTS/0110/01/lkl.00.html.

Swan, Betsy, and Daniel Lippman. "Small group, big headache: Inside DHS' messy Disinformation Governance Board launch." *Politico.com*, May 5, 2022.

Synovitz, Ron. "Afghanistan: Kabul Confirms New Effort To Buy Back U.S.-Built Stinger Missiles." *RadioFreeEurope Radio Liberty*. January 31, 2005. https://www.rferl.org/a/1057196.html

Taylor, Jerome. "Mecca for the rich: Islam's holiest site 'turning into Vegas.'" *The Independent* (London), October 22, 2018.

Terry, Brandon M. "MLK Now." *Boston Review*, September 10, 2018. http://bostonreview.net/forum/brandon-m-terry-mlk-now

Thomas, Skye Arundhati. Review of *The Good Girls: An Ordinary Killing* by Sonia Faleiro. *London Review of Books*, March 10, 2022.

Vallely, Paul. "Isis: Having spent billions, the Wahhabists of Saudi Arabia and Qatar find they have created a monster." Belfast Telegraph, August 25, 2014. Accessed 2021-07-13.

Vasagar, Jeevan. "Niall Ferguson: admirable historian, or imperial mischief maker?" *The Guardian* (London), June 18, 2012. https://www.theguardian.com/books/2012/jun/18/niall-ferguson-bbc-reith-lecturer-radio4.

Victoria, Brian. "Zen terror—Master Nissho Inoue and his band of assassins teach some uncomfortable truths about terrorism, for those who will hear." *Aeon*, July 10, 2019. https://aeon.co/essays/the-lessons-of-nissho-inoue-and-his-cell-of-zen-terrorists.

Viner, Brian. Review of *The Qur'an* (documentary), produced and directed by Antony Thomas. *The Independent* (London), October 23, 2011.

Wade, Francis. "Fleas We Greatly Loathe." *London Review of Books*, July 5, 2018.

Wagner, Peter, and Wendy Sawyer. "States of Incarceration: The Global Context 2018." *Prison Policy Initiative*, June 2018. https://www.prisonpolicy.org/global/2018.html.

Walker, Tom, and Aidan Laverty. "CIA Aided Kosovo Guerrilla Army All Along." *Global Policy Forum*. March 12, 2000. (Originally published in the *Sunday Times*, London.) Accessed 2021-07-11. https://archive.globalpolicy.org/security/issues/kosovo1/ksv17.htm

Wallen, Joe. "'I want a partner with a helipad': India's new matchmakers cater to the super-rich." *The Telegraph* (London), August 29, 2020.

Walmsley, Roy. "World Prison Population List (twelfth edition)." *World Prison Brief*, June 11, 2018. https://www.prisonstudies.org/sites/default/files/resources/downloads/wppl_12.pdf.

Walsh, Bryan. "Japan Mulls Nuclear Revival Not Even 3 Years After Fukushima." *Time*, February 25, 2014.

Ward, Warren. "Sooner or later we all face death. Will a sense of meaning help us?" *Aeon*, May 6, 2020. https://aeon.co/ideas/sooner-or-later-we-all-face-death-will-a-sense-of-meaning-help-us.

Warren, Jenifer. "Terry Cole-Whittaker Says Goodbye to Her Congregation." *Los Angeles Times* (Los Angeles), April 08, 1985.

Watson, James on behalf of 201 signatories. "An open letter to Mehra et al and The Lancet." *Zenodo*, May 28, 2020. doi: https://doi.org/10.5281/zenodo.3871094.

Weigel, David. "How Democrats Plan to Fight Domestic Terror." *The Washington Post* (Washington), January 14, 2021.

Weinberger, Eliot. "One Summer in America." *London Review of Books*, September 26, 2019.

Weiss, Philip. "US watched ISIS rise in Syria and hoped to 'manage' it—Kerry on leaked tape." *Mondoweiss.net*, January 11, 2017. https://mondoweiss.net/2017/01/watched-manage-leaked/.